William J. Fay

JAMES L. CRENSHAW

ECCLESIASTES

JAMES L. CRENSHAW

ECCLESIASTES

A Commentary

THE WESTMINSTER PRESS
PHILADELPHIA

Book design by Gene Harris

First edition

Published by The Westminster Press®
Philadelphia, Pennsylvania

PRINTED IN THE UNITED STATES OF AMERICA

9 8 7 6 5 4 3 2 1

Library of Congress Cataloging-in-Publication Data

Crenshaw, James L.
Ecclesiastes : a commentary.

(The Old Testament library)
Bibliography: p.
1. Bible. O.T. Ecclesiastes—Commentaries.
I. Title. II. Series.
BS1475.3.C74 1987 223′.807 87-16053
ISBN 0-664-21295-6

CONTENTS

PREFACE

In writing this commentary I have received extraordinary assistance from three persons, Marti Steussy, Michael V. Fox, and Judy Matthews Taylor, to whom I hereby express my deepest appreciation. The first two read my manuscript and made valuable suggestions for its improvement, and the third transformed my handwritten text into a typescript that could easily be prepared for publication. In addition, Michael made available to me a copy of his forthcoming commentary on Qohelet, which is especially strong on the linguistic aspects of the book. Roland E. Murphy extended a similar kindness, allowing me to see the typescript of his commentary on Ecclesiastes that will appear shortly in the Hermeneia series. Both Michael and Roland shared offprints with me as well, and in this significant expression of collegiality others have also joined, most notably Robert Gordis (whose commentary on Qohelet was indispensable), R. Norman Whybray, Anton Schoors, Graham Ogden, John Gammie, and Addison D. Wright.

My indebtedness to others, with whom my relationship is less personal, is no less real. Any attempt to list those scholars—living and dead—who have informed my thinking about Qohelet is doomed to fail, but the following deserve special notice: Delitzsch, Barton, and Ginsberg for relentless attention to language and syntax; Podechard for thoroughness, especially the introductory material; Ginsburg for a history of research; Loretz for the study of the ancient Near Eastern parallels; Whitley for philological observations; Hertzberg and Lauha for comprehensiveness; Braun for the Greek background; Ellermeier and Kroeber for special syntactical problems; Lohfink for literary features; Zimmerli for theological insights; Lys for philosophical probings; and Barucq for cautious examination of the status of research on Qohelet.

A major portion of the research during the final stages of writing this book was made possible by a fellowship from the John Simon Guggenheim Memorial Foundation for the academic year 1984–85. That project, "The Depiction of Old Age in Ancient Near Eastern Wisdom Literature," focused on the exquisite poem in Eccl. 11:7–12:7 and enabled me to explore the larger context of Qohelet in a way that would otherwise have been impossible. I wish by this means to express my profound gratitude to Joel

Conarroe, President of the John Simon Guggenheim Memorial Foundation, for its generous support of my research.

This book is dedicated to Austin S. and Grace Rhodes Bobo, who for many years have provided a home away from home for my wife and me.

JAMES L. CRENSHAW

Vanderbilt Divinity School

ABBREVIATIONS

AB	Anchor Bible
ANET	*Ancient Near Eastern Texts Relating to the Old Testament,* ed. by J. B. Pritchard, 2nd. ed., Princeton, 1955
ASTI	*Annual of the Swedish Theological Institute*
ATD	Das Alte Testament Deutsch
BASOR	*Bulletin of the American Schools of Oriental Research*
BDB	*Brown, Driver, and Briggs, *Hebrew and English Lexicon*
BHK	*Biblia Hebraica,* ed. by Rudolf Kittel, 1937
BHS	**Biblia Hebraica Stuttgartensia,* 1978
BHT	Beiträge zur historischen Theologie
Bib	*Biblica*
BKAT	Biblischer Kommentar Altes Testament
BO	*Bibliotheca Orientalis*
BTB	*Biblical Theology Bulletin*
BZ	*Biblische Zeitschrift*
BZAW	Beihefte zur *Zeitschrift für die alttestamentliche Wissenschaft*
CBQ	*Catholic Biblical Quarterly*
E	English (where numbering differs from the Hebrew)
ET	English translation
ETL	*Ephemerides Theologicae Lovanienses*
ExpT	*Expository Times*
FOTL	The Forms of the Old Testament Literature
GKC	*Gesenius-Kautzsch-Cowley, *Hebrew Grammar*
HAR	*Hebrew Annual Review*
HAT	Handbuch zum Alten Testament
HS	*Hebrew Studies*
HSAT	Die Heilige Schrift des Altes Testament
HUCA	*Hebrew Union College Annual*
IB	*Interpreter's Bible,* ed. by G. A. Buttrick, 12 vols., Nashville, 1952–57
ICC	International Critical Commentary
IDB	*Interpreter's Dictionary of the Bible,* ed. by G. A. Buttrick, 4 vols., Nashville, 1962
IDBSup	*Interpreter's Dictionary of the Bible,* Supplementary Volume, ed. by K. Crim, Nashville, 1976
Int	*Interpretation*
ITQ	*Irish Theological Quarterly*
JAOS	*Journal of the American Oriental Society*

JBL	*Journal of Biblical Literature*
JBR	*Journal of Bible and Religion* (now *Journal of the American Academy of Religion*)
JJS	*Journal of Jewish Studies*
JNES	*Journal of Near Eastern Studies*
JPS	*Jewish Publication Society translation *(Tanakh)*
JQR	*Jewish Quarterly Review*
JSOT	*Journal for the Study of the Old Testament*
JSS	*Journal of Semitic Studies*
JTS	*Journal of Theological Studies*
KAT	Kommentar zum Alten Testament
KHAT	Kurzer Hand-Commentar zum Alten Testament
NAB	New American Bible
OLZ	*Orientalistische Literaturzeitung*
OTS	*Oudtestamentische Studiën*
PAAJR	*Proceedings of the American Academy of Jewish Research*
PEQ	*Palestine Exploration Quarterly*
RB	*Revue Biblique*
RHPR	*Revue d'Histoire et de Philosophie Religieuses*
RSV	Revised Standard Version
SAIW	**Studies in Ancient Israelite Wisdom,* ed. by J. L. Crenshaw
SJT	*Scottish Journal of Theology*
SPOA	*Les sagesses du Proche-Orient ancien* (Colloque de Strasbourg, 1962), Paris, 1963
STU	*Schweizerische Theologische Umschau*
TDOT	*Theological Dictionary of the Old Testament,* ed. by G. J. Botterweck and H. Ringgren, Grand Rapids, 1974–
TR	*Theologische Rundschau*
TSK	*Theologische Studien und Kritiken*
TTZ	*Trierer theologische Zeitschrift*
TZ	*Theologische Zeitschrift*
UF	*Ugaritische Forschungen*
VT	*Vetus Testamentum*
VTSup	*Supplements to Vetus Testamentum*
WMANT	Wissenschaftliche Monographien zum Alten und Neuen Testament
WTJ	Westminster Theological Journal
WZLU	*Wissenschaftliche Zeitschrift Leipziger Universität*
ZÄS	*Zeitschrift für ägyptische Sprache und Altertumskunde*
ZAW	*Zeitschrift für die alttestamentliche Wissenschaft*
ZDMG	*Zeitschrift der deutschen morgenländischen Gesellschaft*
ZDPV	*Zeitschrift des deutschen Palästina-Vereins*
ZTK	*Zeitschrift für Theologie und Kirche*

For full details of entries marked * see Bibliography

SELECTED BIBLIOGRAPHY

A. Translations, Texts, Dictionaries, and Grammars

The Revised Standard Version of the Bible.

The New English Bible.

Tanakh: The Holy Scriptures. Philadelphia: Jewish Publication Society, 1985. (Also published in three volumes; vol. 3, *The Writings,* 1982.)

Biblia Hebraica Stuttgartensia. Ed. by Kurt Elliger and Wilhelm Rudolph. Stuttgart, 1967–77.

Septuaginta. Ed. by Alfred Rahlfs. Stuttgart, 1962.

Biblia Sacra. Iuxta Vulgatem Versionem. Ed. by Robert Weber. Stuttgart, 1969.

Baumgartner, Walter, and J. J. Stamm, eds. *Hebräisches und aramäisches Lexicon zum Alten Testament.* 3rd edition. I (1967), II (1974), III (1983). Leiden.

Brown, Francis; S. R. Driver; and C. A. Briggs. *A Hebrew and English Lexicon of the Old Testament, with an Appendix Containing the Biblical Aramaic.* Oxford, 1907.

Gesenius, F. W., *Hebrew Grammar,* rev. by E. Kautzsch; 2nd English edition, ed. and tr. by A. E. Cowley. Oxford, 1910.

Hatch, E., and H. A. Redpath. *A Concordance to the Septuagint and the other Greek Versions of the Old Testament (including the Apocryphal Books).* Oxford, 1897.

Jastrow, Marcus. *A Dictionary of the Targumim, the Talmud Babli and Yerushalmi, and the Midrashic Literature.* New York, 1950.

Joüon, Paul. *Grammaire de l'hébreu biblique.* Rome, 1955.

Köhler, Ludwig, and Walter Baumgartner, eds. *Lexicon in Veteris Testamenti Libros.* 2nd edition, Leiden, 1958.

Williams, Ronald J. *Hebrew Syntax.* 2nd edition. Toronto, 1976.

B. Commentaries, Monographs, and Articles on Qohelet and Related Topics

Allgeier, A. *Das Buch des Predigers oder Koheleth.* HSAT VI, 2. Bonn, 1925.

Alster, Bendt. *The Instruction of Šuruppak.* Copenhagen, 1974.

———. *Studies in Sumerian Proverbs.* Copenhagen, 1975.

Armstrong, J. F. "Ecclesiastes in Old Testament Theology," *Princeton Seminary Bulletin* 94 (1983) 16–25.

Barton, George A. *The Book of Ecclesiastes.* ICC. Edinburgh, 1908 (reprint, 1959).

Barucq, André. *Ecclésiaste.* Paris, 1968.

———. "Qoheleth." *Supplément au Dictionnaire de la Bible,* ed. by Henri Cazelles & André Feuillet. Paris, 1977.

Baumgärtel, F. "Die Ochsenstacheln und die Nägel in Koh 12,11," *ZAW* 81 (1969) 98.

Beentjes, P. C. "Recente visies op Qohelet," *Bijdragen: Tidschrift voor Filosofie en Theologie* 41 (1980) 436–444.

Bertram, Georg. "Hebräischer und griechischer Qohelet," *ZAW* 64 (1952) 26–49.

Bickell, Gustav. *Der Prediger über den Wert des Daseins.* Innsbruck, 1884.

Bickerman, Elias. *Four Strange Books of the Bible.* New York, 1967.

Bishop, E. F. F. "Pessimist in Palestine," *PEQ* 100 (1968) 33–41.

Blank, Sheldon H. "Ecclesiastes," 7–13 in *IDB* II. Nashville, 1962.

———. Prolegomenon to C. D. Ginsburg, *Coheleth.* New York, 1970.

Braun, R. *Kohelet und die frühhellenistische Popularphilosophie.* BZAW 130. Berlin and New York, 1973.

Bream, Howard N. "Life Without Resurrection: Two Perspectives from Qoheleth," 49–65 in *A Light Unto My Path (Jacob M. Myers Festschrift).* Gettysburg Theological Studies 14, 1974.

Breton, S. "Qoheleth Studies," *BTB* 3 (1982) 22–50.

Bruns, J. Edgar. "The Imagery of Eccles. 12,6a," *JBL* 84 (1965) 428–430.

Buccellati, Giorgio. "Wisdom and Not: The Case of Mesopotamia," *JAOS* 101 (1981) 35–47.

Buzy, Denis. "Le portrait de la vieillesse (Ecclésiaste, xii,1–7)," *RB* 41 (1932) 329–340.

———. "La notion du bonheur dans l'Ecclésiaste," *RB* 43 (1934) 494–511.

———. *L'Ecclésiaste.* Paris, 1946.

Camp, Claudia V. *Wisdom and the Feminine in the Book of Proverbs.* Sheffield, 1986.

Castellino, G. "Qohelet and His Wisdom," *CBQ* 30 (1968) 15–28.

Ceresko, A. R. "The Function of Antanaclasis (*mṣ'* 'to find'// *mṣ'* 'to reach, overtake, grasp') in Hebrew Poetry, Especially in the Book of Qoheleth," *CBQ* 44 (1982) 551–569.

Chopineau, Jacques. "L'image de Qohelet dans l'exégèse contemporaine," *RHPR* 59 (1979) 595–603.

Corré, A. D. "A Reference to Epispasm in Koheleth," *VT* 4 (1954) 416–418.

Cosser, William. "The Meaning of 'Life' in Proverbs, Job, and Ecclesiastes," *Glasgow University Oriental Society Transactions* 15 (1953/54) 48–53.

Crenshaw, James L. "The Eternal Gospel (Eccl. 3:11)," 23–55 in *Essays in Old Testament Ethics,* ed. by James L. Crenshaw and John T. Willis. New York, 1974.

———, ed. *Studies in Ancient Israelite Wisdom (SAIW).* New York, 1975.

———. "The Shadow of Death in Qoheleth," 205–216 in *Israelite Wisdom: Theological and Literary Essays in Honor of Samuel Terrien,* ed. by John G. Gammie. Missoula, Mont., 1978.

———. "The Birth of Skepticism in Ancient Israel," 1–19 in *The Divine Helmsman,* ed. by James L. Crenshaw and Samuel Sandmel. New York, 1980.

———. *Old Testament Wisdom.* Atlanta, 1981.

———, ed. *Theodicy in the Old Testament.* Philadelphia and London, 1983a.

———. "Qohelet in Current Research," *HAR* 7 (1983b) 41–56.

———. *A Whirlpool of Torment.* Philadelphia, 1984.

———. "The Wisdom Literature," 369–407 in *The Hebrew Bible and Its Modern*

Interpreters, ed. by Douglas A. Knight and Gene M. Tucker. Philadelphia and Chico, Calif., 1985.

———. "Education in Ancient Israel," *JBL* 104 (1985) 601–615.

———. "The Expression *mî yôdēa'* in the Hebrew Bible," *VT* 36 (1986) 274–288.

———. "Youth and Old Age in Qoheleth," *HAR* 11 (1987).

———. "Ecclesiastes," *Harper's Bible Commentary.* San Francisco (forthcoming).

———. Art. on "Ecclesiastes," *Evangelisches Kirchenlexikon* (forthcoming).

Crüsemann, Frank. "Die unveränderbare Welt. Überlegungen zur 'Krisis der Weisheit' beim Prediger (Kohelet)," 80–104 in *Der Gott der kleinen Leute,* ed. by Willi Schottroff and Wolfgang Stegemann. Munich, 1979a (ET, *The God of the Lowly,* Maryknoll, N.Y., 1984).

———. "Hiob und Kohelet. Ein Beitrag zum Verständnis des Hiobbuches," 373–393 in *Werden und Wirken des Alten Testaments,* ed. by A. Albertz et al. Göttingen, 1979b.

Dahood, Mitchell J. "Canaanite-Phoenician Influence in Qoheleth," *Bib* 33 (1952) 30–52, 191–221.

———. "Qoheleth and Recent Discoveries," *Bib* 39 (1958) 302–318.

———. "Qoheleth and Northwest Semitic Philology," *Bib* 43 (1962) 349–365.

———. "Canaanite Words in Qoheleth 10,20," *Bib* 46 (1965) 210–212.

———. "The Phoenician Background of Qoheleth," *Bib* 47 (1966) 264–282.

———. "The Phoenician Contribution to Biblical Wisdom," 123–148 in *The Role of the Phoenicians in the Interaction of Mediterranean Civilizations,* ed. by W. A. Ward. Beirut.

Delitzsch, Franz. *Koheleth.* Leipzig, 1875. (ET, *Commentary on the Song of Songs and Ecclesiastes,* Edinburgh, 1877.)

Delsman, W. C. "Zur Sprache des Buches Koheleth," 341–365 in *Von Kanaan bis Kerala.* Neukirchen-Vluyn, 1982.

Dhorme, P. "L'Ecclésiaste ou Job," *RB* 32 (1923) 5–27.

Dieterlé, Christiane. "A propos de la traduction de l'Ecclésiaste et de la Bible en français courant," *Etudes théologiques et religieuses* 59 (1984) 377–381.

Driver, G. R. "Problems and Solutions," *VT* 4 (1954) 225–245.

Du Plessis, S. J. "Aspects of Morphological Peculiarities of the Language of Qoheleth," 164–180 in *De Fructu Oris Sui* (Festschrift A. van Selms). Leiden, 1971.

Eaton, M. A. *Ecclesiastes: An Introduction and Commentary.* Leicester, 1983.

Ellermeier, Friedrich. "Das Verbum *Ḥwš* in Koh 2,25. Eine exegetische, auslegungsgeschichtliche und semasiologische Untersuchung," *ZAW* 75 (1963a) 197–217.

———. "Die Entmachtung der Weisheit im Denken Qohelets: Zu Text und Auslegung von Qoh 6:7–9," *ZTK* 60 (1963b) 1–20.

———. *Qohelet.* Teil I, Abschnitt 1. Herzberg, 1967.

———. *Qohelet.* Teil I, Abschnitt 2,7. Herzberg, 1970.

Eppenstein, Simon. *Aus dem Kohelet-Kommentar des Tanchum Jerushalmi.* Berlin, 1888.

Euringer, Sebastian. *Der Massorahtext des Koheleth kritisch untersucht.* Leipzig, 1890.

Fichtner, Johannes. *Die altorientalische Weisheit in ihrer israelitisch-jüdischen Ausprägung.* BZAW 62. Giessen, 1933.

Fiddes, P. S. *The Hiddenness of Wisdom in the Old Testament and Later Jewish Literature.* D.Phil. thesis, Oxford University, 1976.

Forman, Charles G. "The Pessimism of Ecclesiastes," *JSS* 3 (1958) 336–343.

———. "Koheleth's Use of Genesis," *JSS* 5 (1960) 256–263.

Fox, Michael V. "Frame-Narrative and Composition in the Book of Qohelet," *HUCA* 48 (1968) 83–106.

———. "The Identification of Quotations in Biblical Literature," *ZAW* 92 (1980) 416–431.

———. *The Song of Songs and the Ancient Egyptian Love Songs.* Madison, Wis., 1985.

———. "The Meaning of *Hebel* for Qoheleth," *JBL* 105 (1986) 409–427.

Fox, Michael V., and Bezalel Porten. "Unsought Discoveries: Qohelet 7:23–8:1a," *HS* 19 (1979) 26–38.

Frendo, Anthony. "The 'Broken Construct Chain' in Qoh 10:10b," *Bib* 62 (1981) 544–545.

Galling, Kurt. "Koheleth-Studien," *ZAW* 50 (1932) 276–299.

———. "Stand und Aufgabe der Kohelet-Forschung," *TR,* n.s., 6 (1934) 355–373.

———. "The Scepter of Wisdom: A Note on the Gold Sheath of Zendjirli and Ecclesiastes 12,11" *BASOR* 119 (1950) 15–18.

———. *Die Krise der Aufklärung in Israel.* Mainz, 1952.

———. "Das Rätsel der Zeit im Urteil Kohelets (Koh 3,1–15)," *ZTK* 58 (1961) 1–15.

———. *Der Prediger.* HAT I, 18 (1st ed. 1940). Tübingen, 1969.

Gammie, John. "Stoicism and Anti-Stoicism in Qoheleth," *HAR* 9 (1985) 169–187.

Genung, John F. *Ecclesiastes, Words of Kohelet.* Boston, 1904.

Gese, Hartmut. *Lehre und Wirklichkeit in der alten Weisheit.* Tübingen, 1958.

———. "Die Krisis der Weisheit bei Kohelet," 139–151 in *SPOA.* Paris, 1963 (ET in Crenshaw, 1983a, 141–153).

Gibson, J. C. L. *Canaanite Myths and Legends.* 2nd edition. Edinburgh, 1978.

Gilbert, Maurice. "La description de la vieillesse en Qohelet XII,7, est-elle allégorique?" 96–109 in *VT Sup., Congress Volume, Vienna, 1980.* Leiden, 1981.

Ginsberg, H. Lewis. *Studies in Kohelet.* New York, 1950.

———. "Koheleth 12:4 in Light of Ugaritic," *Syria* 33 (1951) 99–101.

———. "Supplementary Studies in Kohelet," *PAAJR* (1952) 35–62.

———. "The Structure and Contents of the Book of Koheleth," *VTSup* 3 (1955) 138–149.

———. "The Quintessence of Koheleth," 47–59 in *Biblical and Other Studies,* ed. by Alexander Altmann. Cambridge, Mass., 1963.

Ginsburg, Christian D. *The Song of Songs and Coheleth.* New York, 1857 (reprint 1970).

Gladson, Jerry A. *Retributive Paradoxes in Proverbs 10–29.* Ph.D. dissertation, Vanderbilt University, 1978.

Glasser, E. *Le procès du bonheur par Qohelet.* Paris, 1970.

Goldin, Judah. "The End of Ecclesiastes: Literal Exegesis and Its Transformation," *Lown Institute for Judaistic Studies* 3 (1966) 135–158.

Golka, Friedrich. "Die israelitische Weisheitsschule oder 'des Kaisers neue Kleider,'" *VT* 33 (1983) 257–270.

Good, Edwin M. "The Unfilled Sea: Style and Meaning in Ecclesiastes 1:2–11," 59–73 in *Israelite Wisdom,* ed. by John G. Gammie et al. Missoula, Mont., 1978.

Gordis, Robert. "Eccles. 1:17: Its Text and Interpretation," *JBL* 56 (1937) 323–330.

———. "Quotations in Wisdom Literature," *JQR* 30 (1939/40) 123–147.

———. "The Social Background of Wisdom Literature," *HUCA* 18 (1943/44) 77–118 (= *Poets, Prophets, and Sages,* Bloomington, Ind., 1971, 160–197).

———. "The Original Language of Qohelet," *JQR* 37 (1946/47) 67–84.

———. "Quotations as a Literary Usage in Biblical, Oriental, and Rabbinic Literature," *HUCA* 22 (1949) 157–219 (= *Poets, Prophets, and Sages,* Bloomington, Ind., 1971, 104–159).

———. "The Translation Theory of Qohelet Re-examined," *JQR* 40 (1949/50) 103–116.

———. "Koheleth—Hebrew or Aramaic?" *JBL* 71 (1952) 93–109.

———. "Was Koheleth a Phoenician?" *JBL* 74 (1955) 103–114.

———. "Qohelet and Qumran—A Study of Style," *Bib* 41 (1960) 395–410.

———. *Koheleth—the Man and His World.* (First published 1951; 2nd ed., New York, 1968).

———. "Virtual Quotations in Job, Sumer and Qumran," *VT* 31 (1981) 410–427.

Gorssen, L. "La cohérence de la conception de Dieu dans l'Ecclésiaste," *ETL* 46 (1970) 282–324.

Graetz, Heinrich. *Kohelet.* Leipzig, 1871.

Hasel, Gerhard F. "Review of Ellermeier's *Qohelet,*" *BO* 26 (1969) 392–394.

Haupt, Paul. *Koheleth oder Weltschmerz in der Bibel.* Leipzig, 1905.

Hengel, Martin. *Judaism and Hellenism.* Philadelphia, 1974.

Hermisson, Hans Jürgen. *Studien zur israelitischen Spruchweisheit.* WMANT 28. Neukirchen, 1968.

Herrmann, W. "Zu Koheleth 3,14," *WZLU* 3 (1953/54) 293.

Hertzberg, Hans Wilhelm. "Palästinische Bezüge im Buche Kohelet," *ZDPV* 73 (1957) 13–24 (= 63–73 in *Festschrift Friedrich Baumgärtel.* Erlangen, 1959).

———. *Der Prediger.* KAT, n.s., xvii, 4. Gütersloh, 1963.

Hessler, B. "Koheleth: The Veiled God," *The Bridge* 1 (1955) 191–206.

Höffken, Peter. "Das Ego des Weisen," *TZ* 4 (1985) 121–135.

Holm-Nielsen, Svend. "On the Interpretation of Qoheleth in Early Christianity," *VT* 24 (1974) 168–177.

———. "The Book of Ecclesiastes and the Interpretation of It in Jewish and Christian Theology," *ASTI* 10 (1975/76) 38–96.

Holzclaw, Brooks. *The Septuagint Book of Ecclesiastes.* Ph.D. dissertation, Hebrew Union College–Jewish Institute of Religion, Cincinnati, 1971.

Horton, Ernest. "Koheleth's Concept of Opposites," *Numen* 19 (1972) 1–21.

Humbert, Paul. *Recherches sur les sources égyptiennes de la littérature sapientiale d'Israël.* Neuchatel, 1929.

Hyvärinen, Kyösti. *Die Übersetzung von Aquila.* Coniectanea Biblica. Lund, 1977.

Irwin, William A. "Eccles. 4:13–16," *JNES* 3 (1944) 255–257.

James, Kenneth W. "Ecclesiastes: Precursor of Existentialists," *The Bible Today* 22 (1984) 85–90.

Japhet, Sara, and Robert Salters. *The Commentary of R. Samuel ben Meir Rashbam on Qoheleth.* Jerusalem, 1985.

Jasper, F. N. "Ecclesiastes: A Note for Our Time," *Int* 21 (1967) 259–273.

Jastrow, Morris, Jr. *A Gentle Cynic.* Philadelphia and London, 1919.

Jenni, Ernst. "Das Wort *'ōlām* im Alten Testament, *ZAW* 64 (1952) 197–248; 65 (1953) 1–35.

Johnson, R. F. *A Form Critical Analysis of the Sayings in the Book of Ecclesiastes.* Ph.D. dissertation, Emory University, 1973.

Johnston, Robert K. "Confessions of a Workaholic: A Reappraisal of Qoheleth," *CBQ* 38 (1976) 14–28.

Johnstone, W. " 'The Preacher' as Scientist," *SJT* 20 (1967) 210–221.

Joüon, Paul. "Notes philologiques sur le texte hébreu d'Ecclésiaste," *Bib* 11 (1930) 419–425.

Kamenetzsky, Abraham S. "Die *P'šita* zu Koheleth," *ZAW* 24 (1904) 181–239.

———. "Die Rätselname Koheleth," *ZAW* 34 (1914) 225–228.

———. "Die ursprünglich beabsichtigte Aussprache der Pseudonyms QHLT," *OLZ* (1921) 11–15.

Kidner, Derek. *A Time to Mourn, and a Time to Dance.* Cambridge, 1976.

Kleinest, Paul. "Sind im Buche Koheleth ausserhebräische Einflüsse anzuerkennen?" *TSK* 56 (1883) 761–782.

Klopfenstein, Martin A. "Die Skepsis des Qohelet," *TZ* 28 (1972) 97–109.

Knobel, P. S. *Targum Qoheleth: A Linguistic and Exegetical Inquiry.* Ph.D. dissertation, Yale University, 1976.

Knoph, Carl S. "The Optimism of Koheleth," *JBL* 49 (1930) 195–199.

Kroeber, Rudi. *Der Prediger.* Berlin, 1963.

———. " 'Der Prediger.' Ein Werk der altjüdischen Weisheitsliteratur," *Altertum* 11 (1965) 195–209.

Kugel, James L. "Ecclesiastes," 236–237 in *Harper's Bible Dictionary.* San Francisco, 1985.

Kuhn, Gottfried. *Erklärung des Buches Koheleth.* BZAW 43. Giessen, 1926.

Lambert, W. L. *Babylonian Wisdom Literature.* Oxford, 1960.

Lang, Bernhard. *Die weisheitliche Lehrrede.* Stuttgart, 1972.

———. "Schule und Unterricht im alten Israel," 186–201 in *La sagesse de l'Ancien Testament.* Gembloux, 1979.

———. *Wisdom and the Book of Proverbs.* New York, 1986.

Lauha, Aarre. "Die Krise des religiösen Glaubens bei Kohelet," *VTSup* 3 (1960) 183–191.

———. *Kohelet.* BKAT 19. Neukirchen-Vluyn, 1978.

———. "Kohelets Verhältnis zur Geschichte," 393–401 in *Die Botschaft und die Boten,* ed. by Jörg Jeremias and Lothar Perlit. Neukirchen-Vluyn, 1981.

Leahy, Michael. "The Meaning of Ecclesiastes 12:2–5," *ITQ* 19 (1952) 297–300.

Lemaire, André. *Les écoles et la formation de la Bible dans l'ancien Israël.* Orbis Biblicus et Orientalis 39. Fribourg and Göttingen, 1981.

Levy, Ludwig. *Das Buch Qoheleth. Ein Beitrag zur Geschichte des Sadduzäismus kritisch untersucht.* Leipzig, 1912.

Lichtheim, Miriam. *Ancient Egyptian Literature.* Berkeley, Calif. I (1975), II (1976), III (1980).

———. *Late Egyptian Wisdom Literature in the International Context.* Orbis Biblicus et Orientalis. Göttingen, 1983.

Lindenberger, James M. *The Aramaic Proverbs of Ahiqar.* Baltimore, 1983.

Loader, J. A. "Qohelet 3:2–8—a 'Sonnet' in the Old Testament," *ZAW* 81 (1969) 240–242.

———. *Polar Structures in the Book of Qohelet.* BZAW 152. Berlin and New York, 1979.

———. *Ecclesiastes.* Grand Rapids, 1986.

Lohfink, Norbert. "Technik und Tod nach Koheleth," 27–35 in *Strukturen christlicher Existenz. Festgabe F. Wulf,* 1968.

———. "War Kohelet ein Frauenfeind?" in *La Sagesse de l'Ancien Testament.* Gembloux, 1979, 259–287.

———. *Kohelet.* Die neue Echter Bibel. Stuttgart, 1980.

———. "*Melek, šallîṭ* und *môšēl* bei Kohelet und die Aufassungszeit des Buchs," *Bib* 62 (1981) 535–543.

———. "Warum ist der Tor unfähig, Böse zu handeln?" *ZDMG* Sup. 5 (1983) 113–120.

Loretz, Oswald. "Zur Darbietungsform der 'Ich-Erzählung' im Buche Qohelet," *CBQ* 25 (1963) 46–59.

———. *Qohelet und der alte Orient.* Freiburg, 1964.

———. "Gleiches Los trifft alle! Die Antwort des Buches Qohelet," *Bibel und Kirche* 20 (1965) 6–8.

———. "Altorientalische und kanaanäische Topoi im Buche Kohelet," *UF* 12 (1980) 267–286.

Ludder, E. "Gott und Welt nach dem Prediger Salomo," *STU* 28 (1958) 105–114.

Lys, Daniel. *L'Ecclésiaste ou que vaut la vie?* Paris, 1977.

MacDonald, Duncan Black. "Eccl. iii 11," *JBL* 18 (1899) 212–213.

———. *The Hebrew Philosophical Genius.* Princeton, 1936.

MacIntosh, A. A. "A Consideration of Hebrew G'R," *VT* 19 (1969) 471–479.

Mack, Burton L. *Logos und Sophia. Untersuchungen zur Weisheitstheologie im hellenistischen Judentum.* Göttingen, 1973.

McNeile, Alan H. *An Introduction to Ecclesiastes.* Cambridge, 1904.

Maillot, A. *La contestation. Commentaire de l'Ecclésiaste.* Lyon, 1971.

Margoliouth, D. S. "The Prologue of Ecclesiastes," *Expositor* 8 (1911) 463–470.

Miller, Athanasius. "Aufbau und Grundproblem des Predigers," *Miscellanea Biblica* 2 (1934) 104–122.

Mitchell, Hinckley G. " 'Work' in Ecclesiastes," *JBL* 32 (1913) 123–138.

Montgomery, James A. "Notes on Ecclesiastes," *JBL* 43 (1924) 241–244.

Muilenburg, James. "A Qoheleth Scroll from Qumran," *BASOR* 135 (1954) 20–28.

Mulder, J. S. M. "Qoheleth's Division and Also Its Main Point," 140–159 in *Von Kanaan bis Kerala* (Festschrift J. P. M. van der Ploeg), ed. by W. C. Delsman et al. Neukirchen-Vluyn, 1982.

Müller, D. "Der gute Hirte: Ein Beitrag zur Geschichte ägyptischer Bildrede," *ZÄS* 86 (1961) 126–144.

Müller, Hans-Peter. "Wie sprach Qohälät von Gott?" *VT* 18 (1968) 507–521.

———. "Neige der althebräischen 'Weisheit.' Zum Denken Qohäläts," *ZAW* 90 (1978) 238–264.

Müller, Hans-Peter, and M. Krause. "Chakham," *TDOT* IV, 364–385.

Murphy, Roland E. "The Pensées of Coheleth," *CBQ* 17 (1955) 304–314.

———. "Qoheleth's 'Quarrel' with the Fathers," 235–245 in *From Faith to Faith* (Donald G. Miller Festschrift), ed. by D. Y. Hadidian. Pittsburgh, 1979.

———. *Wisdom Literature.* FOTL 13. Grand Rapids, 1981.

———. "Qohelet Interpreted: The Bearing of the Past on the Present," *VT* 32 (1982) 331–337.

———. "Wisdom and Creation," *JBL* 104 (1985) 3–11.

———, ed. *Medieval Exegesis of Wisdom Literature: Essays by Beryl Smalley.* Atlanta, 1986a.

———. "Wisdom's Song: Proverbs 1:20–33," *CBQ* 48 (1986b) 456–460.

Neher, André. *Notes sur Qohelet.* Paris, 1951.

Nel, Philip Johannes. *The Structure and Ethos of the Wisdom Admonitions in Proverbs.* BZAW 158. Berlin and New York, 1982.

Nötscher, F. *Kohelet.* Würzburg, 1954.

———. "Schicksal und Freiheit," *Bib* 40 (1959) 446–462.

Ogden, Graham S. "The 'Better'-Proverb (Tôb-Spruch), Rhetorical Criticism, and Qoheleth," *JBL* 96 (1977) 489–505.

———. "Qoheleth's Use of the 'Nothing Is Better' Form," *JBL* 98 (1979) 339–350.

———. "Historical Allusion in Qoheleth IV 13–16?" *VT* 30 (1980a) 309–315.

———. "Qoheleth IX 17—X 20," *VT* 30 (1980b) 27–37.

———. "Qoheleth IX 1–16," *VT* 32 (1982) 158–169.

———. "Qoheleth XI 1–6," *VT* 33 (1983) 222–230.

———. "The Mathematics of Wisdom: Qoheleth IV 1–12," *VT* 34 (1984a) 446–453.

———. "Qoheleth XI 7–XII 8: Qoheleth's Summons to Enjoyment and Reflection," *VT* 34 (1984b) 27–38.

———. "The Interpretation of *dor* in Ecclesiastes 1.4," *JSOT* 34 (1986) 91–92.

Osborn, Noel D. "A Guide for Balanced Living: An Exegetical Study of Ecclesiastes 7:1–14," *Bible Translator* 21 (1970) 185–196.

Pardee, Dennis. "The Semitic Root *mrr* and the Etymology of Ugaritic *mr(r)//brk,*" *UF* 10 (1978) 249–288.

Pedersen, Johannes. "Scepticisme israélite," *RHPR* 10 (1931) 317–370.

Perles, Felix. "A Miscellany of Lexical and Textual Notes on the Bible," *JQR* 2 (1911/12).

Pfeiffer, Egon. "Die Gottesfurcht im Buche Kohelet," 133–158 in *Gottes Wort und Gottes Land. Festschrift H. W. Hertzberg.* Göttingen, 1965.

Pfeiffer, Robert H. "The Peculiar Skepticism of Ecclesiastes," *JBL* 53 (1934) 100–109.

Plöger, Otto. "Wahre die richtige Mitte; solch Mass ist in allen das Beste!" 159–173 in *Gottes Wort und Gottes Land. Festschrift H. W. Hertzberg.* Göttingen, 1965.

Plumptre, E. H. *Ecclesiastes.* Cambridge, 1881.

Podechard, E. *L'Ecclésiaste.* Paris, 1912.

Preuss, Horst D. "Das Gottesbild der älteren Weisheit Israels," *VTSup* 23 (1972) 117–145.

Priest, John F. "Where Is Wisdom to Be Placed?" *JBR* 31 (1963) 275–282.

———. "Ecclesiastes," 249–250 in *IDBSup.* Nashville, 1976.

Rad, Gerhard von. *Old Testament Theology,* 2 vols., London and Edinburgh, 1962.

———. "Das Werke Jahwes," 290–299 in *Studia Biblia et Semitica* (Festschrift Th. Vriezen). Wageningen, 1966.

———. *Wisdom in Israel.* London, 1972.

Rainey, Anson. "Study of Ecclesiastes," *Concordia* (1964) 148–157.

———. "A Second Look at 'amal' in Qoheleth," *Concordia* 36 (1965) 805.

Rankin, Oliver S. *Israel's Wisdom Literature.* Edinburgh, 1936.

———. "The Book of Ecclesiastes," *IB* V. Nashville, 1956.

Ranston, Harry. "Koheleth and the Early Greeks," *JTS* 24 (1923) 160–169.

———. *Ecclesiastes and the Early Greek Wisdom Literature.* London, 1925.

———. *The Old Testament Wisdom Books and Their Teaching.* London, 1930.

Reif, Stefan C. "Review of C. F. Whitley's *Koheleth,*" *VT* 31 (1981) 120–126.

Reines, C. W. "Koheleth on Wisdom and Wealth," *JJS* 5 (1954a) 80–84.

———. "Koheleth VIII,10," *JJS* (1954b) 86–87.

Rofé, Alexander. " 'The Angel' in Qoh 5:5 in the Light of a Wisdom Dialogue Formula" [Hebrew], *Eretz Israel* 14 (1978) 105–109.

Rousseau, François, "Structure de Qohelet I 4–11 et plan du livre," *VT* 31 (1981) 200–217.

Rudolph, Wilhelm. *Vom Buch Kohelet.* Münster, 1959.

Rylaarsdam, J. Coert. *Revelation in Jewish Wisdom Literature.* Chicago, 1946.

Salters, Robert B. "Qoheleth and the Canon," *ExpT* 86 (1975) 339–342.

———. "A Note on the Exegesis of Ecclesiastes 3 15b," *ZAW* 88 (1976) 419–420.

———. "Text and Exegesis in Koh 10,19," *ZAW* 89 (1977) 423–426.

———. "Notes on the History of the Interpretation of Koh 5,5," *ZAW* 90 (1978) 95–101.

———. "Notes on the Interpretation of Qoh 6,2," *ZAW* 91 (1979) 282–289.

Savignac, J. de. "La sagesse du Qôhéléth et l'épopée de Gilgamesh," *VT* 28 (1978) 318–323.

Sawyer, John F. A. "The Ruined House in Ecclesiastes 12: A Reconstruction of the Original Parable," *JBL* 94 (1976) 519–531.

Schiffer, S. *Das Buch Kohelet, nach der Auffassung der Weisen des Talmud und Midrasch und der jüdischen Erklärer des Mittelalters I.* Frankfurt am Main, 1884.

Schmid, Hans Heinrich. *Wesen und Geschichte der Weisheit.* BZAW 101. Berlin, 1966.

———. *Gerechtigkeit als Weltordnung.* BHT 40. Tübingen, 1968.

Schmidt, J. *Studien zur Stilistik der alttestamentlichen Spruchliteratur.* Münster, 1936.

Schoors, Anton. "The Particle *ki,*" *OTS* 21 (1981) 240–276.

———. "Kethibh-Qere in Ecclesiastes," 215–222 in *Studia Paulo Naster Oblata* II. Orientalia Antiqua, ed. by J. Quaegebeur. (Orientalia Lovaniensia Analecta 13.) Louvain, 1982a.

———. "La structure littéraire de Qoheleth," *Orientalia Lovaniensia Periodica* 13 (1982b) 91–116.

Scott, R. B. Y. *Proverbs, Ecclesiastes.* AB 18. Garden City, N.Y. 1965.

Serrano, J. J. "I Saw the Wicked Buried (Ecc 8,10)," *CBQ* 16 (1954) 168–170.

Shaffer, Aaron. "The Mesopotamian Background of Qohelet 4:9–12" [Hebrew], *Eretz Israel* 8 (1967) 246–250.

———. "New Information on the Origin of the 'Three-fold Cord' " [Hebrew], *Eretz Israel* 9 (1969) 159–160.

Shank, H. C. "Qohelet's World and Lifeview as Seen in His Recurring Phrases," *WTJ* 37 (1974) 57–73.

Sheppard, Gerald T. "The Epilogue to Qoheleth as Theological Commentary," *CBQ* 39 (1977) 182–189.

———. *Wisdom as a Hermeneutical Construct.* BZAW 151. Berlin and New York, 1980.

Short, R. L. *A Time to Be Born—A Time to Die: The Images and Insights of Ecclesiastes for Today.* New York, 1973.

Siegfried, K. *Prediger und Hoheslied.* HAT II, 3/2. Göttingen, 1898.

Simpson, W. K., ed. *The Literature of Ancient Egypt.* New Haven and London, 1972.

Skehan, P. W. *Studies in Israelite Poetry and Wisdom. CBQ* Monograph Series 1. Washington, 1971.

Smalley, Beryl. *Medieval Exegesis of Wisdom Literature: Essays by Beryl Smalley,* ed. by Roland E. Murphy. Atlanta, 1986.

Smith, L. L. "Critical Evaluation of the Book of Ecclesiastes," *JBR* 21 (1953) 100–105.

Snaith, Norman H. "Time in the Old Testament," in *Promise and Fulfillment: Essays Presented to S. H. Hooke.* Edinburgh, 1963.

Staerk, W. "Zur Exegese von Koh 10,20 und 11,1," *ZAW* 59 (1942/43) 216–218.

Staples, W. E. "The 'Vanity' of Ecclesiastes," *JNES* 4 (1943) 95–104.

———. " 'Profit' in Ecclesiastes," *JNES* 4 (1945) 87–96.

———. "The Meaning of *ḥepeṣ* in Ecclesiastes," *JNES* 24 (1965) 110–112.

Steinemann, J. *Ainsi parlait Qohèlèt.* Paris, 1955.

Stiglmair, A. "Weisheit und Jahweglaube im Buche Kohelet," *TTZ* 83 (1974) 257–283.

Strobel, Albert. *Das Buch Prediger (Kohelet).* Düsseldorf, 1967.

Taylor, C. *The Dirge of Coheleth.* London, 1874.

Terrien, Samuel. *Till the Heart Sings.* Philadelphia, 1985.

Thilo, Martin, *Der Prediger Salomo.* Bonn, 1923.

Torrey, Charles C. "The Question of the Original Language of Qohelet," *JQR* 39 (1948–49) 151–160.

———. "The Problem of Ecclesiastes IV,13–16," *VT* 2 (1952) 175–177.

Trible, Phyllis. "Wisdom Builds a Poem: The Architecture of Proverbs 1:20–33," *JBL* 94 (1975) 509–518.

Tyler, Thomas. *Ecclesiastes.* London, 1899.

Vawter, Bruce. "Intimations of Immortality in the Old Testament," *JBL* 91 (1972) 158–171.

———. "Prov. 8:22: Wisdom and Creation," *JBL* 99 (1980) 205–216.

———. "Yahweh: Lord of the Heavens and the Earth," *CBQ* 48 (1986) 461–467.

Vergote, Jozef. "La notion de Dieu dans les livres de sagesse égyptiens," *SPOA* (1963) 159–190.

Vischer, Wilhelm. *Der Prediger Salomo.* München, 1926.

———. *Der Prediger Salomo im Spiegel Michael de Montaigne's.* Bethel, 1933.

Volz, Paul. "Koheleth," in *Hiob und Weisheit.* Göttingen, 1911.

Waard, Jan de. "The Translator and Textual Criticism (with Particular Reference to Eccl 2,25)," *Bib* 60 (1979) 509–529.

———. "The Structure of Qoheleth," 57–63 in *Proceedings of the 8th World Congress of Jewish Studies.* Jerusalem, 1982.

Wagner, M. *Die lexikalischen und grammaticalischen Aramäismen im alttestamentlichen Hebräisch.* BZAW 96. Berlin, 1966.

Waldman, Nahum M. "The *dābār ra'* of Eccl 8:3," *JBL* 98 (1979) 407–408.

Walsh, Jerome T. "Despair as a Theological Virtue in the Spirituality of Ecclesiastes," *BTB* 12 (1982) 46–49.

Whitley, C. F. *Koheleth.* BZAW 148. Berlin and New York, 1979a.

———. "Koheleth and Ugaritic Parallels," *UF* 11 (1979b) 811–824.

Whybray, R. N. *The Intellectual Tradition in the Old Testament.* BZAW 135. Berlin and New York, 1974.

———. "Qoheleth the Immoralist? (Qoh 7:16–17)," 191–204 in *Israelite Wisdom,* ed. by John G. Gammie. Missoula, Mont., 1978.

———. "Conservatisme et radicalisme dans Qohelet," 65–81 in *Sagesse et Religion* (Colloque de Strasbourg, October 1976), 1979.

———. "The Identification and Use of Quotations in Ecclesiastes," *VTSup* 32 (1980a) 435–451.

———. *Two Jewish Theologies: Job and Ecclesiastes.* Hull, 1980b.

———. "Qoheleth, Preacher of Joy," *JSOT* 23 (1982) 87–98.

Wilch, John R. *Time and Event.* Leiden, 1969.

Wildeboer, Gerrit. "*Der Prediger,*" in *Die fünf Megillot,* ed. by Karl Budde et al. KHC 17. Freiburg, 1898.

Williams, James G. "What Does It Profit a Man?: The Wisdom of Koheleth," *Judaism* 20 (1971) 179–193 (= Crenshaw, *SAIW,* 1976, 375–389).

———. *Those Who Ponder Proverbs.* Sheffield, 1981.

Williams, Ronald J. "The Sages of Ancient Egypt in the Light of Recent Scholarship," *JAOS* 101 (1981) 1–19.

Winston, David. *The Wisdom of Solomon.* AB 43. Garden City, N.Y., 1979.

Witzenrath, Hagia. *Süss ist das Licht.* St. Ottilien, 1979.

Wölfel, Eberhard. *Luther und die Skepsis.* Munich, 1958.

Wright, Addison D. G. "The Riddle of the Sphinx: The Structure of the Book of Qoheleth," *CBQ* 30 (1968) 313–334.

———. "The Riddle of the Sphinx Revisited: Numerical Patterns in the Book of Qoheleth," *CBQ* 42 (1980) 35–51.

———. "Additional Numerical Patterns in Qoheleth," *CBQ* 45 (1983) 32–43.

Zapletal, Vincenz. *Das Buch Koheleth kritisch und metrisch untersucht.* Freiburg, 1911.

Zimmerli, Walther. "Zur Struktur der alttestamentlichen Weisheit," *ZAW* 51 (1933) 177–204 (ET in Crenshaw, *SAIW,* 175–207).

———. *Das Buch des Predigers Salomo.* ATD xvi, 1. Göttingen, 1962.

———. "Ort und Grenze der Weisheit im Rahmen der alttestamentlichen Theologie," 121–138 in *SPOA,* 1963 (ET in Crenshaw, *SAIW,* 314–326).

———. "Das Buch Kohelet—Traktat oder Sentenzensammlung?" *VT* 24 (1974) 221–230.

Zimmerman, Frank. "The Aramaic Provenance of Qohelet," *JQR* 36 (1945/46) 17–45.

———. "The Question of Hebrew in Qohelet," *JQR* 40 (1949/50) 79–102.

———. *The Inner World of Qoheleth.* New York, 1973.

Zirkel, G. *Untersuchungen über den Prediger mit philosophischen und kritischen Bemerkungen.* Würzburg, 1792.

INTRODUCTION

Life is profitless; totally absurd. This oppressive message lies at the heart of the Bible's strangest book. Enjoy life if you can, advises the author, for old age will soon overtake you. And even as you enjoy, know that the world is meaningless. Virtue does not bring reward. The deity stands distant, abandoning humanity to chance and death.

These views contrast radically with earlier teachings expressed in the book of Proverbs. That book affirms a world in which fear of God and adherence to the insights of previous generations guarantee long life, prosperity, progeny, and honor. God secures well-being for the righteous and self-destruction for the wicked.

Those sages saw society's inequities, but a few inexplicable cracks in the nexus of deed and consequence (Gladson) did not invalidate belief in the overall goodness of a moral God's creation. Then, over time, wisdom teachers lost sight of the anomalies, or found them so threatening that they hardened their dogma in defense. External circumstances absolutely reflect inner worth, went the axiom. But such optimism defies reality. In the resulting religious/intellectual crisis, the voices of Job and Qohelet rose to express alternate perspectives (Gese 1963; Lauha 1960). The unknown author of Job portrays an extreme instance of innocent suffering, but even Job himself assumes a causal connection between deed and consequence. The prose ending to the story endorses this view by restoring Job's fortune.

Qohelet, the author of the book of Ecclesiastes, shows no such conservatism. Qohelet discerns no moral order at all. Humans cannot know God's disposition. This argument strikes at the foundation of the sages' universe.[1]

Qohelet's Teachings

Traditional sages sought advantage in life through rational thought and virtuous deeds. Qohelet declares such effort futile. The fastest runner may

[1]Of the extensive secondary literature on biblical wisdom, the comprehensive treatments by von Rad (1972) and Crenshaw (1981) update older studies by Rankin and Fichtner. Although different in kind, valuable studies derive from Rylaarsdam, Whybray (1974), and Sheppard (1980).

lose a race; and the mightiest warrior, the battle. Smart people may go hungry, skillful ones be ignored. Chance determines everything—riches, fame, power, pleasure, progeny—over it none can exercise control.

In the book of Proverbs (and later in Sirach and Wisdom of Solomon), personified Wisdom speaks directly to people, in her care for human welfare.[2] In Ecclesiastes, the heavens remain silent. Nor does Qohelet identify religious devotion with wisdom (Job 28:28). In Qohelet's belief, God withholds vital information even from the pious.

This leaves the future hidden, utterly mysterious. Mesopotamian wisdom sought to predict events by observing signs.[3] Qohelet declares such effort futile. Even the monotonous cycles of nature defy prediction—*that* they will repeat is sure, but *when* and *how* remain obscure.

Such denigration of intellect is both humble and arrogant. Since Qohelet has been unable to understand reality, he concludes that none can do so. Dismissing the cumulative knowledge of generations, he declares all creation absurd and vexatious. However enlightened the wise person as opposed to a simpleton, they stand equal in the end.

Job attacks God directly, remaining on speaking terms with his adversary and ultimately provoking a dialogue. Qohelet refuses to address the deity, complaining instead to his own heart.[4] (His warning against striving with someone stronger may actually allude to Job.)[5] Qohelet says those attempting to approach God should speak sparingly, and advises worshipers to shun vows, because human weakness may render the promises empty. Be neither excessively virtuous nor overly wicked, he suggests—a superfluous warning, given Qohelet's belief in the ineffectiveness of human will.

To Qohelet, God's activity is as ominous as distant thunder. The sage finds God intent on demonstrating to people that they die just like beasts. The fact that life-breath returns to its source offers no comfort, for the heavenly judge does not keep court appointments. The book's few references to divine judgment disturb both thought and syntax. The forensic notion in the second epilogue (12:13–14) may have influenced references elsewhere. Qohelet himself probably equates divine judgment with death, which defies rational description.

---

[2]The personification of wisdom has evoked considerable discussion in recent literature. The state of the question can be ascertained in Lang (1986), Camp, Trible, Terrien, and Mack.

[3]Buccellati (1981) and Lambert (1960) accentuate the differences between Mesopotamian magical (omen) texts and biblical wisdom literature.

[4]The language may suggest discourse with one's inner being in the same way Egyptian literature describes conversation with one's *ba* (soul). Alternatively, Qohelet may mean no more than that he reflected on something.

[5]The similarities between the books of Job and Qohelet have led several critics to compare them, among the most stimulating Crüsemann (1979), Whybray (1980), and Lauha (1960).

Thunder rumbles even louder when Qohelet mentions God's gifts to human beings. One such gift lodges in the intellect, but sealed so that no one can discover its content. If Qohelet's language echoes Genesis 1–3, aesthetic categories have replaced theological ones: God made everything appropriate for its purpose (3:11). Yet while laughing and crying, speaking and keeping silence, planting and uprooting all have their times under the sun, we cannot discern the concrete occasions for each. Divine gifts resist human manipulation. No action assures divine favor, and indeed no one can even know whether God regards them favorably. Utter mystery prevails, beginning at the portals of life with the miracle of conception and gestation. The sovereign power that grants life may also recall it.

Under such a God, a hierarchy of authority offers no protection from human tyranny. Only once does Qohelet's conscience prompt him to speak out on behalf of the powerless, and there only to bewail the fact that they suffer uncomforted. The selfishness of wisdom literature in general finds full expression in Qohelet. His definitive literary fiction is that of the self-indulgent monarch. He assesses friendship in terms of protection from robbers and warmth on cold nights. He evaluates the world in terms of his own safety and comfort.

Humans have no power to correct divine inequities: "The crooked cannot be straightened, nor the missing counted." Yet this may be just as well, for Qohelet observes that when people do use their ingenuity they pursue wickedness.

The arbitrariness of death troubles Qohelet more than anything else. His predecessors believed in a positive correlation between virtue (or lack of it) and the timing and manner of one's death. They explained rare instances of incongruity by appeal to family or community influence. Qohelet denies any pattern at all in death's timing and choice of victims.

Because death cancels every human achievement, Qohelet concludes that life has no meaning. Death mocks personal ambition and frugality.[6] Qohelet realizes that death grips some people long before they actually die. These individuals may amass fortunes but they cannot enjoy the benefits. Qohelet

[6]Blank (1970, xxiv–xxv) mentions an instance of irony produced by "the last illusion of noble minds," the desire to achieve lasting fame. He recalls C. D. Ginsburg's reference to the immortal Moses Mendelssohn and Graetz's observation that "a century has elapsed since Mendelssohn provided an adequate commentary, which is no longer useful in any respect." Today, says Blank, no scholar gives a second thought to Graetz's solution to Qohelet—that large parts of the book reflect events from Herod's time. Podechard and Ginsburg discuss the history of the interpretation of Qohelet at great length; Holm-Nielsen, Goldin, Smalley, and Murphy (1982) also offer useful insights in this regard. Barucq has provided by far the best dictionary entry on Qohelet. For modern interpretation of Qohelet, five surveys have appeared: Galling (1932; 1934), Breton, Beentjes, and Crenshaw (1983).

considers them less fortunate than stillborns, who at least enjoy rest. Qohelet cites the tradition that "A living dog is better than a dead lion." Context suggests that he doubts the validity of such claims, for he explains the advantage of the living as awareness that they will die, but even that knowledge causes suffering. Qohelet finds in reality itself more cause for grief than celebration.

After death, what? Qohelet concedes ignorance, denying that anyone knows what occurs beyond the grave. In the concluding poem of the book (11:7–12:7) Qohelet compares old age and death to the collapse of an estate and contrasts the stormy, wintry darkness with nature's rejuvenation in the springtime. Literal and symbolic language combine to depict the silencing of the inhabitants of a stately house.[7] The darkness of death affects both slaves and owners, women and men. As professional mourners begin their march, readers perceive that the procession takes place outside their doors too. Nature's callous face turns to the living birds and plants, wholly unmoved by the human plight. Exquisite images portray the actual silencing of humankind: an expensive lamp falling from the wall, spilling its vital liquid, and a pulley breaking at a well, shattering the container into pieces and spilling its contents. Priceless commodities come to ruin: silver, gold, light, water.

Human life ends when its creator recalls the vivifying breath (making human life tantamount to a single act of breathing on God's part). One's brief existence under the sun comes to an end, and the death angel flies off, bearing its reluctant burden into the realm of the night.

The presence of inequities and the permanent sealing of injustice at death prompts Qohelet to despise life. Yet because he cannot welcome the destruction of personal identity he refuses to carry his argument to its logical conclusion. By contrast, comparable skeptics in Egypt and in Mesopotamia openly endorse suicide. "The Dispute Between a Man and His Soul [*ba*]"[8] likens death to—among other things—a sick man's recovery, the fragrance of myrrh and lotus, coming home from battle, the clearing of the sky, and longing for home after many years in captivity. In "A Pessimistic Dialogue Between a Master and Servant"[9] the master asks, "What is good?" and the slave responds: "To break my neck, your neck, throw (both) into the river—(that) is good." When the master retorts that he will break the

---

[7]Several analyses of the poem in 11:7–12:7 have recently appeared, each with a distinctive perspective: Sawyer (1976), Gilbert, Witzenrath, Ogden (1984), and Crenshaw (1987).

[8]The most useful translation of Egyptian texts, the three-volume work of Lichtheim, supplements earlier translations by Pritchard and Simpson. The essay by Williams is enormously helpful.

[9]I have used Lambert for Babylonian wisdom literature, as well as Pritchard. For Sumerian wisdom, I have consulted Alster; Buccellati has written a general essay on Mesopotamian wisdom that contains many good insights.

servant's neck, he hears a poignant question: "(Then) would my lord (wish to) live even three days after me?"[10]

Unlike these authors from other lands Qohelet opts for life. He even recommends the pursuit of pleasure during youth, when one normally has the energy to enjoy life. Qohelet acknowledges that some people lack the capacity to discover pleasure in its various forms—delicious food, desirable women, expensive clothing and perfumes. By disposition or disability, they find it impossible to follow Qohelet's advice, and life passes them by. But to those with ability to enjoy, Qohelet urges pleasure.[11] His language implies that his advice applies exclusively to men.[12] Unless his counsel has completely lost touch with reality (and nothing suggests such a reading of it), Qohelet instructs young *men* ("enjoy the woman you love") of the privileged class. He takes for granted their access to persons in authority and their possession of the means for a comfortable existence in the shade.

One need not assume that Qohelet recommends debauchery, although he tests its true possibilities as part of the royal experiment. He describes the supreme pleasure available to royalty in language that, although unclear to modern readers, is probably metonymic, breasts representing women of delight. In addition, the reference to enjoying the "woman" one loves is unusual if referring to one's wife. Yet Qohelet undoubtedly knows that surrender to passion carries risks, particularly when trifling with the affections of another's wife, so his advice probably falls short of encouraging the extreme licentiousness that the later author of Wisdom of Solomon attacks. Although sensual pleasure appeals to Qohelet, he frequently qualifies the anticipated pleasures with comments about life's brevity and absurdity, and he recommends the place of mourning over the house of revelry.

In recommending these little pleasures to soothe the troubled spirit, Qohelet makes the emancipating claim that God has already approved such drinking and eating. Little room exists here for a scrupulous conscience or for anxiety concerning religious duty. The reminder that God holds people responsible for their actions seems remarkably out of place, therefore, unless it witnesses to ambivalence within Qohelet's mind over the issue of divine justice. Does he believe that God soothes human anxiety about death

[10]Scholarly debate has not resolved the question whether this text is serious or humorous. In any event, it makes the point that a clever sage can relativize any issue, providing a justification for every alternative course of action. The result is resignation and ennui, for the attitude morally cripples.

[11]Gordis (1943/44) advanced the theory that professional wise men belonged to the upper classes; with reference to Qohelet, Bickerman wrote about the "philosophy of an acquisitive society." Crüsemann (1984) took a further step in this direction, describing Qohelet's mentality as calculative, one that measured everything against a monetary standard.

[12]The modern interpreter faces a dilemma: how to use inclusive language without distorting the sense of the original. I have tried to be attentive to both aspects of this problem, believing Qohelet in all probability misogynistic (*contra* Lohfink, 1979).

by allowing people to concentrate on pleasurable memories, or does Qohelet think the deity afflicts them with thoughts of unattainable pleasure? Perhaps the latter possibility comes closer to reality as he sees it.

This, then, Qohelet observes about the human situation. Wisdom's claim to secure one's existence is patently false. No discernible principle of order exists, no heavenly guarantor rewards good conduct and punishes evil deeds. The distant creator, if involved at all, punishes only flagrant affronts such as reneging on religious vows. Since death cancels every imagined gain, rendering life under the sun absurd, one should enjoy a woman, wine, and food before old age and death end even these fleeting pleasures. In sum, Qohelet examines experience and discovers nothing that will survive death's arbitrary blow. He then proceeds to report this discovery of life's absurdity and to advise young men on the best option in the light of stark reality. Such radical views indicate an intellectual crisis in the circle of the wise, at least among those who preserved Qohelet's teachings.

Literary Expression

What medium does Qohelet use for his message? No single genre governs everything spoken. However, the dominant literary type is reflection arising from personal observation. Qohelet seeks out experience of every kind as the most accurate path to insight. He looks, observes, considers, reflects, and testifies to the validity of his conclusions. His language emphasizes both the observation and subsequent reflection; for example, "I said in my heart" (1:16; 2:1, 15; 3:17), "I gave my heart" (1:13, 17; 8:9, 16), "I saw" (1:14; 2:24; 3:10, 16; 4:1, 4, 15; 5:17; 6:1; 7:15; 8:9, 10; 9:11, 13; 10:5, 7), "I know" (1:17; 2:14; 3:12, 14; 8:12), and "there is" (2:21; 6:1, 12; 8:14; 10:5). Repeated use of the personal pronoun *ʾ^{a}nî* (I) thrusts the ego of the speaker into prominence, leaving no doubt about his investment in what is being reported. Because the reflections vary from time to time, some interpreters distinguish between unified critical and broken critical reflections, or between meditative reflection and simple meditation (Ellermeier 1967, 66–79).

In the process of baring his soul Qohelet runs the risk that someone will question his authority to dare such observations. Others can easily dismiss the opinions of an individual as eccentric or palpably false. To counter this sort of response, an editor invests Qohelet with the authority of the wisest sage of all, King Solomon, and identifies him as a professional teacher who spoke reliable and pleasing words to his students (*b^{e}nî,* my son = my student). This secondary effort to create an ethos by consensus reinforces Qohelet's own striving to offer validation. He frequently stresses his firsthand experiences, personal perceptions, and testimony. If asked "How do you know?" Qohelet readily offers the answer, "I saw it."

The highly personal tone and disputative character of Qohelet's teachings lead some commentators to compare the book to a *diatribe* (Lohfink 1980). Although Qohelet does describe an opponent's views, which he proceeds to alter in some way or to oppose in toto, the book presents a monologue rather than a dialogue. Qohelet exposes the debate within his own mind, or to use his word, *lēb* (heart). To be sure, he sets the private interpretations of reality over against conventional wisdom. Because of the limited knowledge of schools in ancient Israel that characterizes biblical scholarship, it seems prudent to use the term "conventional wisdom" rather than refer to the wisdom of the schools.

The prominence of the *royal testament* in 1:12–2:16 (and possibly also in the conclusion resulting from the experiment, 2:17–26) has prompted some interpreters to characterize the entire book in this way (Loretz 1964; von Rad 1972, 226). However, this literary fiction appears limited to the above-mentioned unit, and one can explain the highly personal style apart from this genre. In keeping with Qohelet's abandonment of the fiction of royal authorship after the second chapter, the epilogues ignore it altogether. The royal fiction does not begin the book, as one would expect; instead, a description of natural phenomena and a comparable human situation sums up and evaluates Qohelet's teaching.

On the small scale, Qohelet uses *truth-statements* (often called sentences), "better than" sayings, instructions, traditional sayings, malediction and benediction, autobiographical narrative, example story, anecdote, parable, and antithesis. *Rhetorical questions,* which abound in the book (2:2, 15, 19, 25; 3:9, 21, 22; 4:8, 11; 5:5, 10, 15; 6:8 [twice], 11; 7:13, 16, 17; 8:1 [twice], 4, 7; 10:14), amount to negative truth-statements (that is, denials). The particle of existence *(yēš)* functions likewise to call attention to undeniable facts of life (10:5–7). Two collections of popular truth-statements fit badly into the structure of the book (7:1–12; 10:1–20), making it difficult if not impossible to determine whether Qohelet cites traditional wisdom or composes his own aphorisms. At times it seems that he takes over conventional wisdom and gives it a new twist: "A good reputation is preferable to expensive ointment, and the hour of death, to that of birth" (7:1). Qohelet uses the latter type of truth-statement freely, for the formula "This is preferable to (or better than) that" enables him to pretend to endorse traditional teachings but actually to challenge their veracity by introducing entirely different considerations (4:3, 6, 9, 13; 5:4 [5E]; 6:3, 9; 7:1, 2, 3, 5, 8; 9:4, 16, 18; cf. the emphatic form, "nothing is better than," 2:24; 3:12, 22; 8:15).

Conventional wisdom developed the *instruction* into a significant didactic tool, in both its positive and its negative forms. Exhortations and warnings shaped youngsters' lives in desired ways. Imperatives drew attention to the authority of teachers as they cautioned students against proscribed actions and encouraged them to follow teachings that brought life. Unlike truth-statements, which appealed to general consensus, instructions required supportive arguments. These defenses included, among other things, an appeal to personal authority and accumulated tradition; they consisted of threats, often illustrated by common experience, and of promises rooted in moral and religious tradition. Qohelet rarely uses the instruction, and when he does he grounds it in private experience. Because human efforts ultimately have limited value, and given the powerful role of chance, Qohelet exhorts young people to enjoy life. However, they must not forget God, the distant despot,[13] so Qohelet advises fear when drawing near for worship. Students must exercise similar caution, Qohelet warns, in dealing with earthly rulers whom none dare challenge.

Occasionally, Qohelet resorts to extreme expression of calamity and bliss. He juxtaposes *malediction and benediction* in 10:16–17, which characterizes a country on the basis of its rulers. In 4:10 Qohelet describes the calamitous result of falling when one lacks a companion to offer assistance.

The *autobiographical narrative* (1:12–2:16) forms the basis for conclusions about life (2:17–26). Qohelet uses a literary fiction here, making it difficult to know exactly how much of this derives from personal experience or how much the literary genre demands. He also converses with his heart, a convention in Egyptian literature as well (1:16; 2:1, 15; 3:17, 18; 7:23). Example stories occur in 4:13–16 and 9:14–15. The first story appears to combine typical and actual features (a youth rises from prison to the throne). The second story may be entirely hypothetical, or may actually recall an incident in which a poor, wise man (who had been captured?) used his powers of persuasion to rescue a doomed village. Anecdotes from Qohelet's personal experience appear throughout his observations. He recalls having seen a particularly poignant example of unrelieved oppression (4:1), he remembers a person who accumulated vast wealth but lacked power to enjoy it (6:1–6), and he complains about someone who lost everything in a business venture (5:13–17). The antithesis, which lay at the heart of earlier truth-statements in conventional wisdom, rarely occurs in Qohelet's teachings. A possible exception, 7:16–17, advises a path of moderation, but Whybray (1978) has recently challenged this standard interpretation.

The exquisite poem in 11:7–12:7, best understood as a *parable,* has prompted many interpreters to take it as an allegory. Actually, only 12:3–4a justifies this designation. The symbolism in these verses does not require a transference from the literal to a second object (Gilbert 1981). That is, "keepers of the house" may be just that, and "grinders" may refer to the

[13] Two interpreters have used this language freely—in my judgment, with justification (Pedersen, 360; Lauha 1955; 186; 1978).

women who prepare grain for the daily meal. In the vivid description of youth and old age, Qohelet extends the simple comparison, making it a wrenching account of the victory of darkness over light. The parable emphasizes the advisability of swift action because of the inevitable fate that awaits everyone.

Qohelet's unique style provides a fitting medium for his radical message. In addition to generous use of rhetorical questions, he introduces personal pronouns where the subject already appears in verbal suffixes and prefixes; he uses participles as verbs; and he uses frequent "leading words" (clusters of words, phrases, refrains, thematic statements). His observations contain contradictions, as does life itself (and by means of summary closures they frame his personal life, one characterized by numerous *m^{e}šālîm* [comparisons]). He expresses himself in the niceties of rhetoric such as chiasm, and he creates suspense by delaying interrogatives, holding back a key word and interposing something else between the expectation and the completion to give an unexpected consequent (Good, 72). Qohelet's mixture of poetry and prose suits his wish to comprehend all of reality. His colloquial language may derive from a desire to debunk the proper speech of the sages (Kugel).

This peculiar language marks a transitional stage between classical Hebrew and Mishnaic Hebrew. According to Delsman (1982), twenty-seven hapax legomena occur in the book, together with twenty-six words or combinations of words that appear in the Hebrew Bible only in Qohelet, although Mishnaic texts also have most of them. There are forty grammatical hapax legomena[14] and forty-two Aramaisms,[15] which comprise 3.1 percent of Qohelet's vocabulary. Qohelet conjugates final *alep* verbs like final *he* verbs and fails to assimilate the article in three instances (6:10; 8:1; 10:3). The demonstrative *zōh* takes the place of *zō't;* *'^{a}nî* occurs (29 times) rather than *'^{a}nōkî;* *'^{a}šer* (89 times) alternates with *š^{e}* (68 times); and a decided preference for feminine nouns over masculine forms exists. Qohelet uses numerous words ending in *at, ôn,* and *ût,* and he joins particles together the way they appear in the Mishnah. He employs three rare adverbs *(kbr, 'dn, 'dnh);* others he uses repeatedly (*gam, harbēh,* and *yōtēr;* 32, 14, and 7 times respectively). The adverb *m'd* never occurs in Qohelet. Unusual prepositions also appear, particularly those ending in *at ('al dibrat* and *kol-'ummat š^{e}),* as well as the conjunction *'illû* (6:6) and the interjections *'î* (10:16) and *'îlô* (4:10).

---

[14] *'^{a}biyyônāh, 'zn II, '^{a}suppāh, bwr, bṭl, gûmmāṣ, ḥešrôn, ḥatḥat, ṭaḥ^{a}nāh, y^{e}gî'āh, lahag, māṣôd, m^{e}ṣôdāh, m^{e}qāreh, mērôṣ, sekel, '^{a}bād, '^{a}den, '^{a}denāh, pēšer, r^{e}'ût, r^{e}'ît, šaḥ^{a}rût, šiplût, š^{e}tî, taqqîp,* etc.

[15] *'î IV, b^{e}ḥûrôt, hôlēlôt, hôlēlût, zeh . . . hû', ḥešbôn, yāpeh, yārē' millipnēh, yitrôn, k^{e}bār, kî gam, kišrôn, meh hāyā š^{e}, māh-š^{e}, meh š^{e}, miskēn, siklût, 'ānāh* III, *'inyān, qôhelet, r^{e}'ût, ra'yôn, śiklût, šilṭôn, taḥat haššemeš, tqn,* etc. Wagner identifies 78 Aramaisms.

The Meaning of the Name Qohelet

The Hebrew word Qohelet, from which the name Ecclesiastes derives, has been variously explained as a personal name, a nom de plume, an acronym, and a function. The difficulty of comprehending the meaning of the word Qohelet is compounded by the fact that it seems to be understood differently within the book itself, where Qohelet has the article at least once (in 12:8, although nearly the same sentence occurs in 1:2, where Qohelet lacks the article). In all likelihood, the article also appears in 7:27, where Qohelet takes a feminine verb form, although the word Qohelet is otherwise always construed as masculine. The Septuagint supports a redivision of the consonants in 7:27, yielding *'mr hqhlt* (says the Qohelet).

The name occurs seven times.

1. The words of Qohelet, son of David, King in Jerusalem. (1:1)
2. The ultimate absurdity, says Qohelet, the ultimate absurdity; everything is absurd. (1:2)
3. I, Qohelet, have been king over Israel in Jerusalem. (1:12)
4. Look, I have discovered this—says the Qohelet—(adding) one to one in order to find the sum. (7:27)
5. The ultimate absurdity, says the Qohelet, everything is absurd. (12:8)
6. In addition to the fact that Qohelet was a sage, he also taught the people knowledge. (12:9a–b)
7. Qohelet sought to find pleasing words and accurately wrote down trustworthy sayings. (12:10)

Formally the word Qohelet is a Qal feminine participle. Elsewhere the root *qhl* always occurs in Hiphil or Niphal (causative or reflexive/passive). It means "to convoke," "to assemble" (Hiphil) or "to be gathered" (Niphal). Precedent exists for a masculine personal name with a feminine ending (Alemeth, I Chron. 7:8). This interpretation clearly underlies the identification of Qohelet as son of David, which occurs in the superscription to the book (1:2), but the idea of royal authorship ultimately derives from the book itself (1:12).

David did not, however, have a son named Qohelet who succeeded him. Is Qohelet a nickname for Solomon, who occupied the throne after his father's health failed? The link between "Qohelet" and Solomon could lie in the language of I Kings 8:1–12, where the king assembles *(yāqhēl)* representatives of the people at Jerusalem. But the initiative to look for such a suitable text must surely have sprung from the author's self-presentation in 1:12–2:26, for Solomon's vast wealth supplies the imagined context for the royal experiment comprising these verses. The Egyptian royal testament offers a prototype for this section of the book, but Qohelet did not restrict his sayings to this literary form. Conceivably, the allusion to one shepherd in 12:11 reverts to the royal fiction earlier abandoned by the author, inasmuch as the image of pharaohs as shepherds regularly appears in Egypt (D. Müller). Nevertheless, Qohelet usually speaks as a teacher, not a king. Three other things weaken the argument for viewing Qohelet as a personal name, a substitute for Solomon: (1) the use of the article; (2) the identification of Qohelet as a wise man *(ḥākām)*, presumably a technical term in this instance (12:9); and (3) the point of view from which the author writes. Except for the royal fiction in 1:12–26, the author's perspective invariably suggests a subject powerless to redress the injustices perpetrated by higher officials.

Does the strange form conceal an otherwise unknown identity? Is Qohelet an acronym? Skehan (42–43) has argued that the name for Agur's father in Prov. 30:1a, Jakeh, actually conceals the first letters of a sentence comprising three words *(yqh= yhwh qādôš hû')*. Following this analogy, *qhlt* constitutes the abbreviation of a four-word sentence. But what four words? So far, no satisfactory explanation along these lines has come to light. Some interpreters have thought that Qohelet personifies wisdom, constituting a walking assembly of wise sayings, but elsewhere Dame Wisdom always goes by the name *ḥokmāh*. The most compelling answer to the enigma of the name points to two instances where a feminine participle describes an office (Ezra 2:55, 57; Neh. 7:59). Two different occupations lie behind the personal names in these verses (a scribe and a binder of gazelles). By analogy, Qohelet refers to an office related to assembling people. The Septuagint renders the word this way, associating the noun for assembly with the word for a public gathering *(ekklēsia)*. Jerome continued that line of reasoning in the Vulgate, but stressed the role of speaking in the presence of an assembly. Did Qohelet gather people for a cultic assembly? This understanding led to the Reformers' use of *Prediger* (Preacher) with reference to this book, but no biblical evidence for such a meaning exists. Whatever else Qohelet did, he did not preach, at least in the modern sense of the word.

Did Qohelet assemble people in a school? That kind of activity accords with the epilogist's description in 12:9. School wisdom may have possessed the capacity to criticize itself as in this book. One could even say that Qohelet democratizes wisdom, turning away from professional students to ordinary citizens. The use of *hā'ām* (the people) in 12:9 where one would naturally expect a reference to students favors this interpretation of the situation. Furthermore, if the form *qᵉhillāh* in Neh. 5:7 actually means "harangue," then the word Qohelet might refer to an office of "arguer" or "haranguer." However, the way Qohelet presents his observations does not justify this interpretation of his title.

The verb *qhl* always appears in connection with an assembly of people. If it could also apply to the gathering of objects, then Qohelet might be a "collector of proverbs," as the epilogist remembers the teacher (12:9–11). Qohelet kept an ear in readiness to hear something worthwhile, he searched high and low for appropriate insights, and he grouped the resulting sayings in an understandable way. This instance would not be Qohelet's only departure from ordinary usage of the word. He forged a language and syntax peculiar to this book. Furthermore, he saw no fundamental distinction between humans and animals in death; one could therefore argue that Qohelet assembled sayings rather than people (1:1) and that 7:27 contains a veiled allusion to this understanding of the title ("one to one to discover the sum"). Qohelet collected sayings and in doing so concluded that life amounts to nothing.

Literary Integrity and Structure

We have already mentioned an epilogist who commented on the achievement of the teacher. This introduces the question of literary integrity. Did Qohelet write the complete book, or have several authors contributed to its present form? Answers vary, but four basic responses commend themselves to interpreters: (1) the author wrote the bulk of the book, but editorial glosses entered at a later time; (2) the author cites traditional wisdom and refutes it; (3) the author enters into dialogue with an interlocutor, real or imagined; and (4) the book reflects a single author's changing viewpoints over the years, as well as life's ambiguities.

The earliest written response to Qohelet affirmed conscious design on the part of the esteemed teacher.

> Besides being a sage Qohelet also taught what he knew to ordinary people; he listened, investigated, and *arranged* numerous proverbs.
>
> Qohelet endeavored to find pleasant expressions and faithfully wrote reliable observations (12:9–10).

Several things in the epilogist's remarks invite comment. First, he identifies Qohelet as a professional *ḥākām*. (This term had become a technical one by the time of the epilogue's composition early in the second century B.C.E.)[16] Second, the epilogist claims that Qohelet branched out beyond the school to include the common folk in his assembly of learners. Third, Qohelet made use of the technique which the wise developed through centuries of experimentation: he examined the tradition, searched for its authentic elements, and tried to make sense of its context. Fourth, he appreciated the aesthetic dimension, but in so doing did not sacrifice the

[16] I agree with Whybray (1974) that the majority of references to *ḥᵃkāmîm* in the Hebrew Bible do not refer to professional wise men, but I think the term *ḥākām* (and its plural) eventually came to mean a sage. This meaning is probably present in the superscriptions within the book of Proverbs, the epilogue to Qohelet, and in Sirach. Beyond these instances, one needs to consider each case on its own merits. For example, I believe Qohelet uses the technical term in 8:17.

truth for pleasing sounds. The Hebrew word *tiqqēn,* which I translate "arranged," has this meaning in Sir. 47:9.

> He [David] *placed* singers before the altar,
> to make sweet melody with their voices. (RSV)

Twice Qohelet uses the word in what resemble proverbial expressions; in each instance the sense of "being straight" prevails (1:15; 7:13). In short, the epilogist believed that Qohelet stamped his teaching with recognizable design rather than bequeathing a legacy of random thoughts.

Did this epilogist attempt to assure such a reading of Qohelet by inserting a thematic refrain in 1:2 and 12:8?

> "The ultimate futility!" says Qohelet, "the ultimate futility!
> Everything is futile."

The variant in 12:8, "says the Qohelet," underlines the fact that the third person occurs here instead of the teacher's customary first-person address. This allusion to "the Qohelet" also emphasizes that a title rather than a name occurs here. The gatherer (of wives? of sayings? of people?) sums up his teaching, concluding that all his toil adds up to zero, the supreme nothing. This unforgettable refrain unifies the entire book: from first to last nothing profits those who walk under the sun.

What prompted this admirer to assert that the book has a coherent structure? One answer is that both form and content give the impression of a sustained argument. Qohelet makes effective use of many sapiential forms which occur throughout the ancient Near East, but two set the tone of the book: reflection and royal instruction. The former stamps the conclusions with personal authenticity, while the latter maximizes the impact by attributing such findings to the wisest and richest of men. Who speaks here? One who has subjected all of reality to a test.

What does he conclude? That everything lacks permanence when viewed *coram morte* (in death's presence). The highly personal nature of the self-discourse arouses the suspicion that a single individual has earnestly considered all conceivable alternatives and has retained only that which commends itself to thoughtful persons.

The content also proclaims a coherent message, a single point, which it declares again and again with complete abandon. Since death's shadow threatens all supposed profit, one had best seize what enjoyment opportunity offers.

Opinions differ as to whether emphasis belongs on the circumstantial clause or on the conclusion. To some, a heavy sigh permeates the breadth and length of his observations, even those which encourage youthful pleasure, and wafts the smell of a tomb (Rankin 1936; Galling 1961). A kaleidoscopic demonstration of the inevitable march toward death results. To others, an ecstatic shout arises from gratitude for the divine gift of pleasure when set within its proper context of fear for the free God (Whybray 1982; von Rad 1972, 231).

Choice of vocabulary and motifs enhances this single tone. By frequency of occurrence alone certain words echo throughout the corridors of the edifice fashioned by this skillful teacher: *‘śh/ma‘ăśeh* (62 times), *ṭôb* (51 times), *ḥākām* (51 times), *’ēt* (40 times), *yd‘* (37 times), *‘āmāl* (34 times), *r’h* (30 times), *taḥat haššemeš* (27 times), *kĕsîl* (18 times), *‘inyān* (8 times), *yitrôn* (9 times), *ḥēleq* (8 times). Among these preferred expressions two occur in the Hebrew Bible in Qohelet alone *(‘inyān* and *yitrôn),* while others take on distinctive nuances in this book (*‘āmāl* as labor and its payment, *taḥat haššemeš* as the realm of human activity, *ṭôb* as a designation of favorable fortune). Still others lose their positive sense in juxtaposition with certain expressions *(ḥākām, ma‘ăśeh, ḥēleq).*

To recapitulate, certain features within the book indicate conscious design and thus reinforce the epilogist's judgment concerning the orderly arrangement of dependable truth. These characteristics include form and content, stylistic devices and vocabulary. Can one take a further step toward a theory of design in Qohelet? Walther Zimmerli (1962, 132) has singled out an instance of lively debate where Qohelet actually identifies his opponent.

> I have observed all God's activity—that one cannot find out the work that is done under the sun. He will not discover what he endeavors to find, and even though the sage claims to know, he cannot find it. (8:17)

Such bold language lends credence to the claim that Qohelet endeavored to sustain a thesis over against the wisdom of schools. Precisely what did he intend to say, and what medium did he choose to bear that message?

If this bold attack furnishes any clue, Qohelet challenged the claim that wisdom enabled one to lead a secure existence. The collapse of faith in a God who rewarded virtue and punished vice marks a new turn. Wisdom has lost its power, and *miqreh* (chance) ascends the throne.

Did Qohelet really dare to crush the foundation stone on which sages had built their school? Or did he vacillate from one position to another, at one time endorsing divine reward and retribution, at another denying them? Thus it seems to be—unless Qohelet cites traditional claims in order to refute them. Or unless a redactor has softened the extreme statements of Qohelet by affirming traditional values. Robert Gordis (1939/40; 1968) has proposed that Qohelet quotes "old wisdom," and Norman Whybray (1980) has examined the hypothesis anew. He isolates eight quotations from earlier wisdom (2:14a; 4:5, 6; 7:5, 6a; 9:17; 10:2, 12) on the basis of agreement in form and content with proverbs in the oldest collections attributed to Solomon. Whybray challenges the thesis that Qohelet used citations in order to refute them and ventures the suggestion that he enlisted them as support for his own independent judgments. Some he quoted with full approval (7:5–6; 10:2, 12) but gave them a radically new interpretation. Others he employed to confirm the first stage in the characteristic two-part argument (broken sentences) in which he first posited a truth and then "gravely qualified it by stating a fact of life which runs counter to it." Critics may well wonder whether the independent judgments and radically new interpretations which Qohelet gave to the quotations taken from traditional school wisdom do not amount to refutation.[17]

Do the aphorisms in Qohelet justify the adjective "school" before the noun "wisdom"? If so, did Qohelet represent a rival school? Available evidence does not allow definite answers to these questions. Ben Sira operated a school about 190 B.C.E., but no trace survives of comparable institutions prior to Sirach. Some features of ancient literature indirectly support the hypothesis of an Israelite school in earlier times: (1) the name of a city (Kiriath Sepher); (2) the quality of the literature attributed to sages; (3) the necessity for trained scribes at the royal court; (4) the allusion to Hezekiah's men; (5) the analogy from Egypt and Mesopotamia, where schools flourished; (6) references to the expense incurred in acquiring wisdom; (7) the description of Dame Wisdom as a teacher; (8) Greek influence. Still, this putative school lies shrouded in mystery.[18] Who attended it? The language of Proverbs implies that only males received instruction (cf. the address to sons and the erotic component, written from the standpoint of men). The book of Proverbs would sit equally well in a family setting, a situation altered only slightly in Job and Qohelet (a forensic setting in Job, perhaps the open market in Qohelet).

If a school existed, and if only boys attended its instruction, did they come from wealthy families? That conclusion accords with prevalent notions about the aristocratic nature of Israel's sages, a supposition based largely on the necessity of leisure time. In this case the epilogist's assertion that Qohelet instructed the folk may then possess a polemical thrust, per-

---

[17]Further efforts to fix criteria for discovering quotations are those by Gordis (1981) and Fox (1980). The former identifies four main categories: (1) the verbalization of a speaker or writer's unexpressed ideas or sentiments; (2) the sentiment of a subject other than the writer or speaker; (3) use in argument and debate; and (4) indirect quotations without a *verbum dicendi.* Fox represents a cautious approach, proposing three criteria: (1) the presence of another person besides the primary speaker in the immediate context; (2) a virtual *verbum dicendi* (for example, mouth or speech); and (3) a shift in grammatical number and person. One alternative to quotations, of course, is to recognize redactional glosses. Because editorial glosses touch up many books of the Bible, in all likelihood Ecclesiastes also has such redactional comments, for the radical nature of Qohelet's thoughts invited editorial softening.

[18]Some clarity has emerged as a result of recent studies by Hermisson, Lang (1979), and Lemaire. My own assessment (1986) takes a considerably more cautious position than the preceding studies.

haps even implying that Qohelet functioned as a peripatetic teacher and that part of the pathos of his message arose from this shift to ordinary citizens.

Qohelet owed an enormous debt to the wisdom tradition, despite his attack upon it (Whybray 1979; 1980; Loretz 1984). His speech forms and method of arriving at truth derive from the sages whose optimism he undermines. His teachings often harmonize with theirs, a fact that critics do not always appreciate. But one fundamental difference separated him from the wisdom establishment: Qohelet believed the positive connection between morality and its consequences had snapped.

Scattered bits of evidence indicate that Qohelet also utilized material from beyond the wisdom corpus. Although Forman's claim (1960) that he worked with Genesis 1–11 in hand surely exaggerates things, Qohelet's observation about creation may reflect familiarity with the priestly narrative. Whether or not Qohelet's indictment of women implies a debt to the Yahwist remains unclear, for the sentiment may have characterized many circles (cf. Zech. 5:5–11). Certain remarks seem to indicate knowledge of Job, particularly the dismissing of struggle against a powerful opponent as futile, and perhaps the quoting of a proverb depicting human fate. Some also suppose dependence upon Deuteronomy's interdiction against adding to or subtracting from a written text. But in all these instances, actual use of canonical writings remains in doubt. Qohelet may simply have drawn upon common knowledge, as he certainly did with regard to Greek popular philosophy (Braun, Gammie).

Regardless of the actual source of various ideas, Qohelet fashions them according to his own world view. The resulting teaching placed him on the perimeter of sapiential thought (von Rad 1962, I, 458; Kroeber 1963). Or did it? Zimmerli (1962, 139) has argued that Qohelet returned to "authentic bedrock," to the very heart of Yahwism, divine freedom. From him Qohelet earns the laudable title, "Watchman over God's transcendence." One wonders, however, about the need for such guardians during an era emphasizing the distance separating God and a sinful humanity (an insight which Loader carries too far). Where was divine freedom placed in jeopardy? Granted, Qohelet avoids the idea of personified wisdom; but other reasons for this decision present themselves, primarily the negative verdict on wisdom's accomplishments. The question remains, then: what did Qohelet champion? Interpreters who propose new readings of Qohelet take for granted the assumption that the plan of the book reinforces its message. Most think repetition offers a decisive clue to the book's plan. Norbert Lohfink's recent commentary (1980) admirably illustrates this. In his opinion, Qohelet adopts the Greek rhetorical device known as palindrome, a complete balancing of material so that one can read forward or backward and still achieve the same result. Lohfink envisions the book's structure as follows:

1:1–2	Frame
1:4–11	Cosmology
1:12–3:15	Anthropology
3:16–4:16	Social Criticism I
4:17–5:6 [5:1–7E]	Criticism of Religion (poetic)
5:7–6:10 [5:8–6:10E]	Social Criticism II
6:11–9:6	Ideology Critique (Refutatio)
9:7–12:7	Ethics (poetic at the end)
12:8	Frame

Of course, the scheme lacks perfection; witness the section on criticism of religion. In Lohfink's view, this minor flaw in the palindrome hardly distorts the impression which this Greek stylistic medium leaves. Critics may ask whether sufficient evidence justifies the divisions of units, particularly in light of the vague rubrics. For example, when Qohelet renders his low opinion of women and only slightly higher estimate of men, does he not make an anthropological judgment? Does an ethical concern not permeate much of the book? Interpreters persistently view the second half of the book as ethical conclusions arising from the experiments of the first half.

Lohfink thinks a Greek spirit infuses the book in more than its form, and holds that the message consists of a diatribe. It follows that positive affirmations balance the negative aspects of Qohelet's thought. Failure to recognize the true dialogic character of the book leads to misrepresentation of Qohelet's views. In this fashion Lohfink managed to salvage orthodox understandings of God over against denials of divine justice. Still he listens to the adverse criticism of God, for Lohfink notes that Jesus of Nazareth also rejected the claim that morality secured rainfall for its practitioners.

Two other recent critics have emphasized the view/re-view nature of the book. Borrowing the essential structure proposed some time ago by H. L. Ginsberg (1955), Daniel Lys divides Qohelet into two parts: (I) a view of the human condition, 1:4–4:3; (II) a re-view of the human condition, 4:4–12:7. So far his massive commentary has only dealt with part one, which consists of two subsections: (1) Balance Sheet, 1:4–2:26, and (2) Destiny, 3:1–4:3. The official balance sheet contains an objective and a subjective exposé, while the examination of human destiny meditates upon time and divine justice. The second part includes paradoxes (4:4–6:9) and an ethic (6:10–12:7). Topics covered are work, popularity, the cult, officials, money, grace, and relative ethics (exemplified by woman, philosophy, injustice, success, aging). Lys thinks Qohelet was a philosopher who gave a consistent, lucid analysis of the human condition. The key phrase in this understanding of experience is "emptiness and chasing after wind," which emphasizes the fragility and absurdity of life itself as it glides toward the grave.

Another version of repetition characterizes the monograph by J. A. Loader (1979) on polar structures in the book of Qohelet. He argues that Qohelet linked together form and substance by means of elaborate polar structures. Loader claims to have isolated thirty-eight chiastic structures and sixty polar structures within the book. In all these polarities a negative follows a positive in such a way as to draw attention to the resulting *hebel.* In addition, an intricate system of cross-references joins together numerous lesser polarities and connects the separate verses and larger units. For example, the experiment in 1:12–2:26 yields the following scheme.

> Pole: General *ḥokmāh* / Contra-pole: *kᵉsîl*
> Tension: Relative advantage of the general *ḥokmāh*
> and
> Pole: General *ḥokmāh* / Contra-pole: Occurrences of life
> Tension: Worthlessness of the *ḥokmāh*

From this it follows that Qohelet polemicizes against traditional wisdom. In Loader's view, the tension within the book and that between the form and the subject matter testify to the conflict between Qohelet and school wisdom. In short, internal contradiction represents the opposing viewpoints of Qohelet and traditional sapiential teaching.

Addison D. G. Wright (1968; 1980; 1983) has suggested a different kind of balance between two halves of the book. Taking his cue from the refrain in 1:2, he applies the study of numerology to Qohelet in the same way that Patrick Skehan sought to solve the problem of the unity of Proverbs. Wright notes that the numerical value of *hᵃbēl hᵃbālîm hakkōl hābel* is 216, the exact number of verses in 1:1–12:8. Moreover, *hebel* occurs three times in 1:2, the numerical value being 111 (37 × 3). Assuming that a clear break occurs after 6:9, Wright observes that precisely 111 verses make up the first half of the book. Wright adds that the word *hebel* occurs thirty-seven times in the book, a fact which in his view corroborates Qohelet's preoccupation with numbers. Now there are 222 verses in Qohelet, but the value of the refrain was only 216. What is wrong? In 12:9 the word *wᵉyōtēr* appears at the beginning of the first epilogue. The numerical value of *wᵉ,* six, brings the 216 to 222. On the other hand, the value of the initial word in 1:1 *(dibrê)* is 216. Since the editor of the epilogue used this word three times, Wright thinks he must have appreciated the numerical value of words. Conversely, says Wright, the author of 1:1 (that is, Qohelet) must also have consciously worked with numerical values, for the title forms part of the 111 verses in the first half of the book. Since the second half of the book consists of 105 verses, seven fewer than the first half, Wright proposes a slightly different division by excluding 1:1–18 and 11:7–12:8, which gives 186 verses. Now he can find 93 verses in each half. Returning to 1:2, he notes that *hebel* occurs five times (singular and plural). The sum of 37 × 5 is 185, one short of the 186 arrived at by adding the two 93s. By recognizing the five-*hebel* pattern in the body of the book (2½ *hebel*s in each half, assuming that one *hebel* equals 37, and a half *hebel* 19), Wright accounts for the extra verse. Finally, Wright thinks the editor imposed a six-*hebel* pattern on the entire book.

We should note that this solution to the riddle of the Sphinx, worked out in collaboration with Skehan, seeks to reinforce an earlier attempt using refrains to isolate divisions within the book. According to that analysis, Qohelet consists of two parts.

I. Qohelet's investigation of life (1:12–6:9)
  Double introduction (1:12–15, 16–18)
  Study of pleasure-seeking (2:1–11)
  Study of wisdom and folly (2:12–17)
  Study of the fruits of toil (2:18–6:9)
II. Qohelet's conclusions (6:10–11:6)
    Introduction (6:10–12)
  A. Man cannot find out what is good for him to do
    Critique of traditional wisdom
      On the day of prosperity and adversity (7:1–14)
      On justice and wickedness (7:15–24)
      On women and folly (7:25–29)
      On the wise man and the king (8:1–17)
  B. Man does not know what will come after him
    He knows he will die: the dead know nothing (9:1–6)
    There is no knowledge in Sheol (9:7–10)
    Man does not know his time (9:11–12)
    Man does not know what will happen (9:13–10:15)
    He does not know what evil will come (10:16–11:2)
    He does not know what good will come (11:3–6)

In the first half the six subsections conclude with the refrain, "(all is vanity and) a striving after wind," while the first four subsections in part two end with "not find out" (the last one with a triple occurrence), and the next six subsections conclude with "do not know" (the last one with a triple usage). Bowing to subsequent criticism, Wright has altered his understanding of the number of subsections in 9:1–11:6; he now finds four here to balance the four in 6:10–8:17.

Although J. S. M. Mulder (1982) has endeavored to gain a more favorable response in scholarly circles for Wright's views, it appears that this elaborate hypothesis carries a valid intuition too far. In some instances, the formulaic expression occurs in the midst of a thought unit rather than at the end (for example, 11:2). Moreover, the repeated phrases sometimes do not enter into consideration (4:4, "shepherding the wind"), and other formulaic expressions are ignored altogether ("this is absurd," "under the sun," "I turned and considered"). In addition, the units discussed have such unequal length that one wonders about the utility of such an approach. The decision to concentrate on just three formulaic expressions ("This is absurd and shepherding the wind," "not find out"/"who can find out?" and "can not know") undercuts the claim of objectivity. The many assumptions necessitated by the numerological proof weaken the argument greatly.

Not all critics who think of Qohelet as a treatise showing progress in the structure of thought stress the balance between the two halves of the book. Oswald Loretz recognizes a thematic unity throughout Qohelet, one which the refrain in 1:2 and 12:8 encapsulates. The whole book centers on the sheer emptiness of life, its likeness to fleeting breath. The tensions with the text result from the numerous *topoi* with which Qohelet worked. The inconsistencies cease to count for anything, however, in the light of the ephemeral nature of things.

A similar point is promulgated by A. Glasser, who divides the book into three sections: (1) Personal experience concerning goodness (2:1–26); (2) Inquiry into the goodness in others, its reality and relation to wisdom and justice (3:1–9:10); and (3) Exhortation to make use of lessons acquired from this test (9:11–12:7). Glasser thinks the entire book offers a trial of goodness. The different sections are interwoven, e.g., 2:24–26 introduces the next unit, and 9:7–10 leads directly to the final unit. An introduction (1:12–18) announces the test which Qohelet intends to undertake.

In a recent essay, François Rousseau (1981) applies an analytic method designed for texts which arose in an era of oral tradition. Rousseau thinks the biblical text consists of successive groups of stichoi rather than sequential paragraphs, and that a principle of "twinning" or parallelism existed. Thus an intricate threading of stichoi and subgroups of stichoi according to the same figures and models characterized the text. Rousseau develops an elaborate system of signs to depict the interconnections of various stichoi. Those relationships involve: (1) parallelism between stichoi taken two by two; (2) parallelism within different stichoi; (3) parallelism between subgroups of stichoi in the first instance; and (4) parallelism between subgroups of stichoi in the second instance. This correspondence may take the form of the same word, an equivalent expression, the opposite word or expression, the same idea, or even sequential progression of thought (e.g., from nature to history, natural to human). It may also consist of a correspondence between numbers, and on occasion the parallelism may become quite sophisticated, as in three levels of sensuality, the eye, ear, and taste.

Rousseau takes the prologue in 1:4–11 as the clue for understanding the structure of the book. In his view the prologue consists of an intricately developed system of matching stichoi, in which parallelism and connecting links range from contiguous stichoi to larger units. The entire book includes seven cycles encased within a frame forming a chiasm.

A	Title	1:1
B	Theme	1:2–3
C	Prologue	1:4–11
C′	Epilogue	12:1–7
B′	Theme	12:8
A′	Redactional Note	12:9–14

The seven cycles are:

A	(1)	Solomon's confession (1:12–2:26)
B	(2)	The sage cannot know God's design in general (3:1–13)
	(3)	The sage cannot know what follows death (3:14–22)
C	(4)	Various deceptions and exhortations (4:1–5:19 [20E])
	(5)	Various deceptions and exhortations (6:1–8:15)
B′	(6)	Wisdom's ineffectiveness (8:16–9:10)
C′	(7)	Deceptions and exhortations (9:11–11:10)

Each cycle concludes with a refrain which urges enjoyment; by this means the author throws into relief the optimism of his message. While prologue and epilogue describe human impotency vis-à-vis the natural world and death, the exhortation to eat, drink, and enjoy God's gift of toil naturally reinforces the religious concept of fear before God *(yir'at 'ᵉlōhîm).*

This "twinning of stichoi" or parallelism occurs within the cycles and manifests itself according to several schemes. For instance, it takes place in a stichos (1:4, "a generation comes // a generation goes" a b a′ b′) and in a single cycle.

Cycle 1		Cycle 2	
A	Wisdom is deceptive (1:12–18)	A	Permanence of Yahweh's work (3:14–17)
B	Wealth is deceptive (2:1–11)	A′	Man and beast are alike in death (3:18–21)
A′	Wisdom is deceptive (2:12–17)		
B′	Wealth is deceptive (2:18–23)		

Parallelism may also occur between the cycles.

Cycles	4.	Deception 4:1–16	Hortatory unit 4:17–5:6 [7E]	Deception 5:7–16 [8–17E]	Refrain 5:17–19 [18–20E]
	5.	Deception 6:1–12	Hortatory unit 7:1–22	Deception 7:23–8:14	Refrain 8:15
	7.	Exhortation 9:11	Deception 9:12–17	Hortatory unit 9:18–11:6	Refrain 11:7–10

Even within a subsection of a cycle extensive parallelism may take place.

A Prudence (caution) in speech (9:18–10:3)
B Prudence (caution) in the presence of a king (10:4–7)
C Prudence (caution) in ordinary affairs (10:8–11)
A′ Prudence (caution) in speech (10:12–15)
B′ Prudence (caution) in the presence of a king (10:16–20)
C′ Prudence in ordinary affairs (11:1–2)
D Prudence should not be excessive (11:3–6)

Occasional breaks in the "twinning" do not trouble Rousseau, for he thinks divergences at the beginning, center, or end of a section serve to heighten interest.

The refrain plays a major role in Rousseau's view. In his analysis, largely based on cycles 2, 3, and 5, several components stand out:

1. personal testimony
2. value judgment
3. invitation to joy
4. toil and work
5. God's gift

Rousseau concedes that the refrain occurs slightly fewer times than the "quite short" one about vanity and shepherding the wind, and indeed less often than the question, "What profit does one receive for his work?" These shorter refrains, he thinks, may indicate redactional activity. Rousseau observes that "the appeal to enjoyment is omnipresent and predominant." He continues: "The recalling God's gift is omnipresent. The work of man, mentioned everywhere except in cycle seven, attains the third position. The invitation to enjoy life is primary (29 times); it is clarified in the light of God's gift (17 times) and human work (11 times)." The arbitrary manner in which Rousseau selects the dominant refrain does little to increase confidence in this analysis, aside from the fact that he assumes that oral tradition played a controlling role in the composition of Qohelet. Few interpreters can allow that assumption to pass unchallenged.

Michael V. Fox (1968) defends the essential unity of the book by distinguishing between the author and Qohelet, his persona. The speaker, the frame narrator, tells the story, hence acts as a transmitter. Qohelet is the character through whom the author speaks. This use of an anonymous third person, retrospective frame-narrative encompassing the monologue of a teacher occurs in several Egyptian texts: Kagemni, Ipuwer, and 'Onkhsheshonqy. Fox claims to find the same phenomenon in Ahikar, Tobit, and Deuteronomy. He concludes that the words of Qohelet (1:3–12:7), the motto (1:2; 12:8), and the epilogue (12:9–14) derive from the same person. The epilogue functions: (1) to testify to the reality of Qohelet in the matter-of-fact and reliable voice of a sage; (2) to project and teach readers to have an attitude of respect toward Qohelet; (3) to identify the book as a whole with an indisputably orthodox religious attitude; (4) to set a certain distance between himself and the words of Qohelet, and of other sages as well; and (5) to set Qohelet's words in a broader literary and religious context.

Hans-Peter Müller (1968) discerns an intentional unit in 1:12–3:15.[19] Here a royal travesty (1:12–2:11) includes an experiment with wisdom (1:12–18) and with the folly of joy (2:1–11). Qohelet recommends enjoyment so long as one remembers the limitations expressed in 3:1–9. An inclusio (1:13; 3:10–11) unifies the tractate and gives the enjoyment a theological grounding, which Müller calls "theonomic skepticism."

If such theories concerning an intentional structure of Qohelet have merit, critics should be able to isolate a single theme which the author defends in various ways. Indeed, several interpreters have articulated such themes. They range from "nothing in excess" *(mēden agan)* to the denial of any meaning in life when viewed over against absolute claims. The deception of experience resembles the latter understanding.

By far the most compelling thematic statement concerns the emptiness of life, its lack of profit when all is said and done. This sentiment punctuates the experiments with wisdom, leading to the overwhelming rejection of wisdom's power to probe the dark mysteries of existence. Why, then, do opposing sentiments find expression here and there, prompting several interpreters to see Qohelet as a champion of joy? Ambiguities exist, and they require explanation. Many commentators respond by denying the existence of an intentional structure. For them, Qohelet resembles a loose collection of sentences.

The adjective "loose" seems a bit inappropriate in H. W. Hertzberg's analysis (1963), for he thinks Qohelet consists of twelve smaller units, each of which considers a specific subject. Still, these several collections hardly sustain a single argument; instead they go their separate ways. Robert Gordis (1968), on the other hand, emphasizes the "sentence" character of the book by adopting an earlier suggestion that it represents a teacher's

[19] "Theonome Skepsis und Lebensfreude—Zu Koh 1,12–3,15," *BZ* 1986:1–19.

notebook. This understanding places him alongside Kurt Galling (1969), who isolated 27 separate units.

Aarre Lauha (1978) has recently given this interpretation new vigor. He observes that the book displays no logical plan, although the sentences contain *topoi* which have internal connections. Furthermore, the combination of introit (1:3–11) and epilogue (11:7–12:7) creates a crescendo which underscores the message that nothing new occurs under the sun. Lauha goes so far as to concede to the book a unity of style and thought, but he also postulates two redactors. The first redactor introduced thematic statements (1:1–2; 12:8–11) and rearranged the position of 1:3–11, but he did not alter the content of the book. The second redactor endeavored to negate the force of Qohelet's unorthodox statements, particularly those concerning reward and retribution. To achieve this end, he inserted opposing statements throughout the book and tacked onto the end a sum of the matter that would offend no one but Qohelet.

The thesis that Qohelet lacks any discernible progression in thought rests in part upon outright contradictions within the book. Hans-Peter Müller (1968) has noted that Qohelet juxtaposes a *bonum* and a *malum,* the latter representing the author's own viewpoint. Critics use the phrase *Zwar-aber Aussage* (a "granted, but on the other hand" statement) to describe this phenomenon of broken sentences.[20] Naturally, those who reject a thesis of conscious design appeal to such opposing viewpoints within the book. Does the ambivalence exist in the author himself?

Qohelet affirms divine action, both punishment and reward (3:11, 14; 7:18, 26; 11:5), but he also contends that the deity's remoteness permits no one to comprehend the divine ways (5:1 [2E]; 8:17). Life is better than death (9:4–6), but the dead are more fortunate (4:2), and Qohelet hates life (2:17). Wisdom, unprofitable and empty (1:17–18; 2:13–16), gives one an advantage when accompanied by an inheritance (7:11). Furthermore, it is useful

[20]Hertzberg's commentary makes extensive use of the *Zwar-aber Aussage.* He lists the following texts (30):

Zwar	*Aber*
1:16	1:17–18
2:3–10	2:11
2:13–14a	3:14bff.
3:11a	3:11b
3:17	3:18ff.
4:13–16a	4:16b
7:11–12	7:7 (transposed)
8:12b–13	8:14–15
9:4b	9:5
9:16a	9:16b
9:17–18a	9:18b–10:1
10:2–3	10:5–7

(7:19) and preferable to force (9:16–18). Joy is empty (2:2–3, 10–11), but good (5:19 [20E]; 8:15), for it comes from God (2:24–26). Work is grievous and unprofitable (1:13–14; 2:11, 18; 3:10; 4:6), but God gives it for human enjoyment (5:18). Woman lacks real worth (not one in a thousand, 7:27–28), but a man ought to enjoy the woman he loves (9:9). Retribution does not operate (8:10–14), for the grave treats all alike (9:2–3), but God keeps a tally of merits (7:18, 26) and will eventually judge everyone (11:9).[21]

To be sure, earlier proverbs juxtaposed opposing observations (e.g., Prov. 26:4–5) without detracting from their cogency. In this instance, however, both perspectives accord with reality, for they look at the matter of responding to a fool from two fundamentally different perspectives. Qohelet's contradictions fall into a different category. Which one of the antinomies represents Qohelet's own view? Must interpreters, like Zimmerli (1974), utter a *Zwar-aber Aussage?* Granted, Qohelet displays indications of intentional design; on the other hand, the book has clear manifestations of sentence collections, especially in 9:17–10:20. A lack of coherence extends to subject matter as well as form.

Can one detect, then, two voices in dialogue, as Herder thought, the one stating a thesis and the other its antithesis? Does a single author stand behind the diversity of viewpoint? Do the opposing sentiments represent the inevitable conflict between experience and faith?

This discussion of Qohelet's structure has failed to resolve a single issue, but it demonstrates the complexity of the problem. In my judgment no one has succeeded in delineating the plan of the book, for it certainly has characteristics inherent to a collection of sentences. That is why in the long run even such clever analyses as Wright's numerology must stoop to manipulation in order to make the results correspond to the theory. The study of Qohelet not only comprises the infamous rear entrance through which all sorts of skeptical melancholy enter the religious consciousness (Lohfink 1980, 5). Research into the book also shows that it reflects the interpreter's world view. That is why, I think, opinions vary so widely with regard to such basic matters as Qohelet's optimism or pessimism, his attitude toward women (Lohfink 1979), and his advocacy of immoral conduct (Whybray 1978).

My own analysis of the book's structure,[22] which is tentative, to be sure,

---

[21]On this tabulation of contradictions, see Barucq (1977, 613).

[22]This analysis resembles in many respects that of Schoors (1982b). He suggests the following units:

1:1	title
1:2	general theme of the book
1:3–2:26	Solomon's confession
3:1–22	human beings under the law of time
4:1–16	life in society

consists of the following divisions:

1:1	The Superscription
1:2–3	Motto and Thematic Statement
1:4–11	Nothing New Under the Sun
1:12–2:26	The Royal Experiment
3:1–15	A Time for Everything
3:16–4:3	The Tears of the Oppressed
4:4–6	Proverbial Insights About Toil and Its Opposite
4:7–12	The Advantages of Companionship
4:13–16	The Fickle Crowd
4:17–5:8 [5:1–9E]	Religious Obligations
5:9–6:9 [5:10–6:9E]	The Disappointments of Wealth
6:10–12	A Transitional Unit
7:1–14	A Collection of Proverbs
7:15–22	On Moderation
7:23–29	Seeking and Finding
8:1–9	Rulers and Subjects
8:10–17	The Mystery of Divine Activity
9:1–10	The Shadow of Death
9:11–12	Time and Chance
9:13–18	Wasted Wisdom
10:1–20	A Collection of Proverbs on Wisdom and Folly
11:1–6	The Element of Risk
11:7–12:7	Youth and Old Age
12:8	Thematic Statement (Inclusio)
12:9–14	The Epilogue(s)

In my view, the only secondary materials are the superscription (1:1), the epilogues (12:9–11, 12–14), some glosses (2:26a; 3:17a; 8:12–13; 11:9b; perhaps 5:18 [19E] and 7:26b), and possibly the motto (1:2; 12:8). The first epilogue derives from a close student of Qohelet and reads almost like an epitaph. The second epilogue, less appreciative of Qohelet's endeavors, introduces wholly alien categories as it assesses the radical teacher. I believe the tensions of the book represent for the most part the fruit of a lifetime's

---

4:17–5:8	the advantage of silence over unreflected speech
5:9–6:9	on wealth
6:10–12	transitional unit
7:1–9:10	the experience of life and death
9:11–10:20	wisdom and folly
11:1–6	the necessity of taking risks
11:7–12:7	the necessity of enjoying life
12:8	inclusio: the general theme of the book
12:9–14	epilogue

research. Changing circumstances evoke different responses to conventional wisdom and to one's own former thoughts. Differences in societal concerns also dictate a variety of literary expressions. Qohelet bares his soul in all its twistings and turnings, ups and downs, and he invites readers to accompany him in pursuit of fresh discovery. But the contradictions suggest more than the result of time's passage. They express the ambiguities of daily existence and the absurdity of human efforts to understand it. As in a kaleidoscope, apparently incongruent features of the text come together almost magically, framing many different but meaningful configurations.

The Historical Setting

If all attempts to discern the book's structure are inconclusive, the same verdict characterizes efforts to locate it in a particular time and place. For a brief period, scholars argued that the original language was Aramaic (Zimmerman 1945/46; 1949/50; 1973; Ginsberg 1950; 1952). But fragments of the book in Hebrew from Qumran seem to date to the mid-second century B.C.E. (Muilenburg). Such an early dating of a Hebrew version of Ecclesiastes leaves little time between its composition and the Qumran fragments for its contents to become so popular that translation into Hebrew became imperative. More importantly, translation need not be posited to explain the peculiar style and syntax of the book.

Granted, the book employs an Aramaizing Hebrew, a language with strong Mishnaic characteristics. The high percentage of Aramaisms places Ecclesiastes alongside other late canonical books (Daniel, Esther, Ezra, Nehemiah, Song of Songs). Occasional Persian loanwords also appear, for example *pardēs* (park) and *m^{e}dînāh* (province). Some have seen Greek influence in the phrases "under the sun" and "to see the good" (Ranston 1930), but the former expression occurs in ancient Semitic literature and the latter phrase is authentic Hebrew.

On the basis of certain commercial terms and usages, as well as orthography, Dahood (1952; 1962; 1965; 1966) proposed a Phoenician setting. This theory of the book's origin has made little impact on the scholarly community. Even less convincing has been Humbert's suggestion of Egyptian provenance, based largely on the allusion to natural phenomena in 1:5–7. The references to reservoirs (2:6), leaky roofs (10:18), wells (12:6), farmers' attention to the wind (11:4), the temple (4:17 [5:1E]; 8:10), and bread, wine, and oil as the three primary products of the country suit a Palestinian setting (Hertzberg 1957). But the evidence does not exclude other contexts, for ancient authors were open to receiving material from various sources. The so-called historical references in 4:13–16; 8:2–4; 9:13–15; and 10:16–17 invited use because of their typicality. Therefore, they offer no real assistance in dating the book or in locating its cultural setting.

Many factors point to a relatively late date for the composition of Ecclesiastes. The vocabulary itself shows signs of being very late, for example *sôp, pēšer, māšal* (to rule), *šālaṭ, pitgām, zᵉmān, ʿinyān,* the high frequency of the relative pronoun *šᵉ* attached to the next word, and the exclusive use of the short form of the first-person pronoun *ʾᵃnî.* Moreover, the *waw* consecutive occurs rarely, but of course the literary types in the book do not lend themselves to frequent use of this verbal form.[23] A Hellenistic coloring may rest behind the vocabulary for rulers, perhaps also behind the observations about individuals whose responsibilities brought them into regular contact with the royal court. At least one of the rhetorical questions, a literary device that the author uses nearly thirty times, is attested only in postexilic texts, with one possible exception. This rhetorical question, *mî yôdēaʿ* (who knows?), functions as an assertion that "no one knows" (Crenshaw 1986). The use of participles with accompanying personal pronouns also marks this language as late.

The meager political data that scholars have detected in the book point to a period prior to the Maccabean revolt in 164 B.C.E., for the attitude toward foreign rulers fits best the Ptolemaic period. The Zenon archives reflect a political situation of economic prosperity for the upper echelons of Jewish society about 250 B.C.E. Gordis (1968) and Crüsemann (1979) have argued that Qohelet belonged to the privileged class, although the evidence suggests rather that his students were well to do, hence could act on their teacher's advice about wearing fine clothes and anointing themselves with expensive oils. Such freedom to follow one's inclinations, whether personal or religious, was severely restricted under Antiochus IV's reign (at least for ordinary citizens). Another argument for a date prior to 200 B.C.E. comes from Ben Sira, who knew and used the book about 180 B.C.E.[24] Whitley (1979) has attempted to show that Qohelet actually used Ecclesiasticus, claiming that the language is later than Daniel, that the Mishnaic tongue was widely used in Judea, and that Qohelet wrote before 140 but after Jonathan's appointment in 152 B.C.E. and its accompanying political change. The arguments are unconvincing. A date for Qohelet between 225 and 250 remains most likely.

[23]Barucq (1977, 617–618) cautions against making very much of this phenomenon, for the texts from Qumran witness to competing traditions. The Manual of Discipline uses it freely, in the perfect but rarely in the imperfect, whereas the Damascus Document normally uses the *waw* consecutive even with the imperfect.

[24]Hertzberg (1963, 47–49) and Gordis (1951, 46–48) examine the relationship between Sirach and Qohelet.

The Larger Environment

An intellectual crisis like that in Qohelet struck other cultures also, but not at the same time. One expects, therefore, to find some common themes throughout the ancient Near East (Loretz 1964, 45–134). This phenomenon has led to exaggerated claims of literary dependence. Given the probable date of the book, Hellenistic influence has seemed most likely (Braun). Qohelet's concept of chance *(miqreh)* has been related to *tychē;* absurdity *(hebel)* to *typhos;* profit *(yitrôn)* to *ophelos;* under the sun *(taḥat haššemeš)* to *hypo ton hēlion.* Norbert Lohfink (1980) has postulated competing places of learning in Jerusalem: private schools using the Greek language and temple schools using Hebrew. He argues that Qohelet struck a compromise, expanding Hebrew wisdom with input from Greek thinkers, especially Homer, Sophocles, Plato, Aristotle, and contemporary philosophers. Other interpreters plausibly suggest that Qohelet's knowledge of Greek literature amounts to no more than what any Jew would have absorbed simply by living in Jerusalem during the late third century. The question of the extent of exposure to Greek thought affects every interpretation of the book.

What about literary relationships with ancient Egypt? Qohelet's *carpe diem* resembles the advice of the Harper's Songs (Fox 1985) but then, determination to enjoy sensual pleasure seems universal. Qohelet's preoccupation with death recalls "The Dialogue of a Man with His Soul" and the royal testament form corresponds with the literary type of such Instructions as Merikare. But Qohelet's version does not leave a legacy for a successor, and he drops the royal fiction after chapter 2.

Qohelet also shows thematic similarities with late Egyptian texts, particularly with Papyrus Insinger and The Instructions of ʻOnkhsheshonqy. For example, both Insinger and Qohelet refer to the hiddenness of God and divine determination of fate, while ʻOnkhsheshonqy and Qohelet advise releasing bread (or a good deed) on the waters and promise a profitable return, and both use the phrase "house of eternity." However, the sense of the counsel about releasing bread on water is different, and the euphemism for the grave is widespread.

Perhaps the most striking verbal similarity is with a Mesopotamian text, the Gilgamesh Epic. The alewife Siduri's advice to Gilgamesh that he enjoy his wife, fine clothes, and tasty food closely resembles Qohelet's positive advice. One thing is missing from Qohelet, the allusion to the pleasure that Gilgamesh would receive from his child. The Gilgamesh Epic also deals with the themes of death, life's ephemerality, the importance of one's name, and memory of a person after death.

Another Mesopotamian work, "I Will Praise the Lord of Wisdom," says divine decrees are hidden from humans, a view that Qohelet advocates in 3:11; 8:12–14; and 8:17. The fundamentally pessimistic "Babylonian

Theodicy," differs from Qohelet, who shrinks from blaming all evil on God (cf. 7:29). "The Dialogue Between a Master and His Slave" recognizes the threat posed by women and sets up polarities in a way that commends neither alternative. Qohelet also voices a low opinion of women (7:26) and juxtaposes positive and negative activities (3:1–8).

Canonization

Qohelet's radical views render his teachings an alien body within the Hebrew Bible (Gese 1958). How, then, did the book gain acceptance into the canon? The usual answer, that the attribution to Solomon paved the way for the book's approval as scripture, overlooks the fact that a similar device failed to gain acceptance into the canon for Wisdom of Solomon or for the Odes of Solomon. However, their linguistic medium, Greek, may have canceled the effect of the claim to Solomonic authorship.

A better answer to the question of acceptance points to the second epilogue, which removed the sting from Qohelet's skepticism and advocated traditional views concerning observance of Torah (cf. Sheppard 1977). Evidence from the second century C.E. mentions the book of Ecclesiastes, together with Song of Songs, Esther, Ezekiel, and Proverbs, in a discussion about books that "defile the hands" because of their sacred character. The attitude of Hillel prevailed over the usually conservative Shammaite contingency, who objected to the book. Akiba recognized Qohelet's canonical authority just before the middle of the second century, and the book appears in the list drawn up by the Christian Melito of Sardis about 190 C.E. Objection to its sacred character surfaced again in the early fifth century in a work by Theodore of Mopsuestia. Eventually, worshipers read the book of Ecclesiastes in the synagogue on the third day of the Feast of Booths.

We do not know how soon after its completion Qohelet acquired canonicity. A few verbal similarities between the book and Sirach exist: for example, everything is beautiful in its time (3:11; Sir. 39:16); God seeks (3:15; Sir. 5:3); wise of heart and changed of face (8:1; Sir. 13:24 [25E]); and either for good or for evil (12:14; Sir. 13:24 [25 E]). In addition, verbal echoes also occur in "one in a thousand," and "the end of the matter," but these stock expressions belong to wisdom literature in general. Although Sirach may have known the book of Ecclesiastes, the evidence is not conclusive. A similar situation exists with regard to Wisdom of Solomon, often thought to attack Qohelet's views about enjoying life's sensual pleasures. If the author of chapter 2 has Qohelet in mind, he misreads its teachings, for Qohelet did not advocate robbery (see Skehan).

The Text

The Hebrew text of Qohelet has survived in good condition. Fragments dating from the middle of the second century B.C.E., discovered at Qumran, include part of 5:13–17 [14–18E], substantial portions of 6:3–8, and five words from 7:7–9. The Greek version is thought to be the work of disciples of Aquila, whereas the Syriac translation in the Peshitta seems to rest on a Hebrew text very similar to the Massoretic. The Vulgate strove for faithfulness to the Hebrew, although Jerome completed the translation of Proverbs, Ecclesiastes, and the Song of Songs hastily ("in three days").

A Plea to Readers

For many years I have been fascinated with Qohelet, perhaps because he makes my own skepticism appear solidly biblical. Like him, I observe a discrepancy between the vision of a just world, which I refuse to relinquish, and reality as I perceive it. This radical absurdity gives an urgency and ultimacy to theological probings. But my reading of Qohelet is not necessarily the right one, certainly not the only possible one. I only hope readers will bestow on my understanding of Qohelet the same tolerance that his original audience extended to one whose radical ideas challenged virtually everything they cherished.

From the day I began work on this commentary years ago, two matters have given me much anxiety: translation and documentation. Although I prefer a dynamic equivalence translation for its literary quality, I have hesitated to surrender the pedagogic value of formal correspondence between the source and target languages. I considered offering two different translations but finally abandoned the idea as unworkable. The translation that follows vacillates between formal correspondence and dynamic equivalence; like most compromises, this one does not entirely satisfy me. I urge the reader to consider also the New English Bible, the Revised Standard Version, and the new Jewish Publication Society *Tanakh.*[25] As for the degree to which I acknowledge indebtedness to other interpreters, I have chosen to use minimal documentation, partly because it is pointless to attempt the impossible, and partly because specialists will easily recognize my indebtedness to those who have preceded me. My reading of secondary literature has been extensive, making it impossible to recall who first introduced me to a given idea. The Bibliography will, I hope, direct others to the reading that informed my decision about disputed passages. In those

[25]Believing that no translation adequately renders Qohelet's words, in the discussion I do not always translate a given verse the same way it appears in the translation at the beginning of each section. This practice calls attention to the translator's limits and emphasizes the rich nuances of the biblical text.

cases where my answers do not seem adequate, the Bibliography will offer alternative views that may be more persuasive.

An ancient rabbi quipped that King Solomon wrote Song of Songs in his youth, Proverbs in mature years, and Qohelet in his senility. I do not agree that Qohelet's musings came from an intellect that had lost its sharpness. I think Qohelet's eyes were alert and his powers of observation undiminished. What he taught has remained fresh through the ages, for Qohelet spoke eloquent truth.

COMMENTARY

The Superscription
1:1

1:1 The words of Qohelet, David's son, king in Jerusalem.

Like many other books in the Bible, Ecclesiastes bears a superscription that places it within a larger context. The generalized form of the introductory comment calls to mind prophetic books and collections of proverbs. Even the identification of the author lacks precision, for *ben-dāwid melek* could refer to any number of kings who sat on the throne in Jerusalem, and except for the royal experiment in 1:12–2:26 the book does not adopt a royal perspective.

[1] Similar superscriptions occur in the book of Proverbs: "The words of Agur, Yakeh's son, the Massaite" (reading *hammaśśā'î,*[1] Prov. 30:1) and "The words of Lemuel, the Massaite king, that his mother taught him" (Prov. 31:1). In Prov. 22:17 a superscription ("the words of the wise") seems to have been incorporated in the first line of the text. Although the initial word in Prov. 1:1 is *mišlê* rather than *dibrê,* the entire superscription ("The proverbs of Solomon, David's son, king of Israel") is remarkably close to Eccl. 1:1. In Prov. 10:1 the short form, "The proverbs of Solomon," identifies the second major collection within the book, and Prov. 25:1 expands that brief attribution to read: "These also are proverbs of Solomon that the men of Hezekiah, king of Judah, transcribed."

This type of superscription is not restricted to wisdom literature: "The words of Jeremiah, Hilkiah's son, one of the priests who (lived) in Anathoth in the territory of Benjamin" (Jer. 1:1); "The words of Amos who was among the sheepbreeders from Tekoa . . ." (Amos 1:1). In the latter case the superscription adds the verb *ḥāzāh,* the nominal form of which occurs in Isa. 1:1 ("The vision of Isaiah, Amoz's son, which he saw concerning

[1]Perhaps *hammaśśā'* does double duty, referring both to the literary genre and to the author's country. In any event, the designation of what follows as a burdensome oracle is redundant, for the following *n^{e}'um haggeber* also includes an expression from oracular contexts, even if juxtaposed ironically with a human subject.

Judah and Jerusalem . . .") and in Obad. 1:1 ("The vision of Obadiah").

Egyptian Instructions have similar introductions. The Instruction of Ptahhotep begins: "The Instruction of the Mayor and Vizier Ptahhotep, under the majesty of the King of Upper and Lower Egypt: Izezi, living forever and ever." Other texts of this type preface the technical word *sebayit* (Instruction) with the words "The beginning of." The Instruction for King Merikare, The Instruction of King Amenemhet, The Instruction of Prince Hordedef, and The Instruction of Amenemopet begin with this preface.[2]

The reference to a book of Solomon's *d^ebārîm* (I Kings 11:41) seems to play on the word's ambiguity. Does the allusion presuppose an account of Solomon's words or of his deeds? "Now the rest of Solomon's *d^ebārîm*—everything he did and (all) his wisdom—are they not written in the book of Solomon's *d^ebārîm?*"

The epilogue in Eccl. 12:9–11 virtually equates the respective words, *dibrê* and *m^ešālîm.* During his professional life, it observes, Qohelet listened, searched out, and arranged numerous proverbs, all the time striving for felicitous and reliable expressions. This epilogue also uses the expression "the words of the wise" as a broad category into which Qohelet's *m^ešālîm* fell.

The name *Qōhelet* is a feminine Qal participle from the root *qhl,* meaning to assemble or gather. Because the term has come to designate an occupation, like *hassōperet* in Ezra 2:55 and *pōkeret haṣṣ^ebāyîm* in Ezra 2:57 and in Neh. 7:59, a masculine verb follows. In Eccl. 7:27, the feminine verb probably arose through a mistaken division, when *'āmar haqqōhelet* became *'ām^erāh qōhelet.* This interpretation of the data seems to be confirmed within the book in Eccl. 12:8 ("says the Qohelet") and outside it in the Septuagint. Twice Qohelet functions as a proper name: in 1:12 ("I, Qohelet, was king over Israel in Jerusalem") and in 12:9–10 ("In addition to [the fact] that Qohelet was a sage . . . Qohelet endeavored to discover felicitous words").

Ben-dāwid (son of David) does not necessarily mean one of David's children. In Hebrew usage it can refer to grandchildren or simply to a remote member of the Davidic dynasty. Furthermore, the word *ben* also denotes close relationships of mind and spirit without implying actual physical kinship (sons of the prophets = disciples or guild members; sons of God = servants). Therefore *ben-dāwid* does not require the identification of Qohelet with Solomon, although that association was probably intended.

The appositional phrase "*melek* in Jerusalem" refers to Qohelet, not to David. Proposals for repointing this word as "property-holder" (Ginsberg

[2]The first part of the Instruction of Ani is missing from the surviving text. In all likelihood, the same formula appeared in this lacuna.

1950), or "counselor" (Albright; see Lauha 1978, 2), or *Ratsherr* (Kroeber 1963) have not commended themselves to interpreters. Due to the author's literary fiction of royal authorship in Eccl. 1:12 (abandoned in 2:26), Qohelet was identified with the king of legendary wealth and wisdom. This identification was logical, inasmuch as the author of Eccl. 1:12 had extracted a suitable pen name from the tradition about Solomon's assembling of the people for the dedication of the temple (I Kings 8:1, *yaqhēl*).

The superscription does not come from the author of the book. Although the verse is often credited to the epilogist(s), that unlikely view introduces one difficulty. According to Eccl. 1:1, Qohelet was a king, but in 12:9 he is called a sage, that is, a professional wise man *(ḥākām)*. The purpose of the superscription may have been to strengthen the case for canonical use of the book by attributing its observations to Solomon. The several collections in Proverbs and the Song of Songs bear witness to an effort to enhance the authority of various writings by linking them with Israel's great king whose wisdom was legendary.

Motto and Thematic Statement 1:2–3

1:2 Utter futility! says Qohelet,
Utter futility!
Everything is futile!
3 What does a person profit
From all his toil
At which he works under the sun?

Ecclesiastes opens with a motto and a thematic statement (attributed to Qohelet himself) that brands reality as utterly absurd, transitory, and futile. Consequently, all human toil is wasted effort, completely devoid of profit. The rest of the book justifies Qohelet's unorthodox teaching and draws significant lessons from the unpleasant fact that there is no lasting advantage for humans.

[2] The word *hebel* derives from a root that connotes a breath or vapor.[3] In Ecclesiastes it shows two nuances: temporal ("ephemerality") and existential ("futility" or "absurdity"). The name Abel connotes the first of these. The earliest Greek translations of the Hebrew rendered the word

[3]In this verse, *hebel* appears in an unusual bound form, *hᵃbēl*. The pointing is strange (cf. also 12:8, which forms an inclusio to the book). The form is probably an Aramaizing vocalization similar to *ʿᵃbēd* in Dan. 6:21.

according to this category: *atmis* or *atmos* (breath). Jerome opted for the second category, which he expressed by the Latin *vanitas*. The Septuagint has *mataiotēs*.

The first category, breath or vapor,[4] is reinforced by the image of chasing after or herding the wind (cf. 2:17). Wind, breath, and smoke are insubstantial when viewed from one perspective. Nevertheless, they are very real, even if one cannot see the wind or take hold of any one of the three. Although Qohelet and the person who wrote the inclusio normally prefer the second sense of *hebel*, this preference is not exclusive. Several uses in the book virtually demand the first meaning, that of fleeting appearance and ephemerality.

Hᵃbēl hᵃbālîm is an idiom that expresses the superlative, like *šîr haššîrîm* (the sublime song, song of songs), *šᵉmê haššāmayim* (the highest heaven, I Kings 8:27), *'ebed 'ᵃbādîm* (servant of servants, Gen. 9:26); *qōdeš qodāšîm* (holy of holies, Ex. 29:37). Its preferred position in the sentence and its repetition[5] following the verb and its subject emphasize the negative observation. Whereas the phrase "ultimate absurdity" might have left room for some exceptions, despite its double usage, the final statement "Everything is absurd" makes the judgment universal. Such a bold claim is extraordinary, especially as a thematic statement for the entire book (note its appearances as a summary statement in 12:8). Would not its readers have promptly set to thinking about life's good things that might escape Qohelet's harsh censure? Hence the importance of the identification of Qohelet with Solomon.

The verb *'āmar* in the Qal perfect can be translated by an English perfect ("Qohelet has said"), but it is better to render it like a Greek aorist ("says Qohelet"). This understanding of the verb emphasizes the permanent quality of Qohelet's conclusion about reality. He did not reach this conclusion and quickly abandon it. Instead, Qohelet laid down a shocking verdict and tenaciously clung to that opinion as an accurate assessment of life according to his experience.

Although Qohelet usually speaks of himself in the first person, in this verse and in 7:27 he employs the third person. This alternating persona concentrates the reader's attention momentarily on the source of the weighty judgment and distances the author of the narrative from Qohelet. Therefore the references in the third person are not necessarily secondary glosses. Nor does the intensification of *hebel* in 1:2 and 12:8 require an author other than Qohelet. His facility with language was such that he

---

[4]The word was an appropriate designation for idols, for it declared them inconsequential nonentities.

[5]The inclusio in 12:8 lacks the repeated use of *hᵃbēl hᵃbālîm,* but some manuscript evidence (Peshitta) suggests its originality here.

could easily have varied the usage from the formula that occurs several times (1:14; 2:1, 11, 15, 17, 19, 21, 23, 26; 3:19; 4:4, 7, 8, 16; 5:9 [10E]; 6:2, 9; 7:6; 8:10, 14; 11:8, 10). The function of the motto is to guide the reader toward a proper interpretation of Qohelet's words. He will validate this thesis in what follows, and that includes everything Qohelet says, including his advice to enjoy life insofar as possible.

[3] The rhetorical question of 1:3 explains and justifies the assessment of reality in 1:2 as utter futility. Because nature can achieve nothing new, human activity produces no profit. Such an assertion contradicts traditional teaching, for the sages who composed the book of Proverbs believed that wise conduct brought lasting gain. They subscribed to this conviction so tenaciously that a dogma resulted, often called the theory of reward and retribution. The belief that the deity rewarded virtue and punished vice functioned as a powerful motive for ethical action, but the conviction was eventually absolutized. The result was an encrusted system that admitted few exceptions, and the theological position of the friends in the book of Job demonstrates the extent to which this attitude was taken regardless of its harmful consequences for innocent victims of chance.

The word *yitrôn* (profit) is possibly a commercial term for what is left after all expenses are taken into account. In the Hebrew canon it occurs only in Ecclesiastes, although rabbinic literature uses the word. The fundamental notion is "advantage." What advantage accrues to men and women *(lā'ādām)?* None. The universality of the point is reinforced in two ways.

First, the comprehensive term *b^{e}kol* is used. No work, however devious or noble, secret or public, will have lasting effect. Therefore the claim that everything is futile, ephemeral, is deadly serious. All activity falls under the negative judgment rendered in 1:2. The preposition *b^e* normally means "by" or "in," but it sometimes has the force of "from," as in Ugaritic.[6] Perhaps the clearest instance of this use in Ecclesiastes is 5:14 ("Just as he emerged from his mother's womb, naked he will return, going as he came, and he will take nothing from his toil [wealth?] that he might carry in his hand").

Second, the phrase "under the sun" reinforces the universal sweep of the thematic statement and its rationale.[7] Nothing falls outside the area circumscribed by *taḥat haššāmeš,* except Sheol and heaven, and the underworld

---

[6]Many interpreters view the *bet* as instrumental or *pretii* (of price), but Whitley (52–53) argues forcefully for "from." He adduces II Sam. 22:14 *(min)* and its parallels in Ps. 18:14 *(b^e);* II Kings 14:13 *(b^e);* and II Chron. 25:23 *(min).* He also refers to the Abibaal Inscription ("the King Gebal from [*b*] Egypt") and the Azitawadd Inscription ("and may he not carry me from [*b*] this resting-place unto another resting-place"). For Whitley, a recently published Ugaritic text clinches the case ("Koshar pours spirits from [*b*] the vat").

[7]*taḥat haššāmeš* occurs in the Hebrew Bible only in Ecclesiastes (1:3, 9, 14; 2:11, 17, 18, 19, 20, 22; 3:16; 4:1, 3, 7, 15; 5:12, 17 [13, 18E]; 6:1, 5, 12; 8:9, 15 [twice], 17; 9:3, 6, 9 [twice], 11, 13; 10:5).

brings no advantage to anyone. The expression "under the sun" is attested in the Gilgamesh Epic ("Only the gods [live] forever under the sun. As for mankind, numbered are their days; whatever they achieve is but the wind"), in the Phoenician inscriptions of Tabnit from the sixth century B.C.E., and of Eshmunazar a century later. A twelfth-century Elamite document also uses the phrase. Strictly speaking, therefore, it is not necessary to assume Greek influence on Ecclesiastes *(hyph' hēliō).* A variant *(taḥat haššāmāyim)* occurs three times in Ecclesiastes (1:13; 2:3; 3:1), but there seems to be no difference in meaning between the two expressions, "under the sun" and "under the heavens."

The repetition of the root *ʿāmāl* characterizes existence in the same way the Yahwist did in the story of the Fall, although the vocabulary is different. In his view fallen humanity must eke out a livelihood by the sweat of the brow, always contending with adverse working conditions. The author of Ecclesiastes makes a similar point by choosing the word *ʿāmāl,* which has the nuance of burdensome labor and mental anguish. But not always, for it appears that the word also came to designate the fruit of one's labor (wages), and by extension, wealth.

The second use of *ʿāmāl* is verbal, and it has the relative particle *šᵉ* as a prefix. The shortened form of *šᵉ* occurs sixty-eight times in Ecclesiastes, whereas the longer form *ʾᵃšer* is used eighty-nine times. The short form is ancient, appearing in Hebrew literature of probably northern origin (Judg. 5:7; 6:17; 7:22; II Kings 6:11). However, the particle *šᵉ* came to be used widely in late Hebrew (Lam. 4:9; 5:18; S. of Songs [32 times, except in the superscription]; II Chron. 5:20; 27:27; Pss. 122:3–4; 124:1, 2, 6). It is used exclusively in the Mishnah except for three biblical quotations and one other instance of *ʾᵃšer.*

Out of context, the rhetorical question "What does one profit from all his toil at which he works under the sun?" leaves open the possibility of responding that one reaps a bountiful harvest from a diligent labor. But the juxtaposition of this question with the thematic statement in 1:2 rules out any effort to offer specific instances of advantage from toil. Of course, something does accrue from the various activities that occupy human beings during their waking hours, and some individuals succeed in amassing a fortune by one means or another. Therefore the author must imply something in these two verses that will come to explicit expression later: the finality of death. Implicit within the word *hebel* is the sense of transience. Perhaps the word *yitrôn* points in this direction, for one cannot calculate the profit or loss of individual activity until it ceases. Prior to this final closure all judgments of expenditures and receipts are necessarily provisional.

The thematic statement in 1:2 and its rationale in 1:3 make optimal use of rhetorical devices: two exclamations, an attribution, and an assertion in

1:2; and a rhetorical question in 1:3. The choice of vocabulary and idiom reinforces the sentiment expressed: everything is futile. Together these verses prepare the way for a prologue (1:4–11)[8] that justifies the pessimistic view of life by examining the pointless movement of nature and the meaningless activity of people. Verses 4–7 draw an analogy from observable reality, to which Qohelet responds (1:8), setting forth a conclusion (1:9) that is then reinforced (1:10–11).

Nothing New Under the Sun 1:4–11

1:4 A generation goes, and a generation comes,
But the earth always remains.
5 The sun rises, and the sun sets,
Panting to its place;
There it rises.
6 Blowing southward and circling northward,
Circling, circling, the wind blows,
And on its circuits the wind returns.
7 All streams flow into the sea,
But the sea is never full;
To the place from which the streams flow,
There they flow again.
8 All words are wearisome;
A person is not able to speak them;
The eye is not sated with seeing,
Nor the ear full of hearing.
9 Whatever has happened is what will occur,
And whatever has been done is what will be done;
And there is nothing new under the sun.
10 There is something about which they say,
"Look, this is new!"
It happened already in aeons
That preceded us.
11 No one remembers those who came before.
Nor will anyone recall people who come later;
For them there will be no remembrance
Among those who come after them.

This poem characterizes nature as an endless round of pointless movement, a rhythm that engulfs human generations as well. Oblivious to the

[8]Some critics connect 1:3 with the prologue rather than with what precedes it.

relentless striving of heavenly and earthly bodies, the earth remains unchanged. The sun makes its rounds, as does the wind, and each one returns to start the process again. Streams flow to the ocean in a never-ending process, but they fail to fill the sea. Humans talk incessantly without fully expressing the wearisome nature of things. The eye always increases human desire, and the ear never hears enough. The past repeats itself ad infinitum, so that there is nothing new under the sun. Things only seem new because of a human tendency to forget the past.

[4] The prologue offers a justification for the pessimistic view of things expressed in 1:2–3. It emphasizes the ceaseless activity of the natural world (1:4–7), a constant movement that has no discernible purpose or result. But the prologue also hints that human actions (1:8–11) always fail to reach their goal.

The initial unit (1:4–7) deals with the four elements of the universe as discussed by ancient philosophers: earth, air, fire, and water. The remaining unit (1:8–11) refers to the quality that distinguishes human beings from animals, the capacity for speech, and isolates two aspects of the affective dimension, sight and sound. The section concludes with a denial that novelty occurs anywhere and a bold assertion that everything is destined to oblivion.

The word *dôr,* an appropriate choice because of its ambiguity, suggests both nature and people. The primary sense here is probably the former: the generations of natural phenomena. But the other nuance must also be present, lending immense irony to the observation that the stage on which the human drama is played outlasts the actors themselves.

A traditional response to the earlier question about profit might have pointed to the quest for progeny: it is advantageous to have children, for one's name survives in them. Qohelet undercuts such an argument. Only the earth endures for long, he observes. With these Qal participles for the passing of one generation *(hōlēk)* and the coming of another *(bā')* a significant feature of the book, antithesis,[9] first comes to expression. In this instance the same word is modified by contrasting ideas. One generation dies and another is born.

The participles indicate continuous action; the dying and birthing happen again and again without end. Qohelet's use of *hōlēk* to specify death (cf. 3:20, "All go to one place; everything came from dust and everything returns to dust"; and 5:15, "And this is also a grievous injustice; precisely as he came so shall he depart, and what advantage did he possess that he toiled for the wind?") is an extension of the phrase "to go to his fathers." The verb *hālak* has the sense of dying in several biblical texts outside Ecclesiastes (Ps. 39:14 [13E]; Job 10:21; 14:20; II Sam. 12:23).

[9]Unless *yitrôn* in 1:3 contrasts with *h^{a}bēl* in 1:2.

The sequence (death-birth) is striking, for one normally expects the opposite order. Both the anterior position and the repetition of *dôr* give this word a force equal to the weightier notions of dying and coming into being. But the twofold occurrence of *dôr* already offers a hint of things to come, the monotonous recurrence of purposeless activity. Like generations, which are ongoing and repetitious, nature moves ceaselessly in circuits that are monotonous and futile.[10]

Not everything is caught up in the endless process of going and coming. Whether the endurance of the earth is meant to be contrasted with the transience of generations, in the aggregate or separately, depends on the way one reads the conjunction *w*^e^. It is possible to understand the verse to mean that a generation always succeeds its predecessor, so that (or while) the earth continues for a long time. However, the *w*^e^ probably means "but." Despite continual departures and entries of separate generations, both human and natural, the earth stands intact. The feminine participle *'ōmādet* denotes duration. Jerome perceived the irony in this observation about ephemerality and permanence. He wrote: "What is more vain than this vanity: that the earth, which was made for humans, stays—but humans themselves, the lords of the earth, suddenly dissolve into dust?"

How long did Qohelet think the earth would remain? The word *l*^e^*'ôlām* indicates continuity for a long time, although it lacks the modern sense of eternity, that is, time without end. The idea is that the earth will last as long as the mind can project into the future. Nevertheless, human beings realize no profit, for they pass from the scene forever.[11]

[5] Ancient Egyptians thought of the sun as conveyed on a ship during its nocturnal journey from west to east, and the Greeks pictured Helios driven by steeds on its daily circuit. According to Ps. 19:5 the sun leaves its chamber like a bridegroom and returns like a strong man, having run its course with joy. Qohelet's description lacks this mood of celebration and wonder. Instead of picturing a vigorous champion who easily makes the daily round, he thinks of strenuous panting to reach the destination. Having arrived, an exhausted sun must undertake the whole ordeal again.

Whereas Qohelet placed the subjects before the participles in 1:4, they follow the participles in 1:5. The repetition of the subject in each verse (*dôr* in 1:4; *haššemeš* in 1:5) achieves perfect symmetry in the first four words of these two verses. But the balancing of subject and participle is broken

[10]Elsewhere the perpetual cycle of generations was likened to a tree's shedding its leaves and putting on new ones (Sir. 14:18–19; cf. Homer, *Iliad* 6.146ff.). In anticipation of standing naked before God the blushing trees cast off their garments one by one, while the deity averts the all-comprehending glance until the naked are fully clothed once more.

[11]The Instruction for Merikare has an interesting parallel: "While generation succeeds generation, God who knows characters is hidden; one can not oppose the lord of the land, He reaches all that the eyes can see."

at the level of meaning, for the sense of *bā'* in 1:4 does not extend into 1:5, where the meaning of *bā'* approximates that of *hōlēk* (sets, dies). Furthermore, the extreme brevity of 1:4, which echoes the succinct form in 1:1–3, disappears. The additional phrase "there it rises" advances the thought from exhaustion after an arduous journey to monotonous repetition of drudgery.

Again participles call attention to the durative nature of the action. Although the first *zôrēaḥ* is pointed as a Qal perfect, the prefixed w^e poses a problem. In all probability the original participle *(zôrēaḥ)* lost its *waw* by metathesis, giving rise subsequently to its present pointing. The root *šā'ap* occurs in the sense of panting with anticipation (Ps. 119:131, "With open mouth I pant, because I long for thy commandments") and from exhaustion (Jer. 14:6, "The wild asses stand on the bare heights, they pant for air like jackals; their eyes fail because there is no herbage"; cf. Isa. 42:14, a woman gasping in travail; Job 7:2, a slave longing for a shadow). The accents separate *šô'ēp* from *w^e'el-m^eqômô,* but this is undoubtedly a mistake.

Thus far the prologue has made two sweeping claims. Human beings and natural forces in their individuality and as an aggregate vanish from the scene on which the drama of life is played. The earth alone endures. Moreover, the most visible of the heavenly bodies is consigned to perpetual drudgery. The sun's task is not unlike the punishment imposed on Sisyphus, who was condemned to an eternity of rolling a boulder to the top of a hill only to have it return to the starting place over and over again.

[6] The withholding of the subject is the most striking stylistic feature of this verse. The subject was the opening word in 1:4 and the second word in 1:5, but 1:6 holds it in abeyance until five participles have made an appearance. The immediate effect is to create the illusion that the movement of the sun is still being described. The south-north direction of the wind corresponds to the east-west movement of the sun, thus completing the four points on the compass.

Another stylistic characteristic of this verse is the repeated use of two participles, *sôbēb* and *hôlēk.* The threefold occurrence of *sôbēb* and two fold use of *hôlēk* serve to simulate the feeling of restlessness generated by the constant blowing of the wind. This sense of being caught in a rut reaches its peak in three successive participles *sôbēb sōbēb hôlēk* just before the subject *hārûaḥ* is introduced. Even the next clause returns to this relentless striving for sameness, for it repeats the subject *hārûaḥ* and employs a form of the root *sbb.* [12]

[12]The translation "from its rounds" is based on general Semitic use, a point that Whitley (9–10) has made and for which he has given a number of examples: Esarhaddon ("loyal conduct was taken away from [*'elî*] my brothers"); the Ahiram Inscription ("And may tranquillity flee from [*'alî*] Gebal"); the Moabite stone ("And Chemosh said to me, Go, take Nebo from [*'al*] Israel, and I went by night"); Dan. 6:19 [18E] ("And his sleep fell from him"

Some interpreters have used this verse among others to argue for a Palestinian composition of the book as opposed to an Egyptian setting. The argument is based on the observation that the wind is more tranquil in the land of the Nile. However, a literalistic reading of the verse hardly supports the claim, for the prevailing winds in Israel are from the direction of the Mediterranean Sea, that is, from the west. Poetic imagery must not be pressed in so literalist a fashion. The author engages in a little exaggeration for maximum effect. In his view the relentless blowing of the wind was no more effectual than the sun's daily round or the passing and coming of countless generations.

[7] The fourth example of pointless activity concerns the remarkable fact that countless streams flow into the sea without filling it to overflowing. The Dead Sea offered a particularly striking instance of such a phenomenon, for this small body of water demonstrably had no outlet and still it remained unfilled. From this observable instance, the same conclusion could be reached about other seas. Aristophanes perceived the same thing, writing that "the sea, though all the rivers flow to it, increaseth not in volume" (*The Clouds,* 1294).

This description of the insatiable sea continues the extravagant use of participles, particularly the repeated use of single images. By means of this poetic device, 1:6 reaches a crescendo with three instances of the participle *sōbēb* and another use of the root *sbb;* it now begins to subside in 1:7. But a new twist emerges to fill the gap; an infinitive with a prefixed *lamed* employs the verbal root that occurs in participial form two other times in the verse. The breadth of nuance is remarkable, for *hôlēk* yields the following senses: die (1:4), blow (1:6, twice), flow (1:7, twice).[13]

The rendering in the Septuagint and Vulgate imply that the point of the verse was not the continual flow of streams so much as their constant cycle. Such a view brings the verse into line with the preceding observation about the sun. The final clause can be translated: "and to the place whence the streams flowed, there they returned in order to flow (once more)," but this interpretation requires an assumption of haplography, a putative *mem* having been assimilated from the relative particle *šᵉ* to the preceding *mem.* Of course, this way of understanding the verse precipitated discussions about the function of underground streams, which served to convey the waters back to their place of origin.

[8] Like the wind, which may blow with incredible force, then subside to the point of imperceptibility, the poem has introduced tangible realities against a backdrop of wonders beyond apprehension. The generations of the

[*ᵉlôhî*]); Ps. 16:2 ("I said O Yahweh thou art my God, my good is indeed from thee" [*ʿālеykā*]); the Mishnah ("But if they receive food from him" [*ʿālâw*], *Maas.* 3:1).

[13]Three times counting the infinitive *lālāket.*

universe, the sun running its daily round, the elusive wind—these phenomena lie outside human grasp. With rivers and the sea a rapid shift takes place, for the tiny rivulets, rushing streams, and surging deeps can be seen and touched in a manner that differs appreciably from the way the sun's rays or the breezes are experienced. With this verse the author internalizes ceaseless and pointless movement. What can be observed about nature is also true on the human scene.

The translation "words" may be too restrictive, for Qohelet frequently uses vocabulary that connotes two different meanings at the same time. The translation of "things" provides a fine transition from nature, summarizing what has gone before and anticipating the meaning of the root *dbr* in the rest of the verse. The argument that all other uses of the plural *haddᵉbārîm* in Ecclesiastes (5:1, 2, 6 [2, 3, 7E]; 6:11; 7:21; 9:16; 10:12, 13, 14) connote "words" and therefore this one does too is persuasive only for interpreters who posit absolute consistency of linguistic usage to the author.

This focus on the human arena concentrates on the faculties of speech, sight, and hearing. The sequence is reminiscent of that represented by the generations, the sun, and the wind.[14] One hears the constant talking of endless generations, beholds the sun in the heavens, and listens to the sound of the wind. In the case of the waves, both sight and hearing come into play. The observations about natural phenomena have vacillated between the themes of relentless movement and ineffectual activity. Both ideas continue in the comments on speech, if *haddᵉbārîm* carries this meaning. The insatiable aspect of seeing and hearing is prominent as well; moreover, this endless looking and listening invariably falls short of its goal.

Does Qohelet launch an attack on traditional wisdom at this point? The choice of illustrations certainly fits such an interpretation. The quest for the right word for the occasion is futile, the observations that arise from experience are incomplete, and the "hearing" is insufficient.[15]

[9] An obvious consequence of successive generations, the sun's relentless pursuit of its daily rounds, the cyclical blowing of the wind, and the endless flow of streams to the sea is predictability. The sages before Qohelet had exulted in the universe's orderly pattern. Qohelet does not. His startling conclusion divests the orderly universe, so dear to the sages, of its positive dimensions. The search for analogies between natural phenomena and human conduct retains its validity, but the insights that emerge do not enable the discoverers to extricate themselves from a paralyzing repetition

---

[14]If, that is, one understands *dôr* as deliberately ambiguous. According to Ps. 19:2–4 even natural phenomena are credited with unusual communicative powers, speech that dispenses with words.

[15]The evocative employment of *ʿayin* ("eye," recalling the solar disc?) and *ʾōzen* is not matched by a comparable expression for speech (cf. 8:2, *pî-melek*). *ʾîš* may be chosen to contrast with *ʾādām* in 1:3, hence a specific individual rather than humankind in general.

of the past. Individuals are destined to lives that never achieve fulfillment. Existence under the sun is marked by inadequate speech, insatiable eyes, and partial hearing.

For persons who exalted eloquence—a sense of timeliness, restraint, integrity, persuasiveness—to the status of supreme virtue, the denial that speech can ever be adequate would undercut the entire wisdom enterprise. Furthermore, observation, the technique by which insights into reality were discovered, is judged faulty. But the most burdensome claim must surely have been the assertion that teaching failed to achieve its goal. The hearer did not embody the transmitted teaching, a problem that Egyptian Instructions take into account (cf. Ptahhotep and Ani).

In the view of this poet, present and future are so closely bound with the past that nothing new ever bursts forth. Unlike those who posited golden ages at both ends of the historical time line, Qohelet rejects the thesis that paradise is both a memory and a hope, a past accomplishment and a future possibility. A myth of eternal return does not lurk beneath Qohelet's reminder that the past repeats itself. Rather, the emphasis falls on the burdensome monotony of everything in nature and among human beings.

Modern linguists may differ with Qohelet about novelty, for the use of the interrogative *māh,* coupled with the shortened relative *šᵉ,*[16] itself departs from earlier usage, causing difficulty for the translators of the Septuagint and Vulgate. This late feature of the Hebrew language occurs often in Ecclesiastes (1:9; 3:15, 22; 6:10; 7:24; 8:7; 10:14) and is equivalent to Aramaic *māh-dî* (Dan. 2:28–29) and *māh-zî* in early extrabiblical Aramaic documents. The Mishnah uses *māh-šᵉ* as an indefinite pronoun just as Qohelet does (*Abot* 5:7, "concerning what he has not heard"; and *B. Bat.* 6:7, "whatever he gave, he gave"). Occasionally, *māh* serves as an indefinite substantive (I Sam. 19:3, "and if I see anything I will tell you"; II Sam. 18:22, "and whatever happens I will run"), and occasionally as a relative (I Chron. 15:13, "for that which was at first" [Whitley 1979a, 10–11]; II Chron. 30:3, "to what was sufficient"; Esth. 9:26, "what they saw").

Some biblical authors also believed new things came to pass. They announced that God was about to institute a new covenant and a new exodus, or they envisioned Israel as the grateful recipient of a new heart.

[10] Sages commonly introduced a striking observation by the particle *yēš.*[17] Qohelet uses this protasis often (1:10; 2:21; 4:8, 9; 5:12; 6:1, 11; 7:15; 8:14 [3 times]; 10:5). The Hebrew particle of existence takes on an ironic dimension in his hands, for it calls attention to bogus claims. The labeling of something as new, like the modern fashion, particularly in the arts, of

---

[16]The twofold repetition of *mah-šᵉ* and *hû' šᵉ* reinforces the claim of recurrent phenomena.

[17]Prov. 12:18; 14:12; 15:10; 16:25; 18:24; 20:15; 26:12; 30:11–14. The juxtaposition of the particle of existence and that of nonexistence (*'ên* in 1:9, *yēš* in 1:10) is especially effective.

freely bestowing the adjective "creative," is stripped of its cogency. Qohelet's argument rests on the identity of past and present, a point emphasized by illustrations from nature and human history.

The particle *hinnēh* often signals a shift in point of view.[18] Here Qohelet uses *rᵉʼēh* in a similar manner. Countering the claim to newness, he places the adverb *kᵉbār* (already) in the emphatic position. This word, which seems to indicate duration, occurs in the Massoretic Text only in Ecclesiastes (2:12, 16; 3:15 [twice]; 4:2; 6:10; 9:6, 7). The plural *lᵉʻōlāmîm* is governed by a singular verb here and occasionally outside Ecclesiastes (Whitley lists Isa. 26:4; 45:17; and Dan. 9:24 [1979a, 11; all subsequent references will be to this volume]).

[11] Qohelet ascribes claims of newness to a colossal ignorance of the past, a failed memory.[19] Previous generations are quickly forgotten, and future generations will fare no differently. Although some interpreters relate the *riʼšōnîm* and *ʼaḥᵃrōnîm* to things, particularly to the *ʻōlāmîm* (ages) in 1:10, the usual impersonal form is feminine plural. Therefore, it is better to understand the words as indicating generations past and future.

In this prologue Qohelet has laid down the grounds for reaching his conclusion that life is futile and that there is no profit from endless activity on earth. He supports the intellectual position by appealing to nature's ceaseless movement, which achieves no surplus, and by referring to human striving, which fails to reach its goal. The examples stress the monotony, repetition, and unfulfilled nature of constant activity. The prologue serves as a suitable introduction to the whole book, just as Prov. 1:2–7 introduces the initial collection (1–9), and perhaps the rest of the book as well.

The Royal Experiment 1:12–2:26

1:12 I, Qohelet, was king over Israel in Jerusalem. 13And I determined to search out and to explore by rational means everything that is done under the heavens; it is grievous business God has given people with which to occupy themselves. 14I saw every action that is done under the sun, and everything is futile and shepherding the wind.

---

[18]The accentuation requires a translation such as: "Look at this! It is new" (Adele Berlin, *Poetics and Interpretation of Biblical Narrative;* Eisenbrauns, 1983).

[19]The unusual form *zikrôn* is a construct before the preposition *lᵉ* rather than an absolute (which occurs as *zikkārôn* in the second half of the verse). Gordis lists the following examples of *zikrôn* before *lᵉ*: Hos. 9:6; Ps. 58:5; Prov. 24:9; I Chron. 23:28; Isa. 9:1; Ps. 2:12; *Abot* 5:14.

15 The crooked cannot be straightened,
and the missing cannot be counted.

[16]I said to myself, "Look, I have achieved intellectual superiority over all who preceded me in Jerusalem, and my heart has observed much wisdom and knowledge." [17]I determined to know wisdom and to know madness and folly; I understood that this also was shepherding the wind. [18]For much wisdom is great trouble, and whoever acquires more knowledge increases care. 2:1 I said to myself, "Come, let me test you with pleasure and look on good things"; but this also was futile. [2]Of laughter I said, "Madness!" and of pleasure, "What does this accomplish?" [3]I explored in my mind how to sustain myself with wine—now my mind continued to conduct itself with wisdom—and to lay hold on folly until I could see what was good for human beings to do under the heavens the few days of their lives. [4]I performed impressive feats: I built for myself houses, I planted for myself vineyards. [5]I made for myself gardens and parks, and I planted there fruit trees of every variety. [6]I made for myself pools of water from which to irrigate a forest sprouting with trees. [7]I bought male and female slaves, and their children became my slaves. I also had much cattle, oxen, and sheep, more than all who preceded me in Jerusalem. [8]I collected for myself both silver and gold, as well as the treasure of kings and of provincial rulers; I had for myself male and female singers, also the delights of men—a mistress, many mistresses. [9]I increased greatly, more than all who preceded me in Jerusalem; my wisdom remained with me. [10]I did not withhold anything that my eyes asked for; I did not deny my heart any pleasure, indeed my heart rejoiced in all my earnings and this was my portion from all my toil. [11]Then I turned to all my achievements that my hands had done and to all my wealth that I had worked to acquire; and, oh, everything was futile and shepherding the wind, and there was no profit under the sun. [12]Then I turned to consider wisdom and madness and folly; for what can the person do who comes after the king? What he has already done! [13]Then I perceived that wisdom is superior to folly as light is superior to darkness.

14 The wise person has eyes in his head,
But the fool walks in darkness;

yet I also know that one fate will come upon both of them. [15]And I reflected, "Like the fate of the fool will my fate be, and why then have I been so very wise?" And I reasoned that this is also futile. [16]For there is no remembrance of the wise, as there is never any of fools, because both are already forgotten in the days to come, and the wise die like fools! [17]Then I hated life, for the work that was done under the sun was grievous to me because everything was futile and shepherding the wind. [18]And I loathed all my wealth for which I had labored under the sun because I must leave it to another who will succeed me. [19]And who knows whether he will be wise or foolish; yet he will have control over all my earnings that I toiled for and that I was ingenious for under the sun. This also is futile. [20]So I turned my heart to despair concerning all the toil at which I had worked under the sun. [21]For everyone whose earnings were acquired with wisdom, knowledge, and skill must give them as his portion to an individual who did not work for them. This is also futile and a grievous evil. [22]For what accrues to a person in all his toiling and the striving of his heart at which he works under the sun? [23]All his days are painful and his occupation vexing; even at night his mind cannot rest. This is also futile. [24]There is nothing better for a person than to eat and drink and let himself enjoy good things with his earnings; I have also seen that this is from God's hand. [25]For who can eat and who can have enjoyment if not I? [26]For God gives wisdom, knowledge, and joy to the person who pleases him, but to the one who displeases him God gives the bother of gathering and collecting to give to another who pleases God. This is also absurd and shepherding the wind.

An ancient tradition that kings dispensed wisdom prompts Qohelet to assume the persona of royalty. By this means he can speak authoritatively about the worth of wealth and power. Possessing the resources to experiment with anything he wishes, the king tries a life of pleasure and then tests wisdom's achievements before concluding that everything is futile. He is particularly dismayed because he has no way of assuring that his successor will be wise. In light of these unpleasant facts, he recommends eating, drinking, and enjoying life. But he cannot forget life's absurdity.

The initial subsection (1:12–18) states the royal intent and the conclusion that Qohelet drew from his research. Two proverbial observations punctuate this section, reinforcing the claim that human activity is unpleasant business, futile and unprofitable, like chasing the wind.

The test of pleasure (2:1–11) yields a similar judgment. Things touted far and wide yield no permanent satisfaction; building projects, gardens, servants, wealth, women, leave an empty feeling. In the end Qohelet realizes that everything is futile, like chasing wind, and unprofitable.

It occurs to Qohelet that he should examine wisdom and folly (2:12–17). This test yields nothing but relative good. An aphorism captures this slight advantage of wisdom over folly, and Qohelet finally utters the dreaded word "chance, fate." Because wise and foolish, good and evil, experience the same fate, death, there is no point in striving for wisdom and goodness. This awareness evokes in Qohelet hatred of life, which is futile and chasing wind.

These morbid reflections force him to ponder the matter of inheritance (2:18–23). Who will inherit the fruit of Qohelet's labor? He discovers no assurance that a worthy person will benefit from his sweat. This is absurd.

Then what should one do? Qohelet advises a policy of enjoyment, *carpe diem,* insofar as one is able (2:24–26). But an arbitrary God determines who can have pleasure and who cannot. This extrahuman dimension elicits the oft-used formula that this is also futile and shepherding the wind.

[12] The author introduces himself in this verse.[20] But tradition has not preserved the memory of any king called "Qohelet." The superscription included Qohelet in the line of Davidic rulers, presumably the successor to David. That information is missing from 1:12, although implied in the claim, "king over Israel in Jerusalem," since the Davidic dynasty was virtually uninterrupted from its inception until Jehoiachin's enforced exile in Babylon in 586 B.C.E.

The verb *hāyîtî* (I was, have been) does not imply that Qohelet relinquished the throne prior to writing this verse. Such an interpretation of the Hebrew gave birth to a Talmudic legend that Solomon was forced to give up the kingship to the demon Asmodeus, who reigned until the restoration of a repentant king (*Sanh.* 2:66; *Git.* 68b). The verb has the meaning: "I have been and still am." That is, the action is past, but its effect continues to the present.

Qohelet claims to be a king. However, doubts surfaced very early. In rabbinic times the word for king was here interpreted as "teacher," in agreement with the book's final chapter, which calls Qohelet a professional sage and a teacher.

In the ancient Near East the attribution of wise teachings to royalty is widespread.[21] Qohelet adopts this literary fiction for the moment, discarding it as soon as it has served its purpose. The rabbis perceived the necessity for this "subterfuge"; they reasoned that if a "nobody" claims that he has tested life's good things no one will believe him, but if a monarch says the same thing his words will command respect. Kings have the resources with which to test all pleasures without fear of dire consequences.

While the pen name Qohelet seems to derive from the legend about Solomon, the literary fiction suggests kingship in general. Even the subsequent account of royal achievements, which must surely echo Solomon's grand accomplishments, is silent about his most celebrated innovation, the widespread use of horses and chariots.

---

[20]Qohelet uses the short form *ʾănî* rather than *ʾānōkî,* sharing this feature of style with other late biblical works (Ezra, Esther, Haggai) and the Mishnah. (The Qumran texts manifest a decided preference for *ʾănî* over *ʾānōkî.*) This introduction may resemble ancient Near Eastern royal texts ("I am Kilamuwa, the son of Hayya"; "I am Yehaumilk, king of Byblos"; "I am Azitawadda, blessed by Baal . . . powerful" (Gibson 1978, 34, 95, 47).

[21]The Sumerian Instruction of Šuruppak; the Egyptian Instructions of Merikare and Amenemhet.

This introductory section extends from 1:12 to 2:26. Its two opening statements give conclusions that Qohelet then proceeds to defend (1:12–15, 16–18). In both cases a traditional saying reinforces Qohelet's argument (1:15, 18).

[13] Qohelet undertakes an impossible task: the exploration of everything within human experience. This scope extends far beyond the modest pursuits of earlier sages.

Ancient Israelites considered the heart the center of the intellect, hence the use of the word *lēb.* The initial verb *wᵉnātattî* has the fundamental meaning of giving, but also means to set or place. Accordingly, it suggests a fixed assignment or firm application of reason in pursuing a specific avenue of research.

The verb governs two infinitives, *lidrôš* and *lātûr,* to seek and to spy. The first refers to the length and breadth of the search. Although *dāraš* often appears in liturgical contexts for seeking the divine will or presence, it was not limited to religious settings. The second infinitive, *tûr,* adds the inner depth dimension, the penetration beyond the surface of reality (cf. JPS, "to probe"). The latter word occurs with reference to the spies whom Moses sent into the land of the Canaanites with instructions to assess the terrain and its inhabitants (Num. 13:2, 16, 17). Together, these two words designate the comprehensive nature of Qohelet's search.

Qohelet hoped to achieve his goal by means of *ḥokmāh* (wisdom; cf. 2:3, 9; 7:23).[22] This word has a wide range of meanings, and in poetry it is often linked with near synonyms that offer additional nuances. *Ḥokmāh* itself refers to practical knowledge, skill, cleverness, guile, insight, general intelligence, and wisdom.

Qohelet is fond of speaking in universal terms. The thematic statement in 1:2 already pushes his observation about utter futility to the limit, incorporating *hakkōl* (everything). In the prologue the adjective refers to toil, streams, words, and claims about novelty. Now Qohelet intends to examine everything beneath the heavens, a variant of the earlier phrase "under the sun." Having accomplished his goal, Qohelet concludes that the daily activities of human beings are a heavy burden.

Furthermore, it is God who gives people these odious chores. Repetition of the verb *nātan* almost suggests that Qohelet's search, an arduous mental task, mirrors in miniature the total human effort, God's dubious gift. The noun *ʿinyān* (business) occurs only in Ecclesiastes (2:23, 26; 3:10; 4:8; 5:2, 13 [3, 14E]; 8:16), but it is used in the Talmud (*Qidd.* 6a; *B. Bat.* 114b). The related verb *ʿnh* has four meanings: (1) to answer; (2) to be occupied

[22]Some interpreters (Hertzberg 1963; Ellermeier 1967; Lauha 1978; Lohfink 1980) connect *lidrôš* with *baḥokmāh* and *lātûr* with "everything that is done under the heavens."

with (only in Eccl. 1:13 and 3:10; perhaps also Sir. 42:8); (3) to be oppressed or afflicted; and (4) to sing or chant. Either the second or the third meaning is appropriate in this context.

Qohelet's view of the deity lacks the warmth of the trusting relationship in some parts of the Hebrew Bible. His belief that God imposed a harsh assignment on people resembles a viewpoint occasionally encountered in Mesopotamian texts. Qohelet terms the deity *'ᵉlōhîm* rather than Yahweh, but that preference for the term that refers to the God of all peoples is characteristic of wisdom literature. The expression *bᵉnê hā'ādām* (humankind) reinforces this emphasis on universality. The creator places a heavy yoke on all human beings.

[14] True to the teaching of the sages, Qohelet proceeds by personal observation, eyes open to reality as it presents itself. Unlike his predecessors, however, Qohelet claims that he has taken note of everything that transpires on earth. The word *hamma'ᵃśîm* (the works) occurs often in Ecclesiastes with reference to the deity, but here it concerns human activity also, or even exclusively.

Qohelet again draws a universal conclusion on the basis of what he has seen: "everything (*hakkōl,* the whole, total) is futile and shepherding the wind." The reference to shepherding the wind (cf. 2:11, 17, 26; 4:4, 6; 6:9) conjures up an image of someone chasing the invisible wind, an exercise of utter futility. The root *rā'āh* has two possible meanings in the context of Ecclesiastes: (1) to feed or tend, and (2) to strive or desire. The former suggests a shepherding of the wayward wind: an utter impossibility. Some recent critics prefer the second meaning of *rā'āh* (cf. Whitley, 13). The phrase *rō'eh rûaḥ* in Hos. 12:2 has a parallel *wᵉrōdēp qādîm,* which implies that striving is an appropriate translation of *rō'eh.* In Ezra 5:17 and 7:18 *rᵉ'ût* means will or pleasure, and Prov. 15:14 refers to a fool desiring folly *(yir'eh 'iwwelet).* This meaning also occurs in Ps. 37:3 ("and take pleasure in security"). The plural *rā'ôt* came to mean thoughts (Dan. 2:30, *ra'yônê libbāk;* possibly Prov. 15:28, *yabbîa' rā'ôt*). In some instances the image of shepherding is equally appropriate, and in two cases the context is improved by the pastoral rendering (Hos. 12:2; Prov. 15:14).[23] Both examples mock the behavior of those engaged in shepherding, whether rounding up the wind or feeding on folly.

[15] The previous two verses have argued that God placed a grievous burden on humanity and that individuals have not removed themselves from this odious bondage. Qohelet now quotes an ancient aphorism to the

[23]The first describes Ephraim as herding the wind and pursuing the east wind throughout the day; the second states that "the mind of one who has understanding seeks knowledge but the mouths of fools feed on folly."

effect that it is impossible to improve the human condition, for God's decrees are permanent.[24] The twisted will remain that way, and the missing will resist human calculation.[25]

An Egyptian educational text, The Instruction of Ani, refers to the pedagogic task in similar but more optimistic language. A crooked stick can be straightened (albeit with difficulty), and distorted minds can be corrected. This assertion implies that careful instruction makes a decisive difference in the lives of children. Qohelet has no such optimism.

The word *litqōn* (to straighten) should probably read *littāqēn* or *lᵉhittāqēn,* to be straightened (cf. the Septuagint and Vulgate). This verb occurs in the Old Testament only in Ecclesiastes (1:15; 7:13; 12:9). It takes the Qal form in 1:15; elsewhere it appears in Piel or Hiphil (as it does in the Mishnah). Sirach 47:9 uses the Piel ("he placed"), and in Dan. 4:33 [36E] the Hophal appears ("I was established").

The parallel verb is a Niphal *(lᵉhimmānôt).* It means to be counted, hence the proverb states a truism. How can anyone count the missing elements in a given thing? The noun *ḥesrôn* (loss, deficit) occurs only here, although the form *maḥsôr* (need, poverty) appears in Prov. 6:11; 11:24; Judg. 18:10 (cf. the Talmudic *Qidd.* 32b, "in which there is no monetary loss"). The contrast with *yitrôn* (profit) is striking.

[16] Many scholars argue that Qohelet cites views that he does not share without indicating that he quotes earlier material. Here we do find the Hebrew equivalent of quotation marks *(lē'mōr).* It functions to dramatize inner thoughts. The author carries on a conversation with himself, thinking aloud, weighing the present situation and his own intellectual accomplishments. This self-critique leaves no room for modesty, particularly since Solomon's legendary wisdom and wealth have inspired the royal fiction.

The term *higdaltî* may allude to I Kings 10:23,[26] although the word is a common one and the two texts employ different syntax. The Solomonic legend was broader than implied by this verse in Kings, but later comments by Qohelet include riches as well as knowledge.

The two verbs might also be translated together: "I greatly acquired" (GKC, 120d). (The fundamental sense of *yāsap* is to add or increase.) Qohelet's fondness for verbs with similar meanings is well documented

---

[24]Qohelet characteristically repeats *lō'-yûkal,* and one could make a case for its composition in the course of the argument. However, other poets also used repetition freely. One can read the aphorism as a realistic observation about the necessity of accepting things as they are and going on about one's business. In context it makes an altogether oppressive impact, whatever its original meaning.

[25]Galling thinks it refers to a crooked back and to the shortened spine that caused an old person to be bent over permanently, but Zimmerli relates the phrase to inattentive students.

[26]"Now King Solomon was greater than all the kings of the land with regard to riches and wisdom" (cf. I Chron. 29:25).

(1:13, *drš* and *twr;* 2:26, *'sp* and *kns*). The use of the preposition *'im* with *libbî* is normal, although Qohelet also uses *b^e* (2:1, 15, *b^elibbî*). With *'im* the verb *dbr* is used, and *'mr* is associated with *b^e*. Whitley (14) compares *Ahiqar* 1:25 to the latter use with *b^e*.

Dahood's (1966, 266) attempt to understand the second *'^anî* as a corrupt form of *'ônî* (wealth) is not required by the text. Nevertheless, his translation supplies a parallel to *ḥokmāh:* "I magnified wealth and increased wisdom." Whitley (14–15) writes that the Hiphil of *gdl* is transitive and reflexive, whereas the Qal is intransitive.

Besides this text, only Eccl. 2:12 and 9:13 use the verb *rā'āh* with *ḥokmāh.* The object of Qohelet's observing is ethical and speculative knowledge.

[17] Qohelet uses a *waw* consecutive with imperfect (elsewhere only in 4:1, 7) to indicate that a substantial period has elapsed during which he has observed every kind of wisdom and its practical implementation. Otherwise the expression resembles his determination in 1:13 to search for and probe everything by means of reason. The dual infinitives in 1:13 lend plausibility to the Massoretic accentuation, which implies that the second *da'at* is an infinitive, the *lamed* attached to the first *da'at* governing both. However, the mention of wisdom and knowledge in 1:16 suggests that these words are repeated in 1:17. That is how the ancient versions (Septuagint, Peshitta, Vulgate) understood the verse: the first infinitive governed four objects.[27]

The words for madness (from *hll,* to rage, shout) and folly are doubly perplexing. First, they do not seem to belong here, for Qohelet launches an experiment of wisdom at this point and only later will turn to evaluate madness and folly. Second, *hôlēlôt* is an abstract plural, although *śiklût* is an abstract singular form. In Ecclesiastes *hôlēlôt* appears in 10:13. Outside Ecclesiastes the plural participle *hôl^elîm* (dissolute people) is found in Pss. 5:6; 75:5.

Although *śiklût* is found here, everywhere else in Ecclesiastes the form *siklût* occurs (2:3, 12, 13; 7:25; 10:1, 13), and some manuscripts have *s* rather than *ś* in 1:17. The meaning is therefore "folly" rather than wisdom (the meaning of *śkl*). This confusion of *s* and *ś* was common in late Hebrew.[28] Whitley (16) gives several examples: Job 5:2; 6:2; 10:17; 17:7 (*k'ś* for *k's,* anger); Ezra 4:5 (*skrm* for *śkrm,* hiring). In Biblical Aramaic the tendency continued: *kśdy'* in Dan. 5:30, but *ksdy'* in Ezra 5:12; *śbk'* in Dan. 3:10, 15 but *sbk'* in Dan. 3:5. In extrabiblical Aramaic the shift was intensified (*śkltnw* in Dan. 5:11, 12 but *skl* in *Ahiqar* 1:47).

Jerome comments on this verse: *contraria contrariis intelliguntur* (con-

---

[27]Gordis thinks the meaning is "to know that wisdom and knowledge are madness and folly."

[28]Qohelet gives *maśm^erôt* in 12:11 for *masm^erôt.*

traries are understood by means of their opposites). Qohelet frequently sets opposites over against each other in this manner (2:12; 7:25; 8:16), following a precedent set by the authors of Proverbs, who used antithesis and juxtaposed aphorisms (26:4–5).

The expression *šeggam zeh hû'* occurs in Gen. 6:3 without the *zeh.* Qohelet often uses *hû'* as a copulative. The words *ra'yôn rûaḥ* echo the earlier *rᵉ'ût rûaḥ.*

[18] Acquisition of knowledge is no small achievement. Dense or uncooperative students required extra incentive, so parents and teachers freely applied the cane, believing that the results justified such cruelty. Egyptian and Sumerian scribal texts attest to the prevalence of punishment in schools. Late descriptions of Dame Wisdom agree that her demands are burdensome at first.

Qohelet understood the educational process to be painful, but unlike his predecessors, he found the result equally unpleasant. Open eyes see the injustices of society, and wider awareness of oppression and life's absurdities is disquieting. Furthermore, Qohelet understood the limits that restrict human knowledge, stifling the desire to know and confounding attempts to achieve comprehensive knowledge.

The repetition in this verse is only partly a function of parallelism. On the subconscious level the doubling of terms *(rōb/rob, yôsîp/yôsîp)* and selection of synonyms *(ḥokmāh/da'at; kā'as*[29]*/mak'ôb)* call up the tedium of the learning process. (Only the conjunction *kî* fails to double.) Within the larger unit (1:16–18) the words *ḥokmāh* and *da'at* occur four times each,[30] and the roots *rb* and *ysp* three times. Qohelet's great increase in wisdom brings a surplus of trouble as well.

[2:1] Having concluded that wisdom and reason alone do not satisfy, Qohelet turns to evaluate sensual pleasure, again using the literary device of conversation with himself.[31] (Cf. the Egyptian "Dialogue Between a Man and His Soul.") The Hebrew image is that of rational deliberation, a conversation with one's personified mind. Qohelet urges his heart to launch yet another test. Although the language is polite in the extreme, the imperative lends urgency. Qohelet submits himself to a new test. The word *'ᵃnassᵉkāh* (I will test you) appears to derive from the root *nsh;* the ending is a long form of the second-person pronoun.[32] The means of the test is *śimḥāh* (joy). This word covers pleasures from religious ecstasy to sexual excess. The second imperative, *rᵉ'eh* (see), has the nuance of "experience." Will the pleasures of the body transcend the sober excitement of learning?

[29]*kā'as* is used elsewhere in 2:23; 7:9; 11:10.

[30]*yāda'tî* is used once also.

[31]In 1:16 the variant *dibbartî 'ᵃnî 'im libbî* occurs.

[32]The *plene* spelling was common practice in texts from Qumran, but it is also found in earlier Hebrew (Gen. 10:19, *bō'ᵃkāh;* Jer. 40:15, *yakkekkāh;* II Sam. 2:22, *'akkekkāh*).

Qohelet dispenses with suspense, stating his conclusion at the outset. (Like frequent uses of exclamation points in modern prose, his fondness for particles, particularly for *hinnēh* [look, behold], threatens to become counterproductive.) Pleasure, mentioned here for the third time, does not answer life's enigma. It too is futile.

The purpose of the Queen of Sheba's trip to Jerusalem, according to I Kings 10:1, was to test Solomon with riddles *(l^e^nassōtô b^e^ḥîdôt).* In Eccl. 7:23, Qohelet insists that he has tested all this by means of wisdom *(kol zōh nissîtî baḥokmāh).* We need not, therefore, follow the Vulgate in reading the verb *nsk* (to pour out) and assuming that an object such as wine was implied.

[2] Qohelet proceeds to remove all possibility for misunderstanding his previous comment about the futility of joy, explaining that his test included both frivolity and profound joy, running from one extreme to the other. Now he labels the lighter side sheer madness, and he suggests that the weightier aspect of pleasure achieves nothing substantial.

A similar judgment about laughter occurs in Prov. 14:13 ("Even in laughter the heart is sad, and the end of joy is grief"). Qohelet brands mirth *(ś^e^ḥôq)* a form of madness (cf. Ps. 102:9 [8E], "my enemies taunt me throughout the day, my madmen curse me"). *M^e^hôlāl* is a Pual (Poal) participle from *hll.* In I Sam. 21:14 the Hithpael *wayyithōlēl* ("he played the madman") describes the calculated irrationality which saves the fugitive David's life in enemy territory. Qohelet dismisses frivolity as incompatible with intelligence and psychological stability.

The verdict on joy is equally devastating, although Qohelet does not liken it to incoherent babbling. His quarrel with joy is that it cannot accomplish anything worthwhile. What does this (that is, joy) achieve? The interrogative *mah-zōh* functions rhetorically;[33] it is the equivalent of a denial. The late form *zōh* (for *zōt*) is feminine, modifying *simḥāh* (joy). The usual *zōh* is missing from Ecclesiastes (cf. 2:24; 5:15, 18; 7:23). However, *zōh* has precedents in Biblical Hebrew (Judg. 18:4, *kāzōh w^e^kāzeh;* II Kings 6:19, *lō' zeh hadderek w^e^lō' zōh hā'îr;* Ezek. 40:45, *zōh halliškāh*).

[3] Having pronounced his verdict that sensual pleasure amounts to nothing (2:1–2), Qohelet proceeds to describe his experiment (2:3–8). He carries out this test of pleasure with the same thoroughness with which he tested wisdom; even the same verb recurs (*tûr,* to spy out). The choice of this verb from 1:13 rather than *drš* rests on its reference to the depths, appropriate for studying the labyrinthine corridors of the mind.

The infinitive *limšôk* seems to connote sustained effort, "to prolong," hence "sustain," although the essential meaning of *mšk* is "to draw, pull" (Gen. 37:28, *wayyimš^e^kû wayya^a^lû et-yôsēp min-habbôr,* "and they drew

---

[33]The deity's question in Gen. 3:13 *(mah-zō't 'āśît)* is similar.

and they brought Joseph from the pit"). The psalmist asks the deity to prolong steadfast love (Ps. 36:11), and God declares that divine love is everlasting ("therefore I have prolonged you [by] steadfast love," Jer. 31:3). Others have suggested reading *liśmôk* (to support), assuming a transposed *š* and *m* and taking the *ś* as an orthographical variant of *samek.* This verb occurs in S. of Songs 2:5 (*samm^{e}kûnî bā'^{a}šîšôt,* "sustain me with raisins").[34]

Qohelet uses *b^{e}śārî* as a substitute for the pronominal suffix. If prolongation is the correct nuance of *mšq* here, one would expect the Hebrew word *ḥay* (life). This is another reason to suspect that the sense of prolong has developed into the meaning "sustain."

Lest anyone charge that wine had dulled his critical capacities beyond use, Qohelet adds a circumstantial clause: "my mind *nōhēg* with wisdom." The primary sense of *nhg* is "drive, lead," as in exercising control over animals (II Kings 4:24; Ps. 78:52). The verb means "behave, conduct oneself" in Sir. 40:23 and in the Mishnah (*Abod. Zar.* 3:4; cf. the Targum on Eccl. 10:4). This is the probable meaning in Eccl. 2:3.

Qohelet described the experiment of wisdom with double infinitives (1:13, 17). He does likewise with the test of pleasure. The second infinitive, *w^{e}le'^{e}ḥōz* (to grasp, hold on to), suggests the fleeting nature of sensual pleasure. Qohelet latches onto folly (cf. 7:17, where it is parallel to wickedness; 7:25) for a sustained period so that his judgment will not be skewed by the brevity of his test. He holds folly until he can determine what is good. The expression *'ē-zeh ṭôb* functions interrogatively; a parallel use is in I Kings 13:12 (*'ē-zeh hadderek hālāk,* "which way did he go?"). The final phrase "the number of days of their life" is sharply ironic, for its meaning ("few") stands over against the effort to prolong pleasurable experiences. If one follows the suggested reading in *BHS (w^{e}lō' 'ōḥēz b^{e}siklût),* a parenthetical statement emerges. Qohelet does not take hold of folly.

[4] Like a king, Qohelet did things on a grand scale. The royal fiction undoubtedly draws on the biblical story of Solomon's accomplishments, but the material is developed with considerable freedom. Not one word is whispered about building the temple, although it may be included in the general category of houses. Solomon's achievements in this area are recorded in I Kings 6–10 (II Chron. 8:3–6) and S. of Songs 1:14; 8:11 mentions his vineyards in a not altogether flattering light (cf. I Chron. 27:27).

In this verse and the next five the indirect object *lî* ("for myself") occurs eight times, indicating the king's personal involvement in a life of luxury at any expense. The Egyptian pharaohs built their tombs, the Babylonians

[34]On the basis of Ps. 104:15 (*w^{e}yayin y^{e}śammaḥ l^{e}bab-'^{e}nôš,* "and wine refreshes a person's heart") P. Joüon proposed *l^{e}śammēaḥ,* to make glad. A. D. Corré interprets *mšq* as an instance of epispasm ("removing marks of circumcision"), reading *b^{e}yayin* as *k^{e}yyun* ("like the Greeks").

built their gardens, and Qohelet claims to have performed wonders also. But these impressive accomplishments have already been dismissed as leading to nothing (what do these accomplish? *ʿōśāh* in 2:2, *maʿăśāy* in 2:4).

[5] Israelite kings, like their counterparts throughout the ancient Near East, took great pride in gardens and enclosed parks (S. of Songs 4:12; 5:1; 6:2, 11). These gardens were both aesthetic and practical, providing pleasant shade and delicious food. The parks often were a refuge in which to find a convenient source of wild meat, and they were valued for royal sport. According to Neh. 2:8 the king's enclosure supplied timber for constructing the defensive wall around the city of Jerusalem. The word for parks *(pardēsîm)* is a Persian loanword;[35] Xenophon uses the Greek form *paradeisos* with reference to gardens belonging to Persian kings and aristocracy.

The language of this verse *(ʿēṣ kol-perî)* resembles Gen. 1:11, 29, as if to suggest that Qohelet had access to the pleasures of paradise. But not necessarily, for Israelite eschatology projected a day when houses would be secure and vineyards enjoyed. Naturally, Qohelet makes optimal use of such hopes in describing the royal experiment, for kings could reasonably expect to enjoy multiple houses, numerous vineyards, luxurious gardens, and lush parks.

[6] Considerable documentation exists for royal reservoirs from early times. The Moabite stone records Mesha's boast that he "built Qarhoh . . . its gates . . . its towers . . . the king's houses . . . its reservoirs for water" (*ANET,* 320). The eighth-century Siloam inscription uses the word *brkt* in describing King Hezekiah's awesome accomplishment of engineering. Late evidence is also available to confirm sustained interest in royal reservoirs. Nehemiah mentions the king's pool in Jerusalem (Neh. 2:14), and King Herod's achievements in building reservoirs and aqueducts were impressive.

The addition of *māyim* (water) is typical of Qohelet's style, which often adds words that are not essential to the meaning. (Note the pleonastic [emphatic?] use of *ʾănî* with a verb which has a pronominal suffix, already encountered in 1:16 and 2:1.) Nahum 2:9 also adds *mayim* after *kibrēkat* (pool). The masculine *mēhem* ("from them") does not agree with its feminine antecedent (*berēkôt,* pools), but such lack of agreement (cf. Eccl. 2:10; 10:9; 11:8; 12:1) often occurs in late texts such as Song of Songs, Chronicles, the Qumran Manual of Discipline, and the Mishnah. The use of third-person masculine plural for the feminine also occurs occasionally in earlier texts (Judg. 21:22, *lōʾ ʾattem netattem,* where the antecedent is wives; Job 1:14, *ʿal-yedêhem,* where the referent is *ḥōrešôt,* so Whitley [20]).

The expression *yaʿar ṣômēaḥ ʿēṣîm* ("a forest of sprouting trees") is an accusative of specification, i.e., "a forest sprouting with trees." Trees were

---

[35] The singular form *pardēs* occurs in Neh. 2:8 and S. of Songs 4:13. The plural is used frequently in rabbinic literature. The Septuagint uses *paradeisos* often to translate Hebrew *gan.*

a valuable commodity in the ancient world. The Egyptian Tale of Wenamun refers to a long history of commerce between Egypt and Byblos, which supplied wood for the royal vessel. The Old Testament mentions several uses for timber: shipbuilding, houses, musical instruments, and furniture.

[7] Two kinds of slaves are distinguished here: those whom Qohelet obtained (cf. Gen. 17:12), presumably through purchase, and those born to such slaves (cf. Gen. 15:3). The verb *qānāh* (to get, purchase) refers to buying a commodity with money *(kesep).* The prophet Amos denounced Israelites for buying the poor for a ridiculously small sum (Amos 8:6). The unusual expression for indentured slaves (children of the house) implies that Qohelet profited from the procreational activity of his servants, whose children became his slaves. The singular verb *(hāyāh)* has probably resulted from its attraction to the nearer personal pronoun *(lî)* or the word for house *(bayit).*

After mentioning slaves, Qohelet turns to his other possessions, which were in the slaves' care: herds and flocks; large farm animals and small domestic animals. In some ways this account of wealth is reminiscent of the folk tale about Job, who was greater than all the Easterners (Job 1:3). Qohelet boasts that his possessions were unrivaled by those of anyone before him in Jerusalem. But only David and the Jebusite rulers preceded Solomon in Jerusalem. Once more Qohelet's mask has slipped and revealed the royal fiction for what it is, a rhetorical device.

[8] According to II Chron. 9:27 Solomon had so much silver that it became a common commodity in Jerusalem, and his holdings in fine gold were fabulous (I Kings 10:14–25). The discovery of the treasures of Tutankhamon supports ancient stories about kings who hoarded vast amounts of precious metals.

Although the word *s^egullat* (treasure) can refer to Israel as Yahweh's special possession (Ex. 19:5; Deut. 7:6; 14:2; 26:18), it came to connote a treasure like the one referred to here (cf. I Chron. 29:3, where David provides a treasure in gold and silver for use in the temple). The definite article on the word *hamm^edînôt* has troubled interpreters, for by the rules of standard grammar it ought to be indefinite like *m^elākîm* (kings). It is more natural to read "kings and the prefects," especially now that Ugaritic evidence for this meaning of *mdnt* has surfaced (*Anat* 2.15–16).[36] A similar inconsistency in Qohelet's use of the article occurs in 7:25 *(w^ehassiklût hôlēlôt).*

The reference to singers, both male and female, may represent totality, as seems to be the case in the hapax *šiddāh w^ešiddôt* and the anticipated

---

[36]If one posits an ellipsis of *h^amôn* (wealth), it refers to "the riches of provinces" (Zimmerli 1962, 156, n. 4). The allusion would then be to the payment of tribute by subjugated rulers.

maiden or two for every man in Judg. 5:30 (*raḥam raḥ^a^mātayim,* an obscene allusion?). But the expression in Judges differs both morphologically (a singular and a dual form) and syntactically (a small number) from *šiddāh w^e^šiddôt,* which may be a hendiadys expressing multiplicity like *dôr dōrîm* in Ps. 72:5 (Fox, forthcoming commentary). The context in Eccl. 2:8 seems to demand an erotic interpretation of *šiddāh w^e^šiddôt,* contrary to the translation in the ancient versions: (1) cupbearer (Septuagint, Peshitta); and (2) goblet (Aquila, Vulgate, Targum). Omission of sexual delights in an experiment of sensual pleasure would be strange, and the two words seem to be in apposition with *ta'^a^nûgōt b^e^nê hā'ādām* (man's delights). Comparison with S. of Songs 7:7 [6E] confirms the suspicion that *šiddāh* refers to woman, the supreme delight of man.

Modern critics have followed this lead in proposing two etymologies for *šiddāh: šdd,* to seize (hence those taken in raids, concubines); and *šd,* breast (cf. S. of Songs 7:4 [3E]; 8:1). A letter from Pharaoh Amenophis III to Milkilu prince of Gezer, a document discovered at Amarna, contains an Akkadian gloss on an Egyptian word which can mean concubine. The gloss is *šaditum* (cf. Ugaritic *št,* lady) a form that is probably related to the Hebrew *šiddāh.* Thus the combination *šiddāh w^e^šiddôt* may refer to many mistresses. Nevertheless, such a reading demands that *b^e^nê hā'ādām* be construed as masculine rather than generically. This exclusive reading is entirely appropriate, given Qohelet's attitude toward women.

[9] Qohelet described the experiment with sensual pleasure in 2:4–8. Now he sums up his accomplishments that enabled him to taste life's nectar. Just as Qohelet introduced the experiment in three verses, he concludes it in the same way. To express the success of his first test Qohelet combined two verbs, *gdl* and *ysp* (1:16); he does the same in assessing his progress toward evaluating the life of pleasure. Once more Qohelet mentions his predecessors on the throne in Jerusalem as those with whom he wishes to be compared. He will not allude to this literary fiction again.

The second half of the verse returns to a matter that surfaced momentarily in 2:3, the need to assure others that his experiment with pleasure never fell to the level of mindless stupor. His rational capacity stood by him (*'ām^e^dāh lî*). The verb *'md* appears to have the sense of "remaining" in Eccl. 8:3 (*'al ta'^a^mōd,* "do not remain"; cf. Ps. 102:27 [26E], *hēmmāh yō'bēdû w^e'attāh ta'^a^mōd,* "they perish, but you remain"; Jer. 48:11, *'al-kēn 'āmad ṭa'mô bô,* "therefore his taste remains with him").

[10] The seats of desire, both inner and outer, ruled during the experiment. Neither the eyes nor the heart had cause to complain, for all their desires were fully gratified. According to Num. 15:39 special measures were required to prevent Israelites from following the desires of their eyes and heart. Qohelet pictures himself as a person without restraint, who surrenders to every wish occasioned by inward reflection and focused eyes. As breast represented a desirable woman in 2:8, so eyes and heart stand for the desiring person.

The verb *śmḥ* normally governs the preposition *b*ᵉ (in), but it is occasionally followed, as here, by *min* (from) to designate the source of joy. In Prov. 5:18 one reads *ûśᵉmaḥ mē'ēšet nᵉ'ûrekā* (and rejoice in [from] the wife of your youth). Likewise II Chron. 20:27 has *kî-śimmᵉḥām yhwh mē'ôyᵉbêhem* (for Yahweh had made them rejoice over [from] their enemies).

One of Qohelet's favorite words, *'āmāl,* occurs here for the third time. (Cf. 2:11[2], 18[2], 19[2], 21[2], 22[2], 24; 3:9, 13; 4:4, 6, 8[2], 9; 5:14, 15, 17[2], 18 [5:15, 16, 18(2), 19E]; 6:7; 8:15, 17; 9:9[2]; 10:15). It has the fundamental meaning of toil or burdensome labor, but a derived sense of "wages, wealth" seems appropriate in several contexts. This verse may have two instances of such use, for one could translate *'ᵃmālî* as "my wealth" in both cases (cf. JPS).[37] However, Qohelet's fondness for wrenching more than one meaning out of a word appears to be operative in 2:10. If that is true, the second use of *'ᵃmālî* recalls the expenditure of effort lying behind accumulated wealth. Against this interpretation is the royal fiction, which emphasizes the massive fortune of the experimenter rather than the toil required to collect the gold, silver, and possessions of all kinds.

Portion *(ḥēleq)* is another word that Qohelet seems to have liked (cf. 2:21; 3:22; 5:17, 18 [18, 19E]; 9:6, 9; 11:2). Its essential meaning for him is limitation, a part of something rather than the whole thing. One's portion in life is the share of desirable or undesirable experiences that come along, not as the direct result of good or bad conduct but purely by chance. In a few cases the sense of limitation recedes and the meaning approaches "reward" (2:10; 5:17, 18 [18, 19E]; 9:9). Just how far the gloomier sense remains in the background is debatable, even in 2:10.

[11] The phrase *ûpānîtî 'ᵃnî* ("then I turned") leads one to anticipate an infinitive of "seeing or considering," which actually occurs in the following verse. Instead, Qohelet uses a preposition, again unexpectedly, for the usual one accompanying *pānāh* is *'el* (to). Job 6:28 offers a parallel to Qohelet's rare use of *pānāh* plus *b*ᵉ (*wᵉ'attāh hô'îlû pᵉnû-bî,* "and now turn to me freely"). Qohelet reflects on the results of his test, facing reality after having occupied a dreamland. What has all his striving accomplished?

The self continues to be the measure of all things, as shown by the emphatic use of *'ᵃnî* in this verse. Note also the emphasis on Qohelet's own achievements (*ma'ᵃśay še'āśû yāday,* the works that my hands had per-

[37]Whitley (23) defends the meaning "wealth, gain" in 2:11, 18. He thinks the same use occurs in the Aramaic inscription of Barrakib (*wbyt 'by 'ml mn kl,* which he translates "and the house of my father amassed more than any") and in the Qumran Manual of Discipline (1QS 9:22). The text reads *l'zwb lmw hwn w'ml kpym* ("to leave to him wealth and gain of hands"). This meaning of *'āmāl* is also found in Talmudic literature and Samaritan Aramaic.

formed). Because the test had a dual character, the assessment contains two features. Qohelet faces his accomplishments and his fortune. The unusual phrase *ûbeʿāmāl šeʿāmaltî laʿᵃśôt* can be translated "and my wealth that I had laboriously acquired." A similar use of the infinitive *laʿᵃśôt* is found, for example, in Joel 2:20 (*kî higdîl laʿᵃśôt,* "for he acted mightily") and in Gen. 2:3 (*ʾᵃšer bārāʾ ʾᵉlōhîm laʿᵃśôt,* "that God creatively made").

The last half of 2:11 brings together the distinctive teachings of Qohelet thus far, reiterating the key phrases: "everything is futile," "striving after wind," "there is no profit," and "under the sun." We reach a caesura in the argument, a conclusion that Qohelet substantiates through personal experience. The sages understood this kind of argument, for they based their own teachings on experience and reinforced them by general consensus. Qohelet's question, "What profit does one have for toiling?" evoked this answer: There is no profit, either from the pursuit of wisdom or from reveling in pleasure.

[12] In 1:17 Qohelet introduced, ever so briefly, the topic of madness and folly (the two words appear to be a hendiadys, translatable by "senseless folly"). Now he returns to this subject in relation to wisdom, first considering the relative worth of wisdom and folly (2:13–17), then taking up the matter of successors (2:18–23). The underlying theme in the discussion of both topics is the common end that awaits everyone.

The meaning of 2:12b is unclear. The Septuagint appears to have read *mî ʾādām* ("who is the person?") and *mᵉlēk* (Aramaic for "counsel"; cf. Dan. 4:24, *lāhēn malkāʾ milkî,* "therefore, O king, my advice"). It thus interpreted the Hebrew as an inquiry about the character of the individual who followed advice. Other ancient versions read *hammelek,* "the king" (Vulgate, Peshitta, Targum).

The interrogative *meh hāʾādām* (literally, "who is the person?") reminds one of Ps. 8:5 [4E] (*māh-ʾᵉnôš,* "what is a person?" cf. Job 7:17) and Ps. 144:3 (*yhwh māh-ʾādām,* "Yahweh, what is a person?"). In context, *meh hāʾādām* seems to require a form of the verb *ʿāśāh,* probably *yaʿᵃśeh.* The verb may have dropped out of the Hebrew text by homoioteleuton, the scribe's eye having jumped from the *he* in *meh* to the final *he* of *yaʿᵃśeh.* Or (less likely), *yaʿᵃśeh* may have been suppressed by the similar verb at the end of the verse.

The direct object (*ʾēt ʾᵃšer-kᵉbār,* what already) holds an emphatic position.[38] One expects a singular verb *ʿāśāhû,* for which there is manuscript evidence (Driver lists 68 instances in *BHK*). Or one may read the verb impersonally: "what has been done."

In the Testament of a Heracleopolitan king, The Instruction for King Merikare, a dead king (sic!) says to his son: "May I see a brave man who

[38]The ancient versions do not reproduce the adverb *kᵉbār* (already).

will copy it, who will add to what I have done; a wretched heir would disgrace me" (Lichtheim, I, 103). Qohelet denies the possibility of improving upon the king's deeds. If this is the correct understanding of 2:12, Qohelet continues the practice of posing the topic that follows and stating his conclusions, which he subsequently elaborates.

[13] Qohelet agrees that wisdom is more useful than folly, although he insists that one can never be absolutely certain that intelligent conduct will produce a desirable result. In 2:14 he will qualify the profit of wisdom by stressing its relativity. Qohelet never overturns the sharp polemic in traditional wisdom against various kinds of fools, but he extends the criticism to the sages who confidently claim to possess secret knowledge (cf. 8:17).

Qohelet draws on traditional images of light and darkness to characterize two types of existence. The sages had associated light with the wise (cf. Prov. 6:23, 27, which juxtaposes two flames: the lamp of torah and the fire of passion). Psalm 119:105 describes the divine word as a source of light that illuminates a pathway. Evildoers were thought to wander in the dark (Job 12:25). The final poem of Ecclesiastes (11:7–12:7) stresses the sweetness of light and the inevitability of going to the land of permanent darkness.

[14] The convenient distinction between good and evil, wise and foolish, had been discussed countless times by teachers in the book of Proverbs. Fools squander their energy in dissolute living, waste opportunities through laziness, do not exercise restraint in the face of angry opponents, and spurn sound counsel. They hasten to a land of darkness and gloom. On the other hand, the wise follow a path that leads to long life and well-being. Such was the teaching of the sages.

Qohelet subscribes to portions of this legacy, although he sharply contests some features of it. True, as for the wise, their eyes are in their head, whereas fools grope in darkness. But when Qohelet penetrates beyond the superficial differences between the wise and fools, he realizes that his teachers have overlooked the most important fact of all, a bond that unites villain and hero, fool and sage. Qohelet announces his discovery in an emphatic manner: "Yet I also[39] know that a single happening will befall both of them."

At last the source of Qohelet's dis-ease emerges. The shadow of death relativizes human distinctions. Death alone is absolute; its manner and time of coming register this fact with incontestable accuracy. Chance *(miqreh)*, another of Qohelet's favorite terms (2:14, 15; 3:19 [3 times]; 9:2, 3; the verb

[39]The adversative use of *gam* is typical of Qohelet (cf. 4:8, 14; 6:7; 8:17). So, too, is the emphatic (or pleonastic?) use of *ʾănî* after a verb.

in 2:14, 15; 9:11), refers to events that occur without warning and especially to the event that closes the curtain on a person's life. Although neutral outside the book of Ecclesiastes,[40] both the noun *miqreh* and the verb *qārāh* have an ominous nuance everywhere in Ecclesiastes with the possible exception of 9:11, which emphasizes the unpredictability of events. Qohelet refutes the advantage of wisdom with knowledge that sooner or later everyone must grope in darkness.

[15] If in death there is no distinction among human beings, it makes little sense to undergo the pain of learning. Qohelet concludes that the cosmic order leaves much to be desired.

The emphatic appositional phrase *gam-ʾᵃnî* (also I) modifies the accusative suffix in *yiqrēnî* (it will befall me). Contrary to the fundamental teaching of the sages, wisdom does not postpone the moment of death. Why then bother to be wise?

Interpreters have understood the textually difficult *ʾāz* in two ways: temporally (then) and logically (hence).[41] The adverb *yôtēr,* which Qohelet uses elsewhere in 7:16; 12:9, 12, is taken with the second half of the verse in the Septuagint. One expects another question after *lāmmāh;* for this reason Whitley proposes an original *ʾēy* (where). One could then read *yôtēr* as a predicate adjective: "Where is the advantage?"

In this reflection Qohelet uses two different verbs *(ʾāmar* and *dibber)* with a common object. Both verbs are related to the heart, which is viewed as the seat of the intellect. Qohelet talks within his mind, that is, he reasons and reflects on what he observes with his eyes.

[16] According to Prov. 10:7 the righteous leave behind a blessed memory but fools can count on a rotten reputation. That confident attitude is not shared by Qohelet. In his view death "sinks the wise man, as it does the fool, in eternal oblivion" (Delitzsch, 248). The preposition *ʿim* here functions like *kᵉ* (cf. Job 9:26, *ʿim-ʾᵃniyyôt//kᵉnešer,* like ships//like an eagle).[42]

The combined form *bᵉšekkᵉbār* is equivalent to *baʾᵃšer* (for; cf. 7:2; 8:4) plus *kᵉbār* (already). An accusative of time follows, the days that come after the deaths of the wise and fools. Both *(hakkōl)* are quickly forgotten. This

---

[40]The noun *miqreh* occurs in Ruth 2:3 to describe a fortuitous event that may be wrapped in the blanket of divine solicitude—a hidden act of special providence—in I Sam. 6:9 to distinguish between divine punishment and accidental misfortune, and in I Sam. 20:26 to refer to an unknown happening. The nineteen uses of the verb *qārāh* carry the meaning of chance occurrence.

[41] *ʾāz* is missing from Peshitta, Vulgate, and Coptic versions, and some Greek manuscripts.

[42]In Eccl. 7:11 *ʿim* has the sense of "like," unless "together with" is the nuance. The preposition *ʿim* designates "the common lot" ("together with") in Gen. 18:23 (*haʾap tispeh ṣaddîq ʿim-rāšāʿ,* "will you really destroy the righteous together with [like] the wicked?").

gloomy prospect evokes a strong exclamation: How dies the wise? Like the fool!

In 1:1 Qohelet denied that previous generations would be remembered. From this he now concludes that reputations are insignificant, for everyone will soon be forgotten. Until this point Qohelet used euphemisms for death (*qārāh,* to happen; *hālak,* to pass on), or hinted ever so gently at it (the few days of life; the successor to the king). Now Qohelet hurls the dreaded word *mût* into the center of discussion. The question is not so much query as protest. The exclamatory *wᵉʾêk* (and how) is unusual, but it yields good sense. We need not change the particle to *ʾak* (truly).

[17] Hatred of life is an astonishing attitude for a wise man, for the aim of wisdom was long life (cf. Prov. 8:35, *kî mōṣᵉʾî māṣāʾy ḥayyîm,* "for whoever finds me finds life"; and cf. 3:16, where "wisdom holds long life in her right hand, riches and honor in her left hand"). Qohelet's disdain devolves from his recognition that death fells everyone alike (a resultative *wᵉ,* so, then).

Qohelet's judgment extends to the entire cosmic order. Both the work of the universe and the works of human beings weigh heavily on Qohelet's mind. The preposition and personal suffix *ʿālay* (on me) is a late idiom in Hebrew, common in Aramaic. The preposition *ʿal* occurs in Esth. 3:9 (*ʾim-ʿal-hammelek ṭôb,* "if it seems good to the king"); I Chron. 13:2, *ʾim-ʿᵃlêkem ṭôb,* "if it seems good to you"), and the suffix is added in Ps. 16:6 (*ʾap-naḥᵃlāt šāpᵉrāh ʿālāy,* "yea, I have a beautiful heritage").[43]

The preposition *ʿal* can have the sense of a burden resting on someone's shoulders. That is certainly the meaning of *hāyû ʿālay lāṭōraḥ* in Isa. 1:14 ("they have become a burden to me"). This derived sense of *ʿālay* is possible in Eccl. 2:17; 6:1; 8:6.

Qohelet thus expresses hatred of life, a repugnance resulting from the futility of all things. One expects him to recommend suicide as the logical outcome of such thinking, but the fundamental premise of the teachers (life as the highest good), now thrown into question, still exercised a powerful hold on Qohelet. Human breath was too precious to snuff out, even though in the end one's existence adds up to nothing.

[18] The catchword *wᵉśānēʾtî* (and I hated) functions as transition to the subject of a successor, which Qohelet raised momentarily in 2:12. Having dispensed with the claim that wisdom bestows an absolute advantage over folly, he now exposes the fruitlessness of acquiring great treasure. One must leave everything to another person, but there is no assurance that the heir will be wise. Qohelet implies that fools will squander the inheritance. But

---

[43]Aramaic uses of the preposition with pronominal suffix occur in Dan. 4:24 [27E] (*yišpar ʿᵃlāyk,* "may it please you") and 6:24 [23E] (*ṭᵉʾēb ʿᵃlôhî,* "he was glad"). One may compare *Pirqe Abot* 2:10, "Let the honor (or property) of your friend be as precious to you as your own."

he also is troubled by the fact that death separates persons from the product of their arduous labor. This section (2:18–23) therefore continues the argument in 2:12.

Characteristically, Qohelet repeats the relative *šᵉ* (that, who) and the personal pronoun *ʾᵃnî* (I) three times. Also familiar is the use of a cognate accusative with the verb *ʿāmēl* (to labor). The pleonastic *ʾᵃnî* hardly serves this time to make the verb emphatic, for stress falls on the expression of antipathy. The sentence does not need *taḥat haššāmeš* (under the sun), but Qohelet's fondness for this expression leads him to add it.

Qohelet refers here to royal succession, possibly but not necessarily alluding to Rehoboam, whose folly was the subject of ridicule in the official story that circulated in the southern kingdom. But Qohelet clings only lightly to his literary fiction, for the problem under discussion is universal. At death all individuals bequeath their goods to others, an involuntary separation from toil and its fruits.[44] The Targum universalizes a step further by leaving off the article on *lāʾādām* (the person). Qohelet paves the way for this when he omits the noun *melek* (king) after *šeyyihyeh* (who will be).

The prefixed relative in *šeʾannîḥennû* has the meaning "because." Qohelet uses the relative pronoun in the same way in 4:9 (*ʾᵃšer yēš-lāhem śākār,* "because they have a reward") and in 8:15 (*ʾᵃšer ʾên-ṭôb lāʾādām,* "because there is nothing better for a person"). This use of the relative is found elsewhere (S. of Songs 1:6, *šeʾᵃnî šᵉḥarḥōret,* "because I am dark"; Gen. 30:18, *ʾᵃšer nātattî,* "because I gave"; Gen. 31:49, *ʾᵃšer ʾāmar,* "because he said"). The Hiphil of *nûʾaḥ* means "bequeath" when followed by the preposition *lᵉ* (cf. Sir. 44:8, "There are some of them who have bequeathed a name").

[19] The rhetorical question *mî yôdēaʿ* (who knows) occurs ten times in the Hebrew Bible (II Sam. 12:22; Joel 2:14; Jonah 3:9; Ps. 90:11; Esth. 4:14; Prov. 24:22; Eccl. 2:19; 3:21; 6:12; 8:1). In the first five texts the object of knowledge retains freedom to act unexpectedly. Qohelet (cf. Prov. 24:22) closes the door to surprise. In his hands *mî yôdēaʿ* expresses utter skepticism.

The usual interrogative pair is *hᵃ . . . ʾim* (Gen. 24:21, *hᵃhiṣlîaḥ yhwh darkô ʾim-lōʾ,* "whether Yahweh had prospered his way or not"). But *hᵃ . . . ʾô* occurs in various contexts (Judg. 18:19; II Kings 6:27; Mal. 1:8; Job 16:3; 38:28; Eccl. 11:6). The verb *šālaṭ* is only found in late texts (Neh. 5:15; Esth. 9:1; Ps. 119:133) and in Biblical Aramaic (Dan. 2:39; 3:27; 5:16; 6:25). Qohelet uses *šālaṭ* nine times (2:19; 5:18 [19E]; 6:2; 7:19; 8:4 [twice], 9; 10:5).

---

[44]One could understand *ʿᵃmālî* as "my toil," hence the various projects that brought glory to the king and gave him the reputation of excelling anyone else in Jerusalem. However, it seems better to interpret the word as a reference to wealth.

Again *ʿămālî* functions ambiguously, referring to the fruit of one's labor and the toil itself. Qohelet complains that his projects will fall to someone with neither the interest nor the inclination to look after them, or objects because his hard-earned money will go to someone whose character Qohelet does not know. The verbs *šeʿāmaltî wᵉšeḥākamtî* combine as a hendiadys ("for which I toiled ingeniously"). Even if the successor happened to be wise, that would be little consolation to Qohelet, for the investment in the projects and fortune is his alone. Qohelet finds it unjust that someone else will control what he, Qohelet, earned through hard labor.

[20] The verb *yʾš* occurs only six times in the Bible (including I Sam. 27:1; Isa. 57:10; Jer. 2:25; 18:12; Job 6:26). In all five instances outside Ecclesiastes the Niphal is used, but Qohelet has the Piel, a form presupposed by rabbinic texts (*yeʾuš* in *B. Meṣ* 21b and *tityāʾēš* in *Abot* 1:7; cf. *Kelim* 26:8). Whitley argues for the meaning "disillusion," a stronger sense than the "renounce, give up, despair" of the Niphal. Qohelet abandons all hope.

Sabbôtî seems to function in the same way as *pānîtî,*[45] as a turning from an inadequate perspective. Qohelet recognizes the utter hopelessness of, not just his personal burden, but the human situation. There is no point in working any more.

[21] The particle of existence introduces a condition: if anyone does this . . . . Again Qohelet states a general truth, that everyone who works ably and accumulates a few possessions must pass them on to someone else who has not contributed any effort.[46] The sages' egocentric perspective stands out here, for there is no indication that the donor derives genuine pleasure from bestowing happiness on someone else. The attitude is one of complete self-centeredness; I earned the wages and therefore am entitled to derive satisfaction from them.

The noun *kišrôn* (skill, advantage) is only found in Ecclesiastes (2:21; 4:4; 5:10 [11E]), but the verbal root occurs in Eccl. 10:10; 11:6; and Esth. 8:5. A plural form *kôšārôt* (prosperity) appears in Ps. 68:7 [6E]. A similar word from Ugarit *(kṯr, kṯrt)* means "skilled, expert" at a craft.

Qohelet's tendency to balance an observation with a similar one, or even the same one expressed differently, and to repeat favorite words and expressions dominates this verse. The initial *ʾādām* is balanced by *ûlᵉʾādām,* the nominal *šeʿămālô* by verbal *ʿāmal-bô.* But instead of "and striving after wind" after "this also is futile," Qohelet surprises us by remarking that it is a great evil, a sore injustice.

[45]Delitzsch (249) distinguishes between *pānāh* (to turn clearly around) and *sābab* (to turn away from one thing to another). He sees this latter use of *sābab* in Eccl. 4:1, 7; 9:11.

[46]Jerome summed up the situation as follows: "One has the fruit of another's labor, and the sweat of the dead is the ease of the one who lives."

[22] The participle *hōweh* occurs elsewhere only in Neh. 6:6 (*w^e'attāh hōweh lāhem l^emelek,* "and you will be their king"). It has the fundamental sense of fall or happen, hence "be." Qohelet asks, literally, "For what is to a person?" Although *hāwāh* in late texts resembles *hāyāh* in meaning, especially in the Mishnah, the verb is attested much earlier. The Aramaic inscriptions of Zinjirli (8th century B.C.E.) and Carpentras use *hāwāh.* An imperative form *(h^ewēh)* appears in Gen. 27:29 (*h^ewēh g^ebîr l^e'aḥeykā,* "be mighty over your brothers").

Qohelet includes both physical and mental activity in this assessment. Neither yields any result worth the effort.

[23] Qohelet's question in 2:22 anticipates a negative answer: there is no profit from individual initiative. The *kî* in 2:23 introduces the justification for the implied negative response. One's entire lifetime is characterized by pain and vexation, and this preoccupation with trouble invades even one's evening hours of rest. The image of a mind that is unable to lie down because of disquieting thoughts almost personifies the *lēb.* This idea of troubled thoughts preventing sleep occurs elsewhere in Ecclesiastes (5:11, a rich person's abundance will not allow him to sleep).

One might also translate: "During his days his occupation is painful and vexing." This takes *kol-yāmāyw* (all his days) as an accusative of time like *ballaylāh.* In our translation, the subject, *kol-yāmāyw,* stands at the beginning for emphasis.

Some scholars understand the first half of 2:23 as an aphorism about the unwelcome features of being a merchant. Ben Sira goes so far as to assert that merchants inevitably cheat their customers.

With 2:23 this section comes to an end. Life is full of sorrow and disquiet, exacerbated by the prospect of bequeathing everything to someone else. "This also is futile."

[24] On the basis of Peshitta, Targum, and some Greek manuscripts it appears that haplography has occurred between *bā'ādām* and *šeyyō'kal.* The comparable observation in 3:22 employs a comparative *min* (cf. 3:12 and 8:15, where *kî 'im* rather than comparative *min* occurs). Some earlier interpreters read a question, "Is it not good?" while others added an excluding particle (either *'ak* or *raq*).

Having concluded that both wisdom and an inheritance are ultimately disconcerting, Qohelet offers practical advice for living under the shadow, asserting not so much the goodness of eating and drinking as their relative advantage: not "This is good," but "There is nothing better." The preposition on *'ādām* generalizes the statement ("among human beings"), unless one follows the lead of the Peshitta to read *lā'ādām* ("for a person"). Ecclesiastes 3:12 has *bām* ("among them") in a similar context, which some interpreters think is a mistake for *bā'ādām.*

The combination of an imperfect verb *(šeyyō'kal)* and two perfects *(wᵉšāṯāh, wᵉherʼāh)* places the action in the present. To "look upon good" is to enjoy, with the causative suggesting pampering one's body (cf. 3:13; 5:17 [18E]; 6:6). The phrase *baʿᵃmālô* (in his toil) makes Qohelet's observation more comprehensive. The enjoyment occurs during one's toil as well as afterward. Or the noun *baʿᵃmālô* may refer to wages, making a different point.

Qohelet's positive counsel rests under a cloud. The ability to enjoy life is not in anyone's power, coming as a gift from God. Qohelet relates his own discovery that one cannot enjoy life unless God makes it possible.

[25] Two problems confront the interpreter. What does *yāḥûš* mean, and is the first-person suffix on *mimmennî* correct? The ancient versions do not definitively answer either question. The Septuagint, Peshitta, and Theodotion read *šāṯāh* (drink) for *yāḥûš,* whereas Aquila, Symmachus, and Syro-Hexaplar presuppose *yāḥûś* (the Targum has *ḥᵃšāšāʼ,* feeling or anxiety). The Vulgate's paraphrase presupposes *mimmennî* (and abound in delights "as I"); so does the Targum. The Septuagint, Peshitta, Coptic Versions, and Jerome read *mimmennû* (from him).

What does the verb *yāḥûš* mean? Scholars have suggested the following: (1) enjoy; (2) be anxious, fret; (3) refrain; (4) eat; and (5) consider. They appeal to various verbs from cognate languages: Akkadian *ḫâšu* (to hasten, be worried), Akkadian *ḫss* (to rejoice), Ugaritic *ḫšt* (joy, happiness), Arabic verbs meaning "to be gorged" or "to refrain." After the verb *yōʼkal* (eat) one expects something equivalent to *šāṯāh* (drink), but whether this is the meaning of *yāḥûš* remains unclear.

For *ḥûṣ mimmennî,* found only here in the Hebrew Bible, there are two possibilities. The expression may renew the fiction of royal authorship, boasting that of all people Solomon was most capable of enjoying life. Alternatively, it may return to the previous verse's idea that all enjoyment is a divine gift outside human control. Verse 25 would thus clarify the meaning of the phrase "in the hand of God." No one can find enjoyment unless God wills it.[47]

[26] This verse takes the traditional categories, wise person and fool (sinner), and empties them of moral content. Qohelet's predecessors used *ṭôb* and *ḥôṭeʼ* as ethical terms for good and bad people. Here, the two terms mean simply "fortunate and unfortunate, lucky and unlucky." For Qohelet *ḥôṭeʼ* almost retains its original neutral connotation of errant, missing the mark.

Qohelet's observations transpose the motif, dear to the sages, that wicked

[47]Whitley, following Dahood, has argued that the suffix on *mimmennî* is actually a third-person form. He finds examples in Ps. 16:8 (*mîmînî,* "from his right hand") and 42:5 [4E] (*ʿālay,* "to him"). Whitley adduces Ugaritic and Phoenician parallels for the suffix *y* as a third-person masculine singular ending.

people's wages eventually go to the devout (Prov. 13:22; 28:8; Job 27:16–17). Qohelet turns this cherished belief on its head. Since good people can and do lose their possessions to sinners, the disposer of goods must be indifferent to morality.

The final comment, "this also is futile and striving after wind," sums up the whole business that Qohelet has endeavored to assess rather than issuing a judgment about God's unpredictable treatment of humans. Utter futility characterizes the human endeavor to gain happiness by means of wisdom, pleasure, or achievements. Death cancels the supposed advantages of wisdom over folly, fun over madness, accomplishments over lethargy. One cannot trust that a successor will value wisdom and follow in one's footsteps. The refrain glances ironically at persons busily engaged in storing up earthly possessions without realizing that they cannot hold onto them.

This verse withholds the subject until the very end, just as *hārûaḥ* was delayed in 1:6. Despite repeated references to the lucky person who enjoys divine favor, attention centers on the deity.

A Time for Everything
3:1–15

3:1 For everything there is a season,
And a time for every matter under the heavens.
2 A time to give birth and a time to die,
A time to plant and a time to pull up what has been planted.
3 A time to kill and a time to heal,
A time to dismantle and a time to build.
4 A time to weep and a time to laugh,
A time of mourning and a time of dancing.
5 A time to throw stones away and a time to gather stones,
A time to embrace and a time to refrain from embracing.
6 A time to search and a time to count as lost,
A time to keep and a time to throw away.
7 A time to rip and a time to sew,
A time to be quiet and a time to talk.
8 A time to love and a time to hate,
A time of war and a time of peace.

9 What profit does the worker have from his toil? 10 I have seen the business that God has given humankind with which to occupy themselves. 11 He has made everything beautiful in its time; also he has put the unknown in their mind, because of which no one can find out the

work God has done from beginning to end. [12]I know that there is nothing better in them than to rejoice and to fare well during life. [13]And also that every person should eat and drink and experience good in all his toil—it is a gift of God. [14]I know that everything God does—it will be forever; there will be no adding to it and no subtracting from it, and God has acted so that they will be afraid in his presence. [15]That which is has already been, and whatever will be has been already, and God brings back what has already been pursued.

Ancient sages believed that there was a right time and a wrong time for everything, and they devoted considerable energy to discerning proper times. Qohelet concurs in the view that everything has its own moment (3:1–9), but he insists that humans cannot know those times (3:10–15), for God withholds that information. An arbitrary deity shapes human lives, allowing some persons to participate in pleasure and preventing others from doing so. It does no good to fight against this external control, for God's deeds are permanent, and lest humankind forget that sober fact, the deity acts so that they will possess appropriate fear where God is concerned. Once more Qohelet complains that nothing new ever occurs, for God is caught up in bringing back the past.

[3:1] Qohelet moves beyond the assertion that God freely disposes of human possessions to the claim that every event on earth has a fixed or opportune moment, determined by God and concealed from human eyes. Those caught in the daily round cannot know the predetermined pattern, nor profit by it.

The noun *zᵉmān* occurs only in late Hebrew (Neh. 2:6; Esth. 9:27, 31; cf. Sir. 43:7, seasons of decree, perhaps festival), in Biblical Aramaic (Ezra 5:3; Dan. 2:16; 3:7, 8; 4:33; 7:12), and in the Mishnah (*Zeb.* 1:1, a passover at its appointed time). It is probably borrowed from Aramaic. Both *zᵉmān* and *'ēt* indicate specific points in time rather than continuity.

Qohelet uses both early and late meanings of the noun *ḥēpeṣ* (desire or pleasure, and business).[48] The former occurs in Eccl. 5:3 [4E] (*kî 'ên ḥēpeṣ bakkᵉsîlîm,* "for [God] has no pleasure in fools"); 12:1 (*'ên-lî bāhem ḥēpeṣ,* "there is no pleasure in them"); 12:10 (*dibrê-ḥēpeṣ,* pleasing words). In four instances Qohelet uses *ḥēpeṣ* in the sense of "business" (3:1, 17; 5:7 [8E]; 8:6). In 3:17 *ḥēpeṣ* is used in parallelism with *hammaʿᵃśeh* (work); in 5:7 [8E] *'al-haḥēpeṣ* refers to "any matter." The context in 8:6 ("for to everything there is an appointed time and procedure") resembles that in 3:1, but the differences between these verses reveal the hazards involved in assuming consistency. Qohelet varies both language and style. The particle of exis-

[48]Whitley (30) notes that *ḥēpeṣ* has this meaning of "pleasure" in Judg. 13:23; II Sam. 23:5; and Isa. 44:28. But he also refers to an Aramaic inscription of the eighth century which uses *ḥēpeṣ* in the sense of "business."

tence *(yēš)* appears in 8:6 but not in 3:1. Repetition of *lᵉkōl* occurs in 3:1 only. In 3:1 *zᵉmān* and *ʿēt* are the temporal expressions for *kairos* and *chronos,* while in 8:6 *ʿēt* and *mišpāṭ* (ruling, procedure) are associated with each other. In addition, the variant "under the heavens" appears in 3:1 rather than the more common "under the sun."

[2] A series of fourteen antitheses comes to expression in 3:2–8. These twenty-eight items cover the spectrum of human activity, beginning with birth and death and ending with war and peace. This gives the poem a ring pattern, a closed structure. Most pairs use infinitive verbs prefixed by *lamed;* exceptions occur in 3:4b, 3:5a *(kᵉnôs),* and 3:8 (nouns). The use of opposites to express completeness or totality is frequent in the Hebrew Bible.

Qohelet voices his conclusions about these polarities in 3:9–15. The prefatory judgment in 3:9 rules out any celebration of the deity's orderly universe. The poem's mood recalls the earlier question concerning profit and the description of daily activity as grievous business (1:3, 12); this link is actually made in 3:9–10. Qohelet then objects that human beings cannot discern the times fixed by God (3:11), and that divine activity lasts forever.

The poem opens with life and death, which lie beyond human control. Everything else in the list falls between these critical points. The biblical notion of time as filled with potential does not characterize this poem, for God's determination of everything rules out every attempt to profit from observing the times. Earlier sages searched for the right word or deed for the occasion, but Qohelet pronounces that quest a fruitless chase.

The first infinitive can be translated intransitively on the analogy of Jer. 25:34 *(liṭᵉbōaḥ),* although Qohelet uses a passive form *(hiwwālᵉdô)* in 7:1. A passive rendering, too, parallels *lāmût,* referring to activity over which one has no power. Nevertheless, the active translation "to give birth" provides a better parallel with *laṭaʿat* (to plant). The Qal form of *ʿāqar* is not found elsewhere in the Bible, but the Niphal occurs in Zeph. 2:4 (*wᵉʿeqrôn tēʿāqēr,* "and Ekron will be uprooted"), and the Piel is used for hamstringing animals (Gen. 49:6; Josh. 11:6, 9; II Sam. 8:4; I Chron. 18:4). Both meanings suggest a negative sense for plucking up. An opposite sense, "harvest," has also been proposed,[49] but it is unlikely here.

[3] The first pair of opposites moved from the human to the plant world; the second shifts from humans to one of their activities, the construction of walls or houses. The activities are described from a purely amoral standpoint. Presumably, the killing refers to actions by human beings directed at other persons. Although the parallel between killing and healing is inex-

[49]Whitley (31) mentions an Aramaic inscription from Sefire that uses the noun form of *ʿqr* for offspring, literally offshoot. He also refers to a Phoenician inscription from Karatepe in which the noun has the meaning "storehouses" (*wml' 'nk ʿqrt pʿr,* "and I filled the storehouses of Pa'r"). Hence a translation such as "harvest" seems appropriate for Eccl. 3:2.

act, there is no necessity for changing *lah^{a}rôg* to *lah^{a}rôs* (to injure, tear down).

Execution and violent slaying of enemies were facts of life in Qohelet's world. They were balanced by healing, although feelings toward medicine were ambivalent as late as Ben Sira, who defended the profession on the basis that God created herbs and roots used in healing, and besides, physicians could ask for divine assistance. The ambivalence sprang from the dogma of reward and retribution, which implied that illness was God's punishment of sinners. Physicians risked interfering with divine retribution.

In ancient Palestine construction often required dismantling of existing stone structures. Isaiah speaks of a vineyard owner (God) tearing down its enclosure *(pārōṣ g^{e}dērô),* leaving it exposed for trampling (Isa. 5:5b). Qohelet has in mind human projects requiring breaking through something (the meaning of *pāraṣ*).

[4] The poem makes rapid transition from violence directed against humans and structures to efforts toward healing and building. Like life and history, emotions are uncontrollable. The choice of *r^{e}qôd* rather than *ś^{e}maḥ* was probably occasioned by the similarity in sound between *r^{e}qôd* and *s^{e}pôd.*[50] The last word in 3:3 *(libnôt)* leads naturally to the similarly sounding *libkôt.*

In each of the pairs of antitheses discussed thus far the first opposite resembles the third and the second corresponds to the fourth: being born//planting, dying//uprooting; killing//dismantling, healing//building; weeping//mourning, laughing//dancing.

[5] What was the purpose of discarding stones and collecting others? Interpreters have given several answers to this question, drawing from the realms of warfare, agriculture, business, and affection. During war rocks were thrown on cultivable fields to render the fields useless (II Kings 3:19, 25). In peacetime rocks had to be cleared from a field before cultivation; on hillsides these stones were usually arranged in terraces to prevent erosion, catch the rain, and allow it to penetrate the dry soil (cf. Isa. 5:2). Rocks were also used in the construction of houses in Palestine, both temporary and permanent (a grave heap).

Galling has argued that the discarding and gathering of pebbles refers to the economic realm. Shepherds carried pouches and small pebbles, which represented the number of animals in their care. As the number decreased, they discarded an appropriate number of pebbles, and as it increased, they collected enough rocks to represent the flock. Likewise merchants used stones for recording commercial transactions of various kinds, a possible background for this text. Eissfeldt has pointed to the biblical notion of a

[50]Eaton (79) thinks of the first two references as private emotions and the next two as public, but his interpretation may be forced.

bundle of the living, which he thinks would have been filled with pebbles.

The Midrash Rabbah on Qohelet understands this entire verse in an erotic sense, and in so doing continues the structural pattern of the previous verses. Discarding stones is taken as a symbol for sexual relations, an activity which corresponds to embracing; gathering stones is understood to mean continence, which parallels the last image of keeping far away from embracing. This allusion to stones would be the only metaphor in the poem, which troubles some critics. Furthermore, the verb *ḥābaq* does not necessarily imply erotic embracing. It could refer to the customary embrace of friends or of parents and children.[51]

The actions referred to in both halves of the verse engage the hands and arms. In 3:2b the root *nṭ'* from the previous half verse is repeated, along with another infinitive. Now the repetition mounts up in 3:5 (stones and embrace), making this verse the longest in the poem (it is also the middle verse). Delitzsch (257–258) observed that "the loving action of embracing stands beside the hostile, purposely injurious throwing of stones into a field." But the casting of stones does not necessarily connote a hostile act.

[6] The exact social setting of this verse is unclear, perhaps intentionally, since the poem covers the whole spectrum of existence. The reference may belong to the household, where women searched for something (like the lost coin in Jesus' parable) that had been misplaced. One can easily think of several circumstances where searching was timely and where an unsuccessful search finally justified a decision to consider the object permanently lost.[52]

There were times to save something for future use, but also moments when one needed to squander resources. How does one balance abstemious saving and generous discarding? The repetition of *lᵉhašlîk* from the previous verse is emphatic, for Qohelet could easily have supplied a different verb for throwing something away.

This verse especially illustrates futility. If one could only know whether to invest time in a search, or whether the item is irrecoverable! As it is, one always thinks, "Perhaps if I had looked harder" or "Why did I not just let it go"?

[7] Some interpreters associate the various activities of this verse with mourning and its termination, for on learning of a death individuals tore their garments as an expression of loss. As elsewhere in Qohelet's poem

---

[51]The image of gathering and casting stones is found in Berossus' account of the flood, according to which the survivor repopulates earth by hurling stones over his shoulder. As is well known, the association of reproduction and stones does occur in the Old and New Testaments (for example, "the rock from which you were cut"; "from these stones God can raise up children to Abraham").

[52]The Piel of *lᵉ'abbēd* carries the connotation of perishing or bringing to ruin. In the Mishnah it means to lose (*Tohar.* 8:3, *ham'abbēd,* "if one loses anything").

about time, the first and third infinitives correspond to each other. Job's friends tore their clothes and sat in silence for seven days. The sewing of garments signals the end of mourning, and this event also encourages freedom of expression, especially since speech has been held in check for some time.

One need not restrict the references to mourning and its cancellation, for the verse may simply note that people engage in sewing[53] and ripping garments from time to time, and that they are talkative sometimes and quiet at other times. In any event, Qohelet has already mentioned mourning (3:4b). Ben Sira distinguishes between two types of silence ("There is one who keeps silent because he has no answer, while another keeps silent because he knows when to speak," Sir. 20:6). He goes on to speak about the necessity of knowing the right length of time to speak (20:7). This shows that sages' reflections on silence did not always relate to mourning customs.

[8] The final pair of opposites concentrates on human emotions, on the personal level and in the wider sphere of international relations. After "there is a time to love and a time to hate" one expects the sequence to read "a time to make peace and a time to wage war." Qohelet varies the poem's structure and its syntax, and in doing so he reaches a forceful conclusion. The correspondence between the first infinitive of each pair disappears in this verse, as do the infinitives in the last half verse. The first infinitive (love) is parallel with the last noun (peace), and the second infinitive (hate) corresponds to the third item, the noun (war). The result is a chiastic structure for the whole poem (birth/death: war/peace), and in verse 8 taken alone (love/hate: war/peace). Delitzsch (259) ascribes importance to the fact that the series of pairs expressing opposition comes to rest in "peace."

[9] Qohelet's poem suggests that human beings constantly do things. But does their activity produce anything? (Cf. 1:3 and 5:15 [16 E].) The very form of the poem about the times offers an answer. One thing cancels another. Naturally, Qohelet characterizes people as continually doing things (hence the participle *hāʿôśeh*), but he qualifies their activity when directing a question about the profit of their toiling *(ʿāmēl)*.

The poem focuses entirely on human activity. Nevertheless, Qohelet leaves the impression that the deity controls the right times for all things. Does God relinquish the tight hold on the correct moment for a particular activity? Qohelet addresses that issue in the next section.

[10] Looking back on the ceaseless activity of the poem in 3:2–8, Qohelet declares that he has taken note of the travail, which he attributes to the deity, recognizing the dubious value of the gift all the while. The word for

[53]The verb *tpr* is rare; it is found only here and in Gen. 3:7; Ezek. 13:18; and Job 16:15. However, the verb does appear in the Mishnah (*Šabb.* 13:2; *Kelim* 20:6).

business *(hā'inyān)* derives from the verb *'nh* (to answer, afflict). It retains an oppressive connotation throughout Ecclesiastes, even when the translation appears neutral (task, business). One could translate the final phrase "to afflict themselves with," for that is certainly the effect of the frenetic activity cataloged in 3:2–8.

[11] This difficult verse comments further on the times that make up daily activity under heaven. Qohelet has just said that God bestowed a sorry occupation upon human beings. Now he appears to qualify, then quickly moves to correct this impression. In the end he discovers no comfort in the knowledge that God has made everything appropriate for its particular moment.

The emphatic position of the object (*hakkōl,* everything) admits no exception. But the predicate adjective (*yāpeh,* beautiful) is qualified by the word that lay at the heart of the poem (*bᵉ'ittô,* in its time). If Qohelet has the creation account in mind, he avoids the special verb *bārā',* using instead *'āśāh;*[54] *ṭôb* becomes *yāpeh,* and even then it is qualified with *bᵉ'ittô* rather than *mᵉ'ōd*). When Ben Sira expresses the same idea, he restores the adjective *ṭôb* ("All things are the works of the Lord, for they are very good, and whatever he commands will be done in his time," Sir. 39:16; "The works of the Lord are all good, and he will supply every need in its hour," 39:33). As these verses illustrate, it is impossible to know whether the pronominal suffix on *bᵉ'ittô* refers to the creator or to the abstract idea of time (his time or its time?). Qohelet's point is that an action performed at the right time is appropriate, hence lovely to behold.

God's generosity expresses itself in still another way, according to the next clause. The connective *gam* (also) suggests that what the deity has placed in the human heart (mind) is good. But what is it? Among many possible answers, the most likely are: (1) the world; (2) eternity; (3) darkness. Rabbinic literature uses the word *'ôlām* for the present age and the world to come (compare the Vulgate, *et mundum tradidit disputatione eorum*). This reading presupposes a *lᵉrîbām* (to their strife) for the Hebrew *bᵉlibbām* (in their heart).

Many modern interpreters follow the Septuagint's lead in translating *aiōn* "eternity, duration, the flow of time, incessancy," and the like. Others supply different vowels and interpret the word as "ignorance," "darkness," or "secret." This meaning of the root *'lm* occurs in Eccl. 12:14 (*ne'lām,* hidden); Job 28:21 (*wᵉne'elmāh mē'ênê kol-ḥāy,* "[wisdom] is hidden from the eyes of all the living"); Job 42:3 (*mî zeh ma'lîm 'ēṣāh,* "who is this darkening [hiding] counsel?"). It is supported by the Ugaritic *wglm* ("and it grew dark") and the Phoenician Aḥiram Inscription (10th century

[54]The variation occurs within the account in Genesis; in fact, the summary statement in Gen. 1:31 already uses *'āśāh.*

B.C.E.), where one reads *śth b'lm* ("I laid him in darkness," that is, the grave).[55]

The negative particle *mibbᵉlî* occurs elsewhere in the Old Testament (Ex. 14:11, *hamibbᵉlî,* "is it because?"; cf. II Kings 1:3). There appears to be paronomasia between *bᵉlibbām* and *mibbᵉlî,* which may explain Qohelet's selection of this rare negative particle. Both the Septuagint and Vulgate understood it as a negative of purpose. The two negatives strengthen rather than cancel each other.

The late word *sôp* is attested in Joel 2:20 (*wᵉsōpô 'el-hayyām hā'aḥᵃrôn,* "and its rear to the western sea") and II Chron. 20:16 (*ûmᵉṣā'tem 'ōtām bᵉsôp hannaḥal,* "and you will find them at the end of the valley"). The word *sôp* is also used in Aramaic texts (Dan. 4:8, 19 [11, 22E], "the end of the earth"; 7:28, "the end of the matter"), and the phrase *'ad sôpā'* (to the end) occurs in Dan. 6:27 [26E] and 7:26. In *M. Ber.* 1:1 we read *'d swp h'šmwrh hr'šwnh* ("until the end of the first watch"). Qohelet observes that humans cannot really comprehend anything pertaining to divine activity.

[12] Although Qohelet complains about inability to discover God's secret times, he does claim to possess sure knowledge of a sort. The emphatic declaration, *yāda'tî,* occurs here and in 3:14, each time without the pleonastic *'ᵃnî* that has occurred often to this point. The content of Qohelet's certainty assumes the form of a negative "better" saying.

The plural *bām* (in them) seems to contradict the singular pronominal suffix on *bᵉḥayyāyw* (during his lifetime). One can understand the singular pronoun as referring to the collective; in 3:11, the larger community was represented by a single individual. There is some manuscript evidence for reading *bā'ādām* (as in 2:24, *'ên-ṭôb bā'ādām*), the error resulting from homoioteleuton or perhaps from an abbreviation that was misunderstood (*bām* for *bā'ādām*). The unusual preposition *bᵉ* rather than *lᵉ* also appears in 2:24.

Many interpreters have understood *wᵉla'ᵃśôt ṭôb* ("and to fare well") in the light of the Greek expression *eu prattein.* The parallel in II Sam. 12:18 (*wᵉ'āśāh rā'āh,* "and he will do something bad")[56] does not settle the issue, for other indications suggest that this devotional legend is late (the expression *mî yôdēa'* in verse 22). If this late date is correct, a Greek influence

[55]According to Levy's doubtful reconstruction, Ben Sira uses the noun *'ôlām* in the sense of "world" (3:18, *m'ṭ npšk mkl gdwlwt 'wlm,* "restrain yourself from the glories of the world"). This is the meaning *'ôlām* came to have in rabbinic usage. Although Qohelet uses *'ôlām* in the sense of duration (1:4, "the earth remains unto the ages"; 1:10; 2:16; 3:14; 9:6; and 12:5, "eternal home"), this consistency does not require a translation of something temporal in 3:11, for the vowels may have been different. However, the contrast between *'ēt* and *'ôlām* is a strong argument in favor of reading "eternity" in 3:11.

[56]The sense may be reflexive: "he will harm himself." On the other hand, the meaning may be that David will punish the person who brings bad news to him.

is likely. The meaning would then be "and to succeed [or fare well] in life."

[13] This verse continues the thought expressed in 3:12, as the *w*^{e}*gam* (and also) implies. Qohelet now defines "faring well" with the same formula that he gave in 2:24. Eating, drinking, and experiencing good things by means of one's toil or its wages commend themselves universally. The *kol-hā'ādām* is separated from its referent (literally, "and also that he, specifically every person, should eat . . .").

The two perfect verbs *šātāh* and *rā'āh* are related to the previous verb by *waw* consecutives, rare in Ecclesiastes. Qohelet's capacity for varying his manner of expressing an idea, despite the fondness for formulaic phrases and clauses, is exemplified by the second half of this verse. In 2:24 he concluded the advice about eating, drinking, and enjoying life with the observation that the ability to do these things is within God's control. Now in 3:13 Qohelet remarks that even the power to follow his advice is a divine gift.

[14] The first certitude (3:12) concerned the ultimate source of the ability to derive pleasure from life. Although there is nothing better than to try to enjoy things, whether one can do so or not depends upon the deity's generosity. Qohelet's second certitude (3:14) asserts that there is no way to alter God's ways. If one is unlucky nothing can change that. Reflecting on the implications of this immutability of divine actions, Qohelet concludes that God has planned this way in order to instill fear in human beings.

God's works have a durable quality, described by the Hebrew word *l*^{e}*'ôlām* (unto the ages, forever). The verb *ya*^{a}*'śeh* is imperfect, as if Qohelet speculates about future deeds of God, but by the end of the verse Qohelet shifts to the perfect *('āśāh).* This syntax embraces all *'ôlām,* to which God alone has access.

A formulaic expression of uncertain origin occurs in the observation about adding and subtracting. It is found in Deut. 4:2 (*lō' tōsipû 'al-haddābār . . . w*^{e}*lō' tigr*^{e}*'û mimmennû,* "do not add to the word . . . and do not take away from it") and in Deut. 13:1 [12:32E] (*lō'-tōsēp 'ālāyw w*^{e}*lō' tigra' mimmennû,* "do not add to it and do not subtract from it"). The sayings of Agur have only half of the formula (*'al-tôsēp*[57] *'al-d*^{e}*bārāyw,* "do not add to his words"; Prov. 30:6), for their concern centered on the impact of heterodox views.

The relative *š*^{e} here expresses purpose as *'*^{a}*šer* does elsewhere. For example, Deut. 4:10 reads *'*^{a}*šer yilm*^{e}*dûn l*^{e}*yir'āh 'ōtî,* "that they may learn to fear me" (cf. 4:40, "so that it may go well with you and your descendants"). In Aramaic the relative *dî* similarly expresses purpose (Dan. 4:3 [6E], *dî-p*^{e}*šar ḥelmā' y*^{e}*hôd*^{e}*'unnanî,* "so that they may inform me of the dream's interpretation").

In many contexts within Proverbs, fear before the deity is presented as

[57]Emended text from *tôs*^{e}*p*^{e}.

the correct attitude of a religious person, translatable by something like "to be religious." Qohelet's concept differs greatly, for in a few instances the fear of God comes very close to terror before an unpredictable despot (E. Pfeiffer). Does Qohelet think of the deity as jealously guarding divine prerogatives[58] (an idea that occurs in a few ancient texts, Gen. 3:22; 11:6)?

[15] This verse repeats ideas expressed in 1:9, but ends differently. There Qohelet completed the thought about the sameness of all events with the denial of anything new on earth. Now he introduces the image of God seeking *('et nirdāp).*[59] But what does God seek?

Several answers have been offered: (1) the persecuted; (2) the events of the past; (3) the same; and (4) what God sought previously. The Septuagint, Peshitta, and Targum adopted the first of these, asserting that God seeks out the poor and looks after their interests. But this understanding of the strange expression does not fit the context, even if *nirdāp* means "persecuted" in the Talmud and apparently in Sirach. The inclination to shift this clause to another context demonstrates the weakness of this interpretation.

More likely, Qohelet envisions God pursuing the past in order to bring it back into the present. The masculine ending on *nirdāp,* reflected in the versions except for the Vulgate, poses a problem for this interpretation, but the verse does seem to make the same point as 1:9. There is nothing new. Why? Because God ensures that events which have just transpired do not vanish into thin air. God brings them back once more, so that the past circles into the present.

The other two interpretations are similar, although they are arrived at differently. One appeals to an Arabic cognate of *nirdāp* that means "synonym," hence "the same." The other assumes that *bqš* and *ndp* are synonyms (Ps. 34:15 [14E], *baqqēš šālôm wᵉrādᵉpēhû,* "seek peace and pursue it"; cf. also Deut. 16:20 and Zeph. 2:3).

An interesting text in Sirach (5:3) casts light on the meaning of *nirdāp.* It concerns arrogant boasting by sinners. Ben Sira warns: *'l t'mr my ywkl kḥw ky yhwh mbqš nrdpym.* If the citation ends before the *kî* clause, one can translate: "Do not say, 'Who can have power over me?' for the Lord searches for the persecuted." However, if the citation extends to the end of the verse, it means: "Do not say . . . for the Lord is searching for the past." That is, God is too busy to punish sinners, so I shall take advantage of divine preoccupation with other things.[60]

---

[58]Gordis (233) writes that "only for Koheleth, who has been drained of faith in life's possibilities, does the primitive attitude reassert itself." He adds: "This is not the only instance where the sophisticate reverts to the primitive, so that 'les extrêmes se touchent.' "

[59]The absence of an article is unusual, but Qohelet also omits it in 7:7 *('et-lēb)* and in 4:4 *('et-kol-'āmāl wᵉ'ēt kol-kišrôn).*

[60]Gordis (234) argues that the symmetry of Sir. 5:3–6a demands that the entire verse be understood as the sinner's boast. However, the evidence does not support his claim,

The Tears of the Oppressed
3:16–4:3

3:16 And furthermore I saw under the sun that wickedness was in the place of judgment, and in the place of righteousness, wickedness. [17]I reasoned that God will judge the righteous and the wicked, because there is a time for everything and concerning every deed there. [18]I reasoned about humankind that God is testing them and showing them that they are really beasts. [19]For the lot of humans and the lot of animals is the same; as one dies, so the other dies, and they both have a single life-breath; and human beings have no advantage over animals, for both are transient. [20]Both go to the same place; they were taken from the dust and they return to the dust. [21]Who knows whether the life-breath of humans ascends and the life-breath of animals descends to earth? [22]And I saw that there was nothing better than that humans should rejoice in their accomplishments, for that is their portion. For who can bring them to see what will occur after them? 4:1 Again I turned and saw all the oppressions that were perpetrated under the sun, and oh, the tears of the oppressed, but there was no comforter for them. In the hand of their oppressors there was power, and there was no comforter for them. [2]And I praised the dead who had already died more than the living who were still alive. [3]But better than both of them is the one who still has not been, who has not seen the evil deeds that are done under the sun.

[16] Qohelet denies that any system of justice assures punishment of evildoers and protection of law-abiding citizens. If the meaning of 3:15b were really an assertion of divine solicitude for the poor, this thought would be incomprehensible. Repetition of *hārešaʻ* strengthens and lends poignancy to Qohelet's assertion that judgment is replaced by wickedness. (Qohelet achieved the same effect in 4:1 by repeating the clause *wᵉʼên lāhem mᵉnaḥēm,* "and there was no comforter for them.")

Wᵉʻôd may refer back to *rāʼîtî* in 3:10 or it may be taken as an adverb (wherever). The athnach divides *mᵉqôm* from the verb, implying that *mᵉqôm* is not the direct object. *Šāmmāh* is an emphatic variant of *šām* (there); one need not understand the ending as locative (to there).

Divine arbitrariness would vex us less if God were kindly disposed toward human beings. But Qohelet finds no evidence for this conclusion. In truth, he discovers facts that contradict such an optimistic attitude. Justice is replaced by misconduct. Traditional faith asserts that things will be set right in due time. God tests human beings just to show them that they

---

which requires the omission of 5:6b (cf. also 5:7–8; each piece of advice has supporting rationale).

belong in the same category as animals, for all go to one place. Since the future lies hidden from the eyes of the living, human beings can only rejoice in their work and its benefits.

Unable to discover the future, Qohelet concentrates on the present, where the tears of the oppressed catch his attention. Power belongs to the oppressors, whose victims know no comforters. Injustice leads Qohelet to conclude that the dead are better off than the living, and that the unborn are more fortunate yet, to have been spared the misery of seeing undeserved suffering.

[17] This verse introduces two problems. Did Qohelet really believe that God judged human beings? If so, where did Qohelet think the judgment would take place? To what does the word *šām* refer?

Answers to the first question vary. Many interpreters think Qohelet's emphasis on the miscarriage of justice implies total absence of divine judgment. Others suggest that divine judgment escapes human perception, but God has not relinquished responsibility for judging. If Qohelet adhered to the latter reasoning, his assessment of injustice would be tempered by hope for its adjustment. Such optimism is missing from Qohelet's thought. He complains repeatedly that the same fate befalls evildoers and good people. In light of Qohelet's other comments about judgment, the affirmation of divine judgment appears contradictory. This verse, then, may be a later gloss.

One expects a synonym for *ḥēpeṣ* instead of the word *šām,* but there is no manuscript evidence for something like *z^{e}mān.* If the reading *šām* is original (the Vulgate, Peshitta, and Septuagint[61] confirm its antiquity), it may be understood with reference to divine times or even locally (there with God).[62] Possibly *šām* refers back to *šāmmāh* in 3:16, "the place of perfidy."

Some scholars prefer to read the verb *śām* (to set). This is perfectly plausible from an orthographic standpoint, but the position of the verb at the end of the sentence would be highly unusual. This objection, in turn, is blunted by Qohelet's practice of holding the subject in abeyance (1:6, *hārûaḥ*), a deliberate stylistic device on his part, which he might equally well use with a verb.

[18] Earlier Qohelet used the expression *'al-d^{e}bar* for "concerning, about." Here he uses a form connected with Aramaic *'al-dibrat* (Dan. 2:30). The only other use of *'al-dibrat* in Biblical Hebrew occurs in Ps. 110:4

---

[61]The Septuagint construes the word *šām (ekei)* with the next verse.

[62]Gordis (235) understands *šām* as a cryptic allusion to Sheol, just as Job 1:21 alludes to the netherworld (*'ārōm yāṣātî mibbeṭen 'immî w^{e}'ārōm 'āšûb šāmāh,* "naked I came forth from my mother's womb, and naked I shall return there"; cf. 3:17, 19). The use of a euphemism such as "there" or "over there" is well exemplified in the ancient world. But what would Qohelet have meant by a judgment in Sheol? Elsewhere (9:10) he denies any work to that land of darkness. To get around this difficulty, Whitley (35–36) cautiously proposes that *šām* is an interjection with the meaning "too, also."

(*'al-dibrātî malkî-ṣedeq,* which RSV translates "after the order of Melchizedek"), except for Eccl. 7:14 and 8:2. Its meaning in 7:14 is "so that . . . not," and in 8:2 "concerning."

What does *l^{e}bārām* mean? The root *bārar* means "to separate," hence "choose, select, purify, test." The ending *ām* is the object, and God is the subject, so the word says something about God's testing people. But is the verb an infinitive or a finite verb with an emphatic *lamed?* If one views *l^{e}bārām* as an infinitive, the clause lacks a finite verb, and one must assume that a copula was presupposed by the text.[63] On the other hand, the prefixed *lamed* may be emphatic, and one could translate "whom God indeed chose."[64]

Although the word *w^{e}lir'ôt* is pointed Qal, many interpreters read Hiphil, *lar'ôt* ("show" rather than "see"). In doing so they follow the Septuagint, Peshitta, and Vulgate, among others. The Targum associates *w^{e}lir'ôt* with the initial *'āmartî* ("I said in my heart and saw that . . ."). It seems more natural to view the *w^{e}lir'ôt* as a consecutive infinitive with God as subject and the people as object (*ām* ending on the first infinitive, *l^{e}bārām*).

The final clause is equally difficult. Literally, it can be translated "that they are beasts, they themselves." Because the *hēmmāh* is lacking in the Septuagint, it can be taken as partial dittography from *b^{e}hēmāh.* Perhaps the remaining *lāhem* has an emphatic *lamed,* and the meaning is "that they really are beasts."[65] Alliteration may account for the strange syntax. The questionable *hēmmāh* may be a copula followed by a dative of means. The story of the Fall has a comparable distancing of humans from the divine realm lest men and women seize some of the power belonging to deity.

[19] The present verse and the two verses that follow explain the assertion in 3:18 of similarity between humans and animals: they share a common fate, death.

As pointed, the first part of the observation states that "a fate is humans and a fate is animals—and one fate is theirs." The corrected rendering above, like the ancient versions (Septuagint, Peshitta, Targum, Old Latin), takes *miqreh* as construct, *miqrēh.*

The word *môtar* (advantage) occurs nowhere else in Ecclesiastes, but it

---

[63]Those who view *l^{e}bārām* as an infinitive appeal to Isa. 45:1 (*l^{e}rad,* to subdue) and Jer. 5:26 (*k^{e}šak,* crouching [textually uncertain]).

[64]Whitley (36–37) seems to prefer this understanding of the word, which he defends by offering several other examples of emphatic *lamed* in the Bible: the aphorism in Eccl. 9:4 (*kî l^{e}keleb ḥay hû' ṭôb min-hā'aryēh hammēt,* "for indeed a living dog is better than a dead lion"); Ps. 89:19 ("for indeed Yhwh is our shield"); and S. of Songs 1:3 ("how fragrant are your anointing oils"). The examples are not entirely convincing, particularly the last two.

[65]Whitley (38) appeals to I Sam. 26:11–12 (*w^{e}nēl^{a}kāh lānû . . . wayyēl^{e}kû lāhem,* which he translates "let us go, we indeed . . . and they went, they indeed").

is found in Proverbs (14:23, *bᵉkol-ʿeṣeb yihyeh môtār,* "in all toil there is profit"; 21:5, *maḥšᵉbôt ḥārûṣ ʾak-lᵉmôtār,* "the plans of the diligent surely [yield] a profit"). Elsewhere Qohelet expresses the idea of profit or advantage with *yitrôn* and *yôtēr.* The Septuagint, Symmachus, and Theodotion understood *môtār* as a question (*mî yôtēr,* "what is the advantage?"), with the answer provided by *ʾāyin* ("there is none").

Because the first *lakkōl* refers to both animals and humans, the final clause may use *hakkōl* in the same way. In that case, the meaning of *hābel* would probably be "fleeting," "ephemeral," or "transient." This understanding provides an element of surprise, since the refrain's previous uses had the sense of futility.

[20] Behind this observation stands the ancient story of the Fall, in which God declared to sinful creatures that they were taken from the ground and must return to it, *kî-ʿāpār ʾattāh wᵉʾel-ʿāpār tāšûb* ("for you are dust and you shall return to dust," Gen. 3:19b). Both Job and his young critic, Elihu, recognize the application of the ancient saying to human destiny (Job 10:9, "Remember that you made me like clay and you will return me to dust"; 34:15, "All flesh would perish together, and humans return to dust"). In the same vein Ben Sira asserts that "all things that are from the earth turn back to the earth" (Sir. 40:11a). Likewise, Ps. 104:29 mentions the dreadful consequences of the solar deity's withdrawal: "You hide your face and they are dismayed; you take away their breath, they die and return to their dust."[66]

The dissolution of the body into dust might rule out belief in continued existence in Sheol, but that is not the case. Qohelet affirms the traditional belief that people go to the shadowy abode after death. He harbors no hope that this realm is anything more than unrelieved darkness.

[21] Ancient versions (Septuagint, Peshitta, Vulgate, and Targum) understood the *hāʿōlāh* and *hayyōredet* as indirect questions, thus containing the interrogative *he* rather than the article. Some modern interpreters assume that the Massoretes pointed the two words with articles to dilute the unorthodox sentiment. Yet the equally unorthodox teaching in 3:19 was left unchanged.

Qohelet expresses a caveat about a claim by contemporaries that human beings enjoy a favorable status after death. He does not absolutely rule out the possibility, but he dismisses such speculation as a waste of time. The *mî yôdēaʿ* anticipates a negative response, implying that "nobody knows." Therefore it is pointless to harbor "intimations of immortality." This intellectual position was later branded the teaching of scoundrels (Wisd. of Sol. 2:1–3).

[66]The reference to the ground in Gen. 3:19a is retained in Ps. 146:4, which reads *tēṣēʾ rûḥô yāšub lᵉʾadmātô* ("when his breath goes forth he returns to the ground").

Qohelet's view about the common destiny of animals and humans in Eccl. 3:19–21 does not contradict his distinction in 12:7 between dust that returns to earth and breath that returns to God. Genesis 2:7 identifies two components of human existence (dust and the divine breath). Qohelet remarks that both elements return to their source, a fact from which he drew no comfort (cf. Eccl. 12:8).

[22] Qohelet concludes that the only sensible thing to do is to enjoy what is certain and knowable—human accomplishments. *Maʿᵃśāyw* is here equivalent to *ʿᵃmālîm* in meaning. This verse expresses ideas closely related to those in 2:24 and 3:12, although each verse has its own nuance (eating, drinking, and getting pleasure from toil in 2:24, rejoicing and faring well in 3:12).

The interrogative *mî yᵉbîʾennû* ("who can bring him?") functions like *mî yôdēaʿ* in 3:21, anticipating a negative answer. It is tantamount to saying "no one can bring him." Although the pronominal suffixes are singular, reflecting the singular *hāʾādām,* this word has a collective meaning. The ending on *ʾaḥᵃrāyw* may be a petrified (archaic) suffix on an adverb ("afterward"),[67] but is more likely an ellipsis for "after his death."

What does Qohelet mean by "after death"? In 3:21 he extends the horizon of discussion beyond earthly events, but denies any pertinence to the widening vista. For all humans know death brings everything to an end. This truism sums up the sentiments of 3:19–22. There may be a time for everything, but only God knows the secret. Humans should not think too highly of themselves, linked as they are with animals in a common death. Given this, humans can speculate idly, or enjoy the portion God grants them. Naturally, Qohelet recommends the latter option.

[4:1] Two things stand out in this long verse: its rhetoric and its poignancy. Into the first category go the threefold use of the root *ʿšq* and the repetition of the clause, "and there was no comforter for them." Each occurrence of the root *ʿšq* has a distinctive nuance. The first refers to oppressions, or perhaps the abstract notion of oppression. The third points an accusing finger at the oppressors, and the second mentions the objects of their villainy. Although some interpreters view the second occurrence of *wᵉʾên lāhem mᵉnaḥēm* as dittography,[68] the twofold use of a refrain adds considerable emphasis and should be retained. (Qohelet used the same stylistic device in 3:16, where *šāmmāh hārešaʿ* appears twice. Both verses deal with the miscarriage of justice.)

---

[67]Gordis (238) likens the form to *yaḥᵉdâw.* He appeals to three other instances in Ecclesiastes where *ʾaḥᵃrâw* occurs (6:12; 7:14; 9:3).

[68]Some commentators think verbs may have dropped out of the text, perhaps *môšîaʿ* or *maṣṣîl,* both meaning "deliverer." Other interpreters retain the consonants in the text but understand the word as a shortened Hithpael ("avenger") or derive the verb from *nḥh* (to lead, hence "to free" someone).

Qohelet's usual detachment eases as he reflects on the wasted tears of unfortunate victims. The Hebrew idiom, *wᵉšabtî ᵓᵃnî,* can be translated adverbially ("again I"),[69] indicating that injustice and oppression are not isolated incidents but recurring phenomena. Qohelet juxtaposes the situations of oppressor (a hand of power) and oppressed (tears), lending force to the refrain about the helpless victims. Such misery pained Qohelet, but he suggests no way to comfort the unfortunate persons nor does he urge hearers to correct injustice.

[2] The absence of comforters and the presence of oppressors prompted Qohelet to congratulate those already beyond the grip of violence. Job expresses a similar idea in his initial lament (Job 3:11–19); he thinks the dead are at rest, obliged no longer to hear the voice of taskmasters or to worry about those who excel in bringing calamity. Elsewhere Qohelet declares the day of death preferable to the day of birth (7:1). The aphorism in 9:4b ("For a live dog is better than a dead lion") appears to offer a different view, but context requires that it be understood ironically.

The form *wᵉšabbēaḥ* (and I praised) can only be an infinitive absolute. The use of a personal pronoun after the infinitive is rare, the only other biblical example being Esth. 9:1 (*wᵉnahᵃpôk hûᵓ,* "and which had been changed"). Whitley (40–41) examines the evidence from Phoenician inscriptions, the Amarna tablets, and Ugaritic, without coming to a firm decision. He adduces two examples of infinitive constructs from the Dead Sea Scrolls that have personal subsequent pronouns.[70] Because Qohelet uses the perfect in 8:15 (*wᵉšibbaḥtî ᵓᵃnî,* "and I praised"), some interpreters think *wᵉšabbēaḥ* is an abbreviated perfect, the pronominal suffix having dropped off.

The adverb *ʿᵃdenāh* (still) occurs nowhere else in the Bible; the related *ʿᵃden* in the next verse is also hapax. Both adverbs are probably contractions of *ʿad hēn*[*āh*].[71]

[3] The chief difficulty in this verse is the particle *ᵓēt,* which ordinarily designates an accusative. That it is governed by the distant *wᵉšabbēaḥ* of 4:2 is unlikely. The Vulgate supplied a verb *(judicavi),* which keeps the accusative construction of *ᵓēt,* but the Septuagint and Peshitta understood the form as nominative. The phrase *ᵓēt ᵓᵃšer* is used in I Kings 8:31

---

[69]The verb that follows *(wāᵓerᵓeh)* is one of the few *waw* consecutives with imperfect in Ecclesiastes (cf. 1:17; 4:7). In 4:1 and 4:7 the same phrase introduces the verses *(wᵉšabtî ᵓᵃnî wāᵓerᵓeh).*

[70]Manual of Discipline 7:16 (*lᵉšallēaḥ hûᵓ,* "he is to be sent away") and Damascus Document 9:1 (*lᵉhāmît hûᵓ,* "he is to be put to death").

[71]Whitley (41) posits distinct origins for *ʿᵃdenāh* (from *ʿādāh,* "up to, till, until") and *ʿᵃden* (from *ʿādad,* "at the same time, during, while, when").

in the sense of "if," but the Peshitta and Vulgate seem to have read *'im* (cf. II Chron. 6:22). These are the only two uses of *'ēt 'ašer* in the Bible.[72]

Qohelet's use of *'ēt 'ašer* resembles the use of *'et-šᵉ* in the Mishnah. Whitley (42) lists two examples of *'et-šᵉ: Dem.* 2:5 (*'t-šdrkw lhmdd,* "whatever is measured") and *Git.* 9:7 (*'t-šh'dym nqryn 'mw kšr,* "the signatories which can be read together—that is legal"). Gordis had earlier mentioned *Git.* 9:5 *('t-šh'dym nqryn bw kšr); Ber.* 3:1; *Šeqal.* 8:7 (1968, 239; all subsequent references are to this volume).

This preference for the nonexistent over the dead or the living suits the hatred for life that Qohelet expressed in 2:17. Such loathing of the conditions under which life must be carried out arises from a vision of the way things should be in a perfect world. Qohelet shared the sages' conviction that a just moral order should accompany belief in the Creator, but sees no evidence to confirm the conviction. Instead, oppression dominates. The resulting suffering incites Qohelet to praise the dead and the unborn. Ben Sira also gives voice to the power wielded by circumstances in evaluating death (Sir. 41:1–2). He observes that death is bitter indeed when one is living at peace in the lap of luxury, but welcome to one who is old and incapacitated.

Proverbial Insights About Toil and Its Opposite 4:4–6

> 4:4 And I saw that all the toil and all skillful activity is one person's jealousy of another; this is also absurd and shepherding the wind. [5]The fool folds his hands and consumes his flesh. [6]A handful of rest is better than two hands full of toil and shepherding the wind.

Qohelet observes that human industry grows out of envy and accomplishes nothing permanent. He supports this thesis by quoting two aphorisms that comment on the way of an indolent person and the advantage of a present possession, however meager, over something that may be obtained at the expense of considerable labor. If the observation about the sluggard who consumes his flesh does not suggest that he lives off his body fat, it

[72]Jer. 38:16 (*'ēt 'ašer 'āśāh-lānû,* "who made us") and 6:18 (*ûdᵉ'î 'ēdāh 'et-'ašer-bām,* "and know, O congregation, what [will happen] to them") are questionable cases. The first has an alternative reading (the Qere) and the second is the object of the imperative *(ûdᵉ'î).*

attacks an unfair system in which the person has plenty of meat despite his laziness. The other proverb comes perilously close to stifling individual initiative, for it urges contentment rather than encouraging the taking of risks for worthy goals.

[4] The word *kišrôn* occurs in Biblical Hebrew only in Ecclesiastes (2:21; 5:10; 10:10 [11E]; 11:6), Esther (8:5), and Psalms (68:7 [6E]),[73] but it is common in later Aramaic and in Mishnaic Hebrew. Gordis (240) observes that this word may relate to the Canaanite deity of crafts, Kothar. *Hamma'ᵃśeh* (the work) echoes the previous verse, where the work is qualified as evil *(hārā')*. The implication of the dual objects in 4:4 is that some types of toil produce discernible results, but Qohelet thinks such productive work stems from envy.[74]

Qin'at (envy, jealousy) is usually followed by the prepositions *lᵉ* or *bᵉ*. Here we find *min* (cf. *miggābōah yirā'û* in 12:5). The preposition *min* expresses reciprocity, rivalry that fragmentizes society. Rivalry is not necessarily counterproductive; this positive aspect of *qin'at* is recognized in *B. Bat.* 21a (*qn't swprym trbh ḥkmh,* "the rivalry of scholars increases wisdom"). The word has a negative sense in Isa. 11:13 (*wᵉsārāh qin'at 'eprayim . . . 'eprayim lō'-yᵉqannē' 'et-yᵉhûdāh,* "Ephraim's jealousy will depart . . . Ephraim will not be jealous of Judah"), proceeding to link jealousy and violence. On Qohelet's personalization of the national problem of jealousy and violence, Delitzsch remarked: "All the expenditure of strength and art has covetousness and envy, with which one seeks to surpass another, as its poisoned sting" (275).

[5] A natural conclusion from Qohelet's harsh judgment about work is that toil commends itself so little that one should follow the path of inactivity. The aphorism in 4:5 rules out that option. In Prov. 6:10 (24:33), folded hands suggest idleness that eventuates in poverty.

The phrase *wᵉ'ōkēl 'et-bᵉśārô* ("and eats his flesh") is difficult. Elsewhere the Bible does refer to actual and metaphorical cannibalism. Micah 3:3 alludes to those "who eat the flesh of my people" *(wa'ᵃšer 'ākᵉlû šᵉ'ēr 'ammî),* chopping up the flesh and bones like meat in a pot. Isaiah 49:26 warns oppressors that God will make them eat their own flesh *(wᵉha'ᵃkaltî 'et-mônayik 'et-bᵉśārām),* and they will be drunk with their own blood as with (like, *kᵉ*) wine. The phrase *le'ᵉkōl 'et-bᵉśārî* ("to consume my flesh") has the nuance of slander in Ps. 27:2. Proverbs 30:14 refers to devouring

---

[73]The form *kišrôn* occurs only in Eccl. 2:21; 4:4; 5:10. In 10:10 *hakšêr* occurs and *yikšar* in 11:6. Esther 8:5 has *wᵉkāšēr haddābār lipnê hammelek* ("and if the thing seems right before the king"), and Ps. 68:7 [6E] has *môṣî' 'ᵃsîrîm bakkôšārôt* ("he leads out the prisoners in prosperity").

[74]Murphy describes the phenomenon of envy as the dark side of human activity where *homo homini lupus.*

the needy *(le'ᵉkōl ʿᵃniyyîm mē'ereṣ wᵉ'ebyônîm mē'ādām*[*āh*], "to eat the poor of the earth and the needy of the ground").[75]

But Qohelet's aphorism may have quite another meaning, pointing out a paradox that in an imperfect world even fools who refuse to join the rat race resulting from jealousy sometimes have adequate meat. The translation of *bᵉśārô* as "his meat," meaning animal meat, is certainly appropriate. Whether this word can mean "the meat that he owns" is another matter. But is anyone who beats the system this way really a fool?

[6] Juxtaposition of the two previous verses has left the impression that both work and idleness are undesirable, the former because it springs from rivalry and the latter because it produces nothing. Qohelet now judges that a little rest is preferable to much effort, or (if the *ʿāmāl* signifies wealth rather than toil) that such possessions are not worth the effort. Qohelet sympathizes more with the fool than with one who toils endlessly to acquire more possessions than the neighbors. Here Qohelet concurs with the sages who preferred a small morsel with peace to an elaborate meal accompanied by strife (Prov. 15:16; 16:8; 17:1). Qohelet imagines a single open palm versus two hands cupped to hold the maximum amount. This interpretation involves reading *kap nāḥat* and *ḥopnayim ʿāmāl* as construct chains, the final *mem* on *ḥopnayim* being enclitic.[76] Alternatively, the *nāḥat* and *ʿāmāl* may be adverbial accusatives, and one could translate "with rest . . . with toil." The Septuagint seems to have understood the Hebrew as construct chains, but the Targum followed the alternative interpretation. If the verse contains an ancient aphorism, the final phrase *ûrᵉʿût rûaḥ* is Qohelet's addition.

The Advantages of Companionship 4:7–12

4:7 And again I saw futility under the sun. [8]There was a person without a second; he had neither son nor brother; and yet there was no end to all his toil, also his eyes were not satisfied with wealth; and for whom am I toiling and depriving myself of good? This is also futile and unpleasant business. [9]Two are better than one, because they have a good reward in their work. [10]For if the one falls, the other lifts up his

[75]The Massoretic Text has "from humankind."

[76]Whitley (42–43) gives various examples of the *mem* enclitic from the Hebrew Bible (Deut. 33:11; Gen. 14:6; Isa. 10:5), Phoenician (*'lm nrgl,* "the god Nergal"), the Karatepe Inscription (*yrdm 'nk, ysbm 'nk,* "I brought down, I settled"), and Ugaritic (*lhtmn bʿl,* "O son-in-law of Baal"; *bnm 'yl,* "son of Il"). Delsman (360–361) lists the following verses in which enclitic *mem* occurs: 4:6; 10:15, 18.

companion; but unfortunate is anyone who falls without having another to help him up. [11]Moreover, if two lie together they are warm, but how can a person be warm alone? [12]And if they overcome one person, two can withstand together; and a threefold cord is not easily broken.

This section opens with an observation about a man who had no close relative but who toiled unceasingly and never asked why he did so and deprived himself of pleasure. Three examples underscore the stupidity of such conduct: a traveler needs a friend in case he falls into a pit or off a cliff; a person needs a companion to stay warm at night; and a victim in a robbery needs assistance from a friend. Qohelet concludes the unit by citing an aphorism about the strength of a threefold cord, which forsakes the thematic words "one" and "two" for an even larger number.

[7] This verse makes transition from observations about envy and laziness to reflections on avarice. Qohelet's language is punctuated by a pleonastic use of the personal pronoun *'ănî,* together with stereotypical phrases.

[8] Verses 8–12 converge on a single point, the advantage of having a companion. Qohelet has already complained about having to leave his possessions to a person who might be a fool (untutored or evil). Now he discusses the practical advantages of having someone who can benefit from one's toil and who can help an individual in trouble. Sapiential egocentrism, which soared to new heights in the royal experiment, weakens appreciably in this unit.

The particle of existence introduces a hypothetical case, perhaps even an example from daily observation. Qohelet has observed a loner who worked without pausing long enough to ask whether it was worth the energy expended. This person had no spouse (or friend?)[77] and no son or brother (no family), but he labored continuously and hoarded possessions. Qohelet interjects a first-person query,[78] demonstrating an identity with this person, at least in sympathy: "Why am I toiling and depriving myself of good?" Although the loner does not stop to ask this significant question, Qohelet asks it for him. Or, the example may end at the middle of the verse (riches), the rest being Qohelet's personal application.

Not only does the man work ceaselessly, but he is never content with what he earns. The eye, the organ of desire, cannot be satisfied. No motive is given for the person's endless desire, whether greed or the fear of growing old and having no means to subsist. The preponderance of monosyllables in this long verse is striking, lending emphasis to the actual content. Here form enhances content nicely.

---

[77]Qohelet's references to one's wife are strange, if they are such (4:9, *šēnî,* "a second"; 9:9, *'iššāh 'ăšer-'āhabtā,* "a woman whom you love").

[78]Gordis (242) views this as an example of a quotation without any identifying marks.

[9] The example of a person with no companion prompts Qohelet to observe that it is better to team up with another individual for mutual profit. The statement that two persons receive a higher yield from their work does not mean that their wages are necessarily greater. Rather it refers to the way each person's work complements the other's efforts and therefore enables them to complete more tasks with less effort.

The articles on *haššᵉnayim* (the two) and *hāʼeḥād* (the one) individualize two persons and one person. Qohelet uses *ʼᵃšer* (because) as a conjunction here and in 8:11–12 and 10:15.

[10] Qohelet's first illustration that two are better than one concentrates on the perils of traveling, specifically the danger of falling into a concealed pit (although the verb *nāpal* is not otherwise used of falling into a pit) or slipping on treacherous terrain. A person journeying alone would probably perish from exposure or injury, whereas one who had a companion could count on a speedy rescue. (Alternatively, the expression for falling may stand for adversity in general.)

The plural verb *yippōlû* (he falls) is partitive. Other examples of this usage are Gen. 11:3 and Judg. 6:29 ("A man said to his companion," *wayyōʼmᵉrû ʼîš ʼel-rēʻēhû,* and Isa. 47:15 ("each errs, according to his way," *ʼîš lᵉʻebrô tāʻû*). The ancient versions (Septuagint, Peshitta, Vulgate) read *wᵉʼîlô,* a shortened form of the woe cry (*ʼôy-lî,* "woe to me," Isa. 6:5); only the Targum seems to have read *ʼillô (ʼim lû),* "if" (cf. Eccl. 6:6). The form *ʼî* occurs in the Hebrew Bible only in Eccl. 4:10 and 10:16 (*ʼî-lāk ʼereṣ,* "woe to you, O land"), but it also appears in the Mishnah (*Yebam.* 13:7, "woe to him on the loss of his wife, and woe to him on the loss of his brother's wife"). The Mishnah also has a form *wᵉʼîlû* (but, on the contrary).

[11] During the cold night hours, body heat, whether the warmth of an animal or that of a companion, helped to ward off the evening chill. The verse states this truism, following it with a rhetorical question. Thus Qohelet emphasizes the plight of a lonely person, unable even to stay warm at night.

Qohelet refers not to husband and wife or lovers, but to any two people who lie together for mutual warmth.

[12] This third example comes from the world of travel, where one might fall prey to lurking bandits, while two people could successfully fight off attack.

As in 4:10, the pronominal suffix anticipates the appositional *hāʼeḥād* (the one). (Literally, the protasis states: "And if one overcomes him, the individual.") The verb *tqp* occurs only in late Hebrew (Job 14:20, *titqᵉpēhû lāneṣaḥ wayyahᵃlōk,* "you overcome him forever and he dies"; 15:24, *titqᵉpēhû kᵉmelek ʻātîd lakkîdôr,* "you overcome him like a king prepared for the onset"), in Aramaic (Dan. 4:8, 17; 5:20), and in the Mishnah (*Abot* 3:8, "even if his study is too difficult for him"). Qohelet uses the verb also in 6:10.

One need not interpret the aphorism in the second half of this verse as an allusion to the birth of a son. It is better taken as a general comment. Note the x/x + 1 pattern (one/two, two/three), a favorite in the ancient world. It seems to have implied fullness or completion. If two people provide a real advantage, then three are even better.

The Fickle Crowd
4:13–16

4:13 Better is a poor youth—and wise—than an old king—and foolish—who does not know how to be enlightened any longer. [14]For from a prison he emerged to be king, although he had been born poor in his kingdom. [15]I saw all the living who were walking under the sun, along with the second youth who will succeed him. [16]There was no end to all the people, to all who were before them; also those who come later will not rejoice in him; indeed this is also absurd and shepherding the wind.

Qohelet discusses the speed with which people forget rulers, regardless of their achievements. Although a poor but intelligent king is better than an old fool who sits on the throne, the people soon forget even those who accomplish remarkable feats, such as rising from poverty to the throne, or even from prison. This anecdote, which echoes the story about Joseph, lacks clarity, for one cannot determine how many characters, two or three, to envision. The author may be guilty of imprecise syntax, or the story may describe a fickle crowd that readily welcomes new rulers. The introduction of a "second" may reflect the influence of the previous unit, which also moves unaccountably from two to three.

[13] The word "second" *(šēnî, šᵉnayim)* occurs five times in the previous unit (4:8, 9, 10, 11, 12). This word may provide the link with the anecdote about a poor youth, for *haššēnî* (the second) appears in 4:15. Although this rags-to-riches story has some affinities with the Joseph narrative, 4:13–16 contains no specific historical references.

In ancient wisdom, poverty and youth were less desirable by far than maturity and kingship. Youth was vulnerable to sensual allurement, and poverty resulted (so the teaching went) from laziness. Age, by contrast, brought wisdom and honor, with kingship the ultimate reward for exemplary conduct. Of course, not every case of poverty and youth fitted the negative assessment, nor did every instance of kingship and age result in its opposite. Now Qohelet virtually reverses the traditional values, exalting youth and decrying old age. This astounds us until we hear the final qualifying adjectives (wise and foolish). The initial contrasts, poor youth and aged king, ambiguous as they are, leave open the expected response.

The word *miskēn* (poor) is unique to Qohelet within the Bible (4:13; 9:15–16), but Ben Sira uses it (Sir. 4:3; 30:14), as does the Talmud. A similar word occurs in the laws of Hammurabi and the Mari documents (*muskenum,* state's dependents, underprivileged). The final verb is also late (Ezek. 3:21; 33:4, 5, 6; Ps. 19:12 [11E]). The root *zhr* in the Niphal occurs elsewhere in Ecclesiastes only in 12:12. The form *z*ᵉ*hîrîn* appears in Ezra 4:22 ("[be] careful"); Ben Sira uses the verb in the sense of being instructed (42:8). The verb is also found often in the Mishnah. Qohelet might mean that the old king can no longer take care of himself, but this interpretation robs the statement of its sting. The phrase *'ašer lō'-yāda'* ("who does not know") points to the unconscious aspect of the king's behavior. Refusing to take advice has become second nature to him.

[14] The antecedents in this verse, although unclear, seem to continue the story about the poor youth and the old king. The first "he" refers to the youth, as does the last "he." But what about the pronominal suffix on *b*ᵉ*malkûtô* ("in his kingdom")? It seems to allude to the old king, whose throne the poor youth rose from bondage to occupy.

The word *hāsûrîm* does not refer to rebels (from *sûr*) but is a short form for *hā'ᵃsûrîm,* the *alep* having dropped out and a compensatory *kameṣ* having been placed under the article. The house of bonds (=prison) did not prevent the youth from putting his knowledge to effective use. In due time his expertise was recognized and he rose to rule over a kingdom in which he had been born poor.

There is no need to understand *hāsûrîm* as an allusion to the maternal womb, although such a reading would provide a parallel for *nôlad rāš* ("he was born poor"). Nor is it necessary to read *l*ᵉ*melek* for *limlōk,* construing the *lamed* as emphatic ("even a king [goes forth from the womb]"). The ancient versions (Septuagint, Peshitta, Vulgate) understood the *hāsûrîm* to be a form of *hā'ᵃsûrîm* (prisoners). The Targum renders the word by "idol worshipers."

[15] The word *haššēnî* ("the second") links this verse loosely with the previous unit (4:7–12), but the reference to a second youth has struck many interpreters as incomprehensible. Solutions vary: excising it (or *hayyeled,* the youth) as a gloss; transposing the half verse to some other place (for example, after 4:10a); viewing "the second" as apposition;[79] and envisioning a youth in addition to the one mentioned in 4:14.

The simplest view is to understand the allusion as a solemn reminder that

---

[79]Gordis (245) finds an exact parallel in Hos. 2:9 [7E] ("I will return to my husband who was first" [*'îšî hāri'šôn*]), but this interpretation rests on an assumption that Hosea uses exact language about husbands and lovers.

even the youth who emerged from prison to sit on the throne will be replaced by someone else. The passage then illustrates the endless recurrence of events. If the participle (*hamᵉhallᵉkîm,* "who were walking") carries the slightest hint of death, which it does in some instances in Ecclesiastes, the point about a successor becomes all the more emphatic. Then the scope of Qohelet's vision is wide indeed: the living, the dying, the coronation of a new ruler.

[16] The phrase, "to all who were before them" is difficult. (The Vulgate and Peshitta have a singular pronominal suffix, which can be taken as a reference to the youthful ruler.) One could perhaps interpret the plural suffix as an allusion to both rulers, the old king and his young successor. However, Hebrew normally portrays a king as being before his subjects rather than vice versa.

Qohelet argues that endless people older than the king(s) were unmoved by the achievements of the youth. Likewise, those younger than the monarch found no pleasure in someone who did not belong to their own generation. Neither the past nor the future generations cared that the young man achieved so much.[80] The sentiment echoes the opinions expressed earlier about successive generations and the forgetfulness of humankind.

Religious Obligations 4:17–5:8 [5:1–9E]

4:17 [5:1E] Watch your step when you go to the house of God, for drawing near to listen is preferable to a sacrifice that fools give, because they are not aware that they are doing wrong. 5:1[2] Do not be quick to speak and do not think hastily to cause a word to go forth before God, for God is in heaven and you are on earth, so let your words be few. 2[3]For as dreams come with much business, so the voice of a fool accompanies many words. 3[4]When you vow a vow to God do not delay paying it, for he has no pleasure in fools; pay what you vow. 4[5]It is better that you do not vow than that you vow and do not pay. 5[6]Do not let your mouth cause you to sin, and do not say before the messenger that it was a mistake; why should God be angry against your voice and destroy the work of your hands? 6[7]Yes, in a multitude of dreams and futility and many words—still fear God. 7[8]If you see oppression of the poor and violation of justice and the right in the province, do not be astonished by the matter, because an official watches over

[80]Whitley (46–47) understands *qēṣ* (end) as the referent of the pronominal suffix *(bô).* In his view, Qohelet says that future citizens will not rejoice in the fact that there is no end to the masses.

another official, and executives are over them. [8[9]]And an advantage of a land in everything is this—a king for a field that is being worked.

Because of the distance separating human beings from the deity, Qohelet recommends a policy of restraint in speech. Moreover, the few words should be truthful, for calling attention to one's lack of integrity incurs risk. Although Qohelet adopts traditional language about vows, he discourages their use. Recourse to the excuse of unintentional sin when confronting a priestly messenger who has come to collect a defaulted pledge will not extricate one from danger. If the messenger connotes the angel of death, such protests fall on deaf ears. Qohelet believes that talkativeness increases the chances for affront, just as dreams generate anxiety. One's primary obligation, to fear God, includes an acknowledgement that the deity has no special fondness for fools. The unit ends with an attack against the prophetic voice of protest over oppression, for a hierarchy of responsibility rises to the supreme earthly ruler, perhaps ascending a step higher to God.

[4:17 (5:1E)] Earlier sages warned their students to hold their foot back *(m*ᵉ*naʿ ragl*ᵉ*kā)* from the paths of evildoers (Prov. 1:15; cf. 4:26) and to make their foot rare in the house of a neighbor (Prov. 25:17, *hōqar ragl*ᵉ*kā mibbêt rēʿekā*). The Qere of Eccl. 4:17 [5:1E] also has the singular "foot," and the ancient versions confirm this reading. Qohelet warns against thoughtless rushing into the temple.

The second clause may be understood as a continuation of the imperative *š*ᵉ*mōr* (watch). In this case, *w*ᵉ*qārôb,* an infinitive absolute, functions as an imperative (and draw near). The admonition then reads: watch your step . . . and draw near to listen. But the sequel is awkward: fools sacrifice a gift. Perhaps it is better to understand *w*ᵉ*qārôb* nominally and to assume an ellipsis of *ṭôb* before comparative *min* (cf. 9:17). Nevertheless, the expression is awkward, especially the use of *zābaḥ* (sacrifice) with *mittēt* (gift).

The final clause is also difficult. What do fools not know? How to do evil? To say that the fools' stupidity renders them incapable of doing anything bad would indeed be a comment full of contempt and irony. Or do they not know that they are doing evil? Alternatively, does the *lamed* denote a circumstance, a result, or a time, so that they do not know when they do wickedly?

Some critics think the text has suffered loss, perhaps *kî ʾim* (cf. Eccl. 3:12; 8:15) or *min* before *la*ᵃ*śôt.* Both would mean that fools know nothing else but doing evil.

Qohelet's first admonition is anticipated in the prophetic statement that obedience is better than sacrifice (I Sam. 15:22, "Behold, to obey is better than sacrifice, and to listen is better than the fat of rams"). The same sentiment occurs in wisdom literature, both Egyptian and Israelite (Prov. 15:8, "The sacrifice of the wicked is an abomination to the Lord"; 21:3, "To do righteousness and justice is preferred by the Lord over sacrifice"; 21:27, "The sacrifice of the wicked is an abomination").

Qohelet advises caution lest one's actions incur divine wrath. This advice neither recommends nor discounts traditional piety, although Qohelet suspects the motives and conduct of some who approach the sacred place. The "house of God" probably refers to the second temple, although it might denote a synagogue.

[5:1 (2E)] Traditional wisdom advocated thought before speech so as to avoid rash remarks. Qohelet also warns against precipitate speech. He implies that thoughtful consideration of what to say before God will result in fewer words, as one realizes the distance between speaker and addressee. Psalm 115:3 completes the observation that God is in heaven by declaring that God does everything that God desires. Qohelet may be similarly emphasizing God's power, or perhaps he focuses on God's distance and indifference.

The verb *bhl* in the Piel means "hasten" in several late texts. In II Chron. 35:21 one finds "For God has commanded me to hurry" *(wē'lōhîm'āmar lᵉbahᵃlēnî),* and in Esth. 2:9 the king is said to have provided Hadassah with ointments, food, and maidens quickly *(wayᵉbahēl).* Equally late and rare is *mᵉʻaṭṭîm* (few) as a predicate adjective. It occurs only in Ps. 109:8 (*yihyû-yāmāyw mᵉʻaṭṭîm,* "may his days be few").

Does Qohelet refer to prayer or to vows in this verse? A similar text in Sir. 7:14 mentions speech before elders as well as prayer before God ("Do not prattle in the assembly of the elders, nor repeat yourself in your prayer"). The Aramaic expression *lᵉhanpeg imra'/'mr qᵒdom* means "speak to," and this use suggests that Qohelet simply refers to speech rather than to prayer.

[2 (3E)] The mention of a fool and words links this aphorism to its context. Dreams (the article is generic) are remote from the subject under discussion, unless Qohelet thinks of the practice of incubation. In this case, the point is that the activity associated with lying down at a holy place in anticipation of a vision will be successful. But such an interpretation does not accord with the rest of the verse. Therefore it is better to view the first half as a comment that frenetic business has lingering effects that disturb sleep, causing dreams (cf. Sir. 31:1–4).

The second half of the verse affirms that loquacity marks a fool. The truth of this assertion is not obvious, for the mark of folly is surely the substance of the speech rather than its quantity. Perhaps there is simply a greater possibility for foolish words when speech flows freely. This aphorism belongs with the ancients' other warning against idle chatter. In Eccl. 10:12–14 Qohelet takes up the topic again, asserting that the fool multiplies words *(wᵉhassākal yarbeh dᵉbārîm).*

[3 (4E)] The first part of this verse quotes Deut. 23:22a [21E] almost exactly *(kî-tiddōr neder layhwh ʼᵉlōheykā lōʼ tᵉʼaḥēr lᵉšallᵉmô,* "when you vow a vow to the Lord your God, do not delay fulfilling it"). Qohelet drops both the name Yahweh and the second-person pronominal suffix on God. Deuteronomy recommends prompt payment of vows because the Lord will consider failure to pay one's debt a serious sin. Qohelet offers a similar motive, although he is reluctant to mention God, a tendency also encountered in the New Testament era. (When Qohelet says that there is no delight in fools, he means that God takes no pleasure in them.) But while Deuteronomy encourages the making of vows, Qohelet discourages them.

The danger of promising something to God during difficult times, subsequently forgetting the vow, was recognized in various settings. Proverbs 20:25 observes that such unreflective vows constitute a trap, and Ben Sira warns: "Let nothing prevent you from paying a vow promptly, and do not wait until death to be released from it" (Sir. 18:22). This counsel from Ben Sira occurs in a context that emphasizes careful consideration before speaking and before entering various situations.

[4 (5E)] Once a sacred oath was uttered, it was difficult to extricate oneself from the obligation. Of course, there were circumstances that made it desirable to do so, and religious authorities invented the means of getting around such commitments. Qohelet suggests that one does better to avoid vows in the first place. He does not absolutely rule them out, but advises against vows that one cannot or will not fulfill.

[5 (6E)] Presumably, the subject is still vows. Qohelet advises against uttering a promise that is not kept, for sooner or later one will have to offer an excuse for the delay in fulfilling the vow. One's speech may lead one's whole person into an offense against the deity. The striking images (mouth and flesh) stand for tangible realities: speech and the whole person.

To whom would one give an excuse? The Septuagint and Peshitta translate God *(hāʼᵉlōhîm).* This may be original, since otherwise it is difficult to explain how this reading found its way into both texts. The lame excuse, "It was a mistake," would simply call attention to the offense and prompt the deity to deal destructively.

The Massoretic Text now reads "messenger." In context it probably refers to a priest or an emissary from the temple who came to inquire about the failure to pay one's vows into the temple treasury. The reading "angel" may have arisen as a distancing of God from the human arena. The messenger of death in Egyptian wisdom is a suggestive parallel.[81]

The language of the protest is taken from priestly legislation. The word *šᵉgāgāh* (mistake) connotes an offense committed without knowledge or

---

[81] "When your envoy comes to fetch you . . . do not say, 'I am young to be taken.' For you do not know death. When death comes he steals the infant who is in his mother's arms, just like him who reached old age" (The Instruction of Ani, Lichtheim, II, 138).

intention, hence inadvertent sins (cf. Num. 15:22–31; Lev. 4:2–35). The interrogative *lāmmāh* (why) functions in the same way *pen* does; it can be translated by "lest." There is strong support for the plural "works," but the meaning is not affected.

[6 (7E)] The syntax of this verse is difficult to understand. The conjunction *waw* (and) joins three words—"dreams," "futility," and "words"—which have no direct relationship with the final imperative to fear God. No solution seems entirely satisfactory.

On the basis of Ps. 94:19 (*b^{e}rōb śar'appay b^{e}qirbî,* "when my inner concerns multiply"), Gordis translates the preposition *b^{e}* "in spite of," to get the sense, "Despite many dreams, futilities, and copious words, fear God." He understands the *kî* as asseverative ("indeed"). But the *bet* in Ps. 94:19 is probably not concessive, for the usual meaning, "in the midst," makes good sense there.

Another effort to grasp the intent of this verse in Ecclesiastes is based on asseverative use of *waw:* "For in a multitude of dreams and futilities there are indeed many words." Whitley adopts this reading, offering several examples of an emphatic *waw* in the Bible (II Sam. 3:38, *w^{e}gādôl* [truly great]; Ps. 49:21 [20E], *w^{e}lō'* [certainly not]; Ps. 90:2, *ûmē'ôlām* [yea, from eternity] and one example from Ugaritic (*št 'alp qdmh mra' wtk pnh,* "set an ox before him, a fatling right in front of him").

Despite the ambiguous syntax, the final command leaves nothing to the imagination. This imperative, "Fear God," concludes Qohelet's remarks about cultic obligations. Fear of God results in few words, faithfulness in paying vows if one ever resorts to them, and generally in conduct that does not invite punishment.

[7 (8E)] Qohelet has already described the plight of the oppressed: there was no one to deliver them. Here he takes for granted the inequities of daily existence and advises against dismay. The various levels of authority insulate officials from discovery and punishment. In the provincial government the officers extract as much revenue as possible from lesser officers, who turn to the peasantry for their annual dues. Officials caught between superiors and underlings look out for their own welfare. Heavy taxation of the people provides revenues for bribing higher authorities.

The use of *šōmēr* (watchman) for an officer occurs in S. of Songs 3:3 and 5:7 (*m^{e}ṣā'unî haššōm^{e}rîm hassōb^{e}bîm bā'îr,* "the watchmen who went about the city found me"). Although the verb *šāmar* is frequently applied to God who watches over Israel, that is not the implication of this verse (the highest official being God).[82] The verb also has a hostile meaning (Ps. 56:7 [6E], *hēmmāh 'ᵃqēbay yišmōrû,* "they watch my steps").

---

[82]Nevertheless, *g^{e}bōhîm* can be a plural of majesty. It then refers to the highest official, the king.

Israel's prophets held the king responsible for ensuring justice. Qohelet sees evil as immutable. Therefore there is no point in getting upset over the perfidy.

[8 (9E)] The meaning of this verse is totally obscure. One expects an observation that partially resolves the tension of a never-ending hierarchy of officials who squeeze revenues from those below them. Does a king who guarantees agriculture bring profit to everybody, since a cultivated field yields produce that can be converted into cash for the payment of taxes?

The main difficulty lies in the second half of the verse, although *bakkōl* also poses a minor problem. Does it refer to persons or to things? The reading "in every respect [in everything]," based on Gen. 24:1 ("The Lord had blessed Abraham in every respect [*bakkōl*]") understands the Ketib *hî'* as neuter (this).

The Niphal verb *ne'ᵉbād* in the second half of the verse ordinarily means "tilled" or "cultivated" (Deut. 21:4, a valley "that is neither tilled [*lō'-yē'ābēd*] nor sown"; Ezek. 36:9, *wᵉne'ᵉbadtem,* "and you [mountains of Israel] will be tilled"; 36:34, *tē'ābēd,* "[the land that was desolate] will be tilled"). This usage suggests that the word *ne'ᵉbād* modifies *lᵉśādeh* (for a field). Or one may relate the word *ne'ᵉbād* to *melek,* rendering "a king served by a field." Whitley (51) argues that the Niphal has a middle use here, and that the *lamed* prefix on "field" can be translated "from": "a king benefits from a field." But evidence for translating *lamed* "from" is hardly convincing (Ps. 29:10, *yhwh lammabbûl yāšāb,* "the Lord sits enthroned over the flood"; I Chron. 9:27, *wᵉhēm 'al-hammaptēaḥ wᵉlabbōqer labbōqer,* "and they open the door every morning").

The Disappointments of Wealth 5:9–6:9 [5:10–6:9E]

5:9 [10E] Whoever loves money will not be satisfied with money, and whoever loves wealth gets no gain. This is also absurd. 10[11]When goods increase, those who consume them multiply, and what advantage does their owner have except that his eyes look on them? 11[12]Sweet is the sleep of the laborer whether he eats little or much, but the satiety of the rich person does not permit him to sleep. 12[13]There is a serious evil that I have seen under the sun; riches were kept by their owner to his own harm. 13[14]Specifically, those riches were lost in an unfortunate venture, and he begets a son, but he possesses nothing. 14[15]Just as he came forth from his mother's womb, naked he shall again go as he came, and he will not bear anything from his wealth that he can carry with him. 15[16]This is also a serious injustice; exactly as he came so shall he go, and what profit does he have that he toils for the wind? 16[17]Also all his days he eats in darkness and much vexation, sickness, and resentment. 17[18]This is what I have seen to be good, that is appropriate, to eat and drink and to look on good things in the toil that one toils at under the sun the few days of life that God has given, for that is one's portion. 18[19]Also every person to whom God gives riches and possessions and whom God empowers to eat from it and to have a portion and to rejoice in one's toil: this is a gift of God. 19[20]For he will not long remember the days of his life, because God keeps him occupied with the joy of his heart. 6:1 There is an evil that I have seen under the sun, and it is burdensome to human beings: 2a man to whom God gave riches, possessions, and honor, and he lacked nothing of all he wanted, but God did not empower him to consume any of it, for instead a stranger devoured it; this is also absurd and grievous sickness. 3If a person begets a hundred children and lives many years—and if the days of his years are many—but he is not satisfied with good things, then even if it does not have a burial, I say that the stillborn is better off than he. 4For in futility it comes and in darkness it goes, and with darkness its name is covered. 5Indeed, although it does not see the sun or know anything, this person has more rest than that one. 6And if someone lives a thousand years twice over but does not enjoy the good—do not both go to a single place? 7All toil of human beings is for their appetite, but the appetite is never filled. 8For what advantage does the wise person have over the fool; what does the poor person have who knows how to get along with the living? 9Better is the sight of the eyes than the roving of the appetite; this also is futile and shepherding the wind.

Various factors over which we have no control lead to disenchantment with wealth: bad investments, sickness, increasing overhead costs, worry, and an inability to take wealth with us at death. Qohelet exposes human jealousy to public scrutiny, the grasping to have more than our neighbors possess and the insatiable lust for possessions. Those who love money will see it slip through their fingers like quicksilver. In some respects, therefore, poor laborers have an advantage, for they sleep soundly while rich people lie awake from overeating or anxiety. Qohelet recalls a specific instance of someone who acquired wealth and lost it, much to the chagrin of the heir. The echo of Job 1:21 gives way to a description of miserly existence. God's role remains unclear, either afflicting individuals with memories of better things or enabling them to survive from a rich store of memory. In Qohelet's view, longevity does not solve the problem, for some people live a long time but do not have the capacity to enjoy life. A stillborn child fares better.

[9 (10E)] The topic of the insatiable appetite of humans appears for the third time. In 1:8 and 4:8 Qohelet observed that the eyes were never satisfied with seeing or with possessions. Now he dispenses with the image of insatiable eyes, using the language of passion. The lover of money will never find satisfaction in the wealth that results from an acquisitive lust. The observation takes an aphoristic form, repeating *kesep* (and *'ōhēb*) for emphasis.

The next clause is unclear for two reasons. First, only here is the verb *'āhab* construed with the preposition *b*ᵉ (the participle *'ōhēb* plus *behāmôn*). Second, there is no verb. Should *lō'-yiśba'* (will not be satisfied) be supplied from the previous clause? Or is it preferable to follow the Peshitta and repoint *lō' tᵉbû'āh* (gain, increase, produce) to *lō' tᵉbô'ēhû* (it will not come [to him])?[83]

The preposition *b*ᵉ seems to have been added through dittography of the final *bet* on the participle *'ōhēb.* The difficult *lō' tᵉbû'āh* can be understood as ironic ellipsis: anyone who loves wealth . . . no increase! The language derives from agriculture (yield, produce, harvest). By his choice of language in both aphorisms, Qohelet covers a wide range of topics: convertible cash *(kesep),* possessions of all kinds from cattle to real estate *(hāmôn),* and the land's bounty *(tᵉbû'āh).* None will satisfy those who love riches. The saying does not deny that the acquisitive person obtains money, but that he or she will find satisfaction. The next verse offers a reason for the absence of pleasure despite an increase in possessions.

[10 (11E)] Increased possessions require many people to watch over the wealth and to see that it continues to yield dividends. Slaves must be fed and clothed, employees reimbursed, and an ever-increasing band of dependents arrive at the door of the person with riches. As a result, the only positive value that the owner derives from increased wealth is the joy of beholding it, yet Qohelet has already observed twice that the eyes can never be filled with seeing.

The word *haṭṭôbāh* (the good) signifies every desirable thing and comprehends the three different words for wealth in 5:9 [10E]. The image of devourers *('ôkᵉleyhā)* powerfully portrays the drain on resources that accompanies expansion in agricultural holdings, real estate, or mercantile ventures. The plural form for owner *(lib'āleyhā)* has precedent in Ex. 21:29 ("and its owner is warned") and in Ex. 22:10 [11E] ("and its owner shall accept"). Qohelet uses the plural form several times (5:12 [13E]; 7:12; 8:8).

The final phrase, *rᵉ'ût* (Qere) or *rᵉ'iyyat* (Ketib) *'ênāyw,* "the seeing of his eyes," suggests that the owner merely gets to watch as his wealth is consumed by others.

[11 (12E)] Qohelet contrasts the ease with which an exhausted worker falls asleep, even on a partially empty stomach, with the troubled thoughts of the wealthy. Does the sleeplessness derive from overeating or anxious worry? The ambiguity may be intentional. The proverbial tradition exam-

---

[83]The Septuagint seems to have read *lō' lô* (not to him), a reading that the Targum also has *(lêt lêh).*

ines both ideas (cf. Prov. 25:16, which advises against gorging oneself on honey lest one vomit, and Sir. 31:1–4, which describes the different experiences of the rich and the poor with respect to sleep and food). Ben Sira states that anxiety about wealth prevents slumber, but the rich man fills himself with dainties while the poor works hard and watches as his possessions diminish. The leisure of the two is very different: the rich person, who can afford to rest, eats dainties, but the poor becomes poorer when pausing from labor.

The Hiphil participle *mannîaḥ* (permit) is a late form. The psalmist (Ps. 105:14) declares that God did not permit anyone to oppress them (the Israelites; *lōʾ hinnîaḥ ʾādām lᵉʿošqām*). Elsewhere Qohelet registers a less optimistic opinion about the plight of the worker; the lot of humankind is one, specifically an absence of rest by day or night. What kind of worker does Qohelet have in mind? The evidence for reading *hāʿebed* (the slave) is weak (Septuagint, Symmachus, Theodotion), although this reading provides a contrast with the person who has wealth. If *hāʿōbēd* is an abbreviation for *ʿōbēd hāʾᵃdāmāh,* the reference is to agricultural labor (cf. Gen. 4:2; Prov. 12:11). The latter text understands working the land as a positive endeavor ("Whoever tills his land [*ʿōbēd ʾadmātô*] will have plenty of bread, but whoever pursues empty things lacks intelligence"). The word for satiety (*yiśbaʿ,* "he will have plenty") does not here possess the negative overtones that Qohelet usually bestows on it.

[12 (13E)] The particle of existence joins hands with the verb of observation to call attention to an especially painful instance of riches that did not bring happiness (5:12–17 [13–18E]). The Qal participle *ḥôlāh* (sick, ill) modifying the noun *rāʿāh* (evil) suggests a serious malady. The same use occurs in Eccl. 6:2, but with noun and adjective reversed (*wāḥᵒlî rāʿ,* "and grievous affliction"). Jeremiah describes his own affliction in similar syntax, although with different vocabulary (Jer. 10:19, *naḥlāh makkātî,* "my wound is serious"; 14:17, *makkāh naḥlāh mᵉʾōd,* "a very serious blow").

The *lamed* on *bᵉʿālāyw* (their owner) has given rise to opposing interpretations: the riches were guarded for their owner or by their owner. The latter interpretation is strengthened by a similar use of *lamed* after a passive participle in Gen. 14:19 (*bārûk ʾabrām lᵉʾēl ʿelyôn,* "blessed be Abram by El Elyon"). Qohelet's point seems to be that rich people are consumed by anxiety lest they lose their accumulated wealth, and the concern eats away at them, causing mental and physical distress.

[13 (14E)] The explicative *waw* attached to the initial verb identifies this verse as an elaboration of the point about the grievous evil, an expression that occurs again in 5:15 [16E]. The anxious care in guarding the wealth was fruitless, for the money was depleted in a risky business venture. In this instance the owner only watched as the wealth disappeared. The timing was especially bad because the unfortunate man begat a son, an event normally signaling good fortune, but now there was no money in the father's possession nor in that of the son.[84] The pronominal suffix on "money" may be purposefully ambiguous. The essential point is that the money was lost.

Qohelet's fondness for opposites is evident in the juxtaposition of riches and utter poverty in this verse. The negation (*wᵉʾên . . . mᵉʾûmāh,* and there was nothing) stands out after the mention of opulence. The next verse repeats this word *mᵉʾûmāh,* as well as the specific reference to an absence of anything in his possession *(bᵉyādô).*

[14 (15E)] The idea that one emerges from the womb naked and returns to mother earth the same way also occurs in Job 1:21 (*ʿārōm yāṣātî mibbeṭen ʾimmî wᵉʿārōm ʾāšûb šāmāh,* "naked I came from my mother's womb, and naked I shall return there"). The notion was probably widespread in Qohelet's day (Ps. 139:15; Sir. 40:1). Whereas the expression in Job seems to allude to the underworld by using the euphemism "there" *(šāmāh),* Qohelet prefers the euphemism for dying "to go" (the verb *hālak*).

The subject of this coming and going is unclear. It seems more natural to take it as a reference to the son, but the pronominal suffix on *baʿᵃmālô* ("from his toil [wages]") requires a shift from son to father, which may argue for taking the father as the subject. Throughout Qohelet points to the common lot of the once-rich father and the poor son, both born with empty hands and both destined to die that way.

Many interpreters think *baʿᵃmālô* contains the *bet* of price or instrumentality. The translation above takes the *bet* in the sense of "from," for which Whitley (52–53) gives considerable evidence. From the Bible he points to parallel passages which replace *bᵉ* with *min* (II Sam. 22:14//Ps. 18:14 [13E]), "Yahweh will roar from heaven"; II Kings 14:13//II Chron. 25:23, "from the Ephraim Gate to the Corner Gate"). Whitley also adduces evidence from Phoenician and Ugaritic.

[15 (16E)] The expression *rāʿāh ḥôlāh* (serious evil) is carried over from 5:12, which refers to the hoarding of wealth in vain. Now Qohelet reiterates the observation in 5:14 [15E] that no one can take anything more in death than was brought at birth. As individuals arrive (naked, empty-handed), so they depart. The peculiar *kol-ʿummat* (exactly) is an Aramaizing misreading of the prepositions *kᵉ* plus *lᵉ* and *ʿummat.* Its present form results from the influence of a comparable Aramaic expression *qol-qᵒbēl dî* (because; cf. Dan. 2:40).

The final phrase "that he toils for the wind" varies the usual expression for herding the wind or striving after the wind. The image of working for something as intangible as wind has extraordinary power, for the wealth that the rich man had managed to acquire slipped through his fingers exactly as wind eludes those who hope to capture it in their hands. With

[84]Gordis (252–253) thinks the *bᵉyādô* is a phonetic misspelling of *bᵉʿᵃdô* (for him).

the recurrence of the question about profit Qohelet reiterates the earlier denial that anyone gains a profit from working (1:3).

[16 (17E)] Qohelet describes his hours as characterized by darkness and its minions—sickness, irritation, and resentment. He already has a foretaste of the long darkness yet to come. Because of his stinginess, he even consumes his food in the dark. The word *yō'kēl* (he eats) may have the wider sense of "spend" as in Amos 7:12 (*we'ekol-šām leḥem,* "and eat bread there," that is, "earn your living"). However, Qohelet's fondness for expressions like coming and going in darkness (2:14; 6:4) may have led him to characterize the one positive possibility as negated by darkness.

The Septuagint has *kai penthai* ("and grief") instead of "he eats." This reading of *'bl* for *'kl* continues in the Syro-Hexaplar and Coptic versions. The syntax, thus understood, lacks a verb but includes five nouns: "Also all his days are in darkness, grief, considerable vexation, sickness, and resentment."

Literally, the second half of the verse reads: "and he is much vexed, and his sickness and anger." The preposition *b^e* carries over from *haḥōšek,* and the pointing of [*w^e*]*kā'as* should be changed from that of a verb to yield a noun *(ka'as).* Moreover, the pronominal ending on *w^eḥolyô* (and his sickness) seems to have arisen through dittography (or possibly through loss of a *lamed* from *lô* ("to him"). These changes produce a far more coherent reading.

[17 (18E)] Having considered the example of the wealthy person who neither enjoyed his wealth nor retained it for his son's benefit, Qohelet advises on the best way to avoid such misery and resentment of that unfortunate individual (5:17–19 [18–20E]). As the verb of observation *(rā'îtî)* introduces the negative example, so begins the positive counsel, although the language of the latter is cumbersome.

Earlier interpreters suggested that *ṭôb 'ašer-yāpeh* ("good that is beautiful") translated the Greek expression *kalos kagathos,* but this view no longer commends itself to most critics.[85] The adjective *yāpeh* has the sense of "appropriate, proper, becoming" in rabbinic literature ("silence is becoming to the wise," *Pesaḥ.* 99a). In Eccl. 3:11 Qohelet uses *yāpeh* in this sense of "appropriate."

The word *mispar* (few) is an accusative of time; it has the meaning of paucity (2:3; 6:12). In the translation above, the Massoretic pointing of *ṭôb* has been ignored. Note that the accentuation of this long verse includes no *athnach* (as in Gen. 21:9; Num. 9:1; Isa. 36:1; Jer. 13:13; 51:37; Ezek. 42:10; Amos 5:1; I Chron. 26:26; 28:1; II Chron. 23:1).

[18 (19E)] Not everyone has the power to enjoy wealth, for some people

[85]The only biblical parallel is Hos. 12:9 [8E] (*'āwôn 'ašer ḥēṭ',* "iniquity that is sin").

are by nature stingy, or otherwise prevented from taking advantage of good things. Qohelet claims that the capacity to eat and benefit from wealth lies in God's hands. The late verb *w^{e}hišlîṭô* (Hiphil of *šlṭ,* "to rule," hence "empower") also occurs in 6:2, which refers to one whom God does not enable to eat anything from the goods in his possession. Elsewhere the Hiphil of *šlṭ* occurs only in Ps. 119:133 (*w^{e}'al-tašleṭ-bî kol-'āwen,* "and do not allow any iniquity to gain power over me"), but the Haphel is found in Dan. 2:38, 48 (*w^{e}hašl^{e}ṭāk, w^{e}hašl^{e}ṭēh,* "and making you [him] rule").

Qohelet's claim that the ability to enjoy wealth is a divine gift has its positive dimensions, but the actual phrasing ("everyone[86] to whom God gives") implies that some people who are not so favored by God therefore spend their days in dark misery. This knowledge that life's pleasures cannot be earned through diligence and good conduct undercuts the fundamental premise of wisdom thinking. Ironically, Qohelet achieves this tour de force by emphasizing another feature of ancient wisdom: religious faith. In Qohelet's affirmations about God, the notion of divine gift loses its comforting quality. The gift comes without rhyme or reason; it falls on individuals indiscriminately. Those who do not receive it can do nothing to change their condition.

[19 (20E)] The meaning of this verse depends on the interpretation of *ma'^{a}neh.*[87] What does God do? The verb *'ānāh* in the Qal means "to answer," "be occupied with," and "afflict." Although one could understand the sense to be that God afflicts the person by the constant presence of thoughts about the good life, most interpreters choose the second option: "to keep one occupied with." Perhaps both nuances are present, for preoccupation with pleasure is vexing to those who are unable to participate in the good life. Qohelet has described two kinds of people, those who cannot enjoy life and those who can. If this verse is a summary statement, it ought to refer to both groups. If it refers only to the person who enjoys divine favor, it means that pleasures keep one's mind off the brevity of life.

Another way of rendering the first part of the verse is to understand *lō' harbēh yizkōr* as "he will not think much." There is little difference between this idea and the one represented in the above translation ("he will not long remember"). The difference lies in orientation; in the former, anticipation is meant, and in the latter, it is retrospection.

The word *lēb* (heart, mind) may carry a cognitive meaning here rather than an emotive one, but probably refers to sensual enjoyment.

[6:1] Qohelet gives another example of misfortune (6:1–6). The earlier

---

[86]The article is attached to *'ādām* (person) despite the preceding *kol* (all).

[87]The correct reading was probably *ma'^{a}nēhû;* that is what the Septuagint, Peshitta, and Targum read.

one may have been brought on by the rich man's folly, but this example illustrates the undesirable features of having to rely on the divine gift. Here is a person who has everything the heart can desire, but who lacks the capacity to enjoy these good things. In such circumstances, the person is less fortunate than an aborted infant.

The particle of existence *(yēš)* generally introduces a new idea (4:8; 5:12 [13E]; 8:14; 10:5), but *yēš* in 8:6 and the second *yēš* in 8:14, perhaps also that in 2:21, do not appear to function this way. Some manuscripts have *ḥôlāh* (sickness) after *rā'āh,* a scribal attempt to bring the language in line with 5:12 [13E].

In 8:6 the expression *rabbāh 'ālāyw* also occurs. Its meaning is "great, serious upon him," hence heavy or burdensome. The article on *hā'ādām* (the man, humans) does not necessarily anticipate the specific individual to be discussed as the example of misfortune but may refer to people in general.

[2] Unlike the man in 5:12–14 [13–15E], who did not enjoy his wealth or pass it along to an heir, but lost it through some calamity, the person in 6:1–2 lacked the power to enjoy his vast fortune, whether because of poor health, his preoccupation with business, or some other unspecified reason. Qohelet's interest centers on stating the ultimate cause of the misfortune: God.

In the book of Proverbs, the foreign woman robs young men of their share in long life by offering stolen water and bread eaten in secret (Prov. 9:17). Qohelet may play on this idea of a stranger devouring the fortune of the rich man. But the word *nokrî* (stranger) does not necessarily indicate a foreigner. For Qohelet, it may simply describe the "someone else" who enjoys what a rich man worked to acquire.

II Chronicles 1:11 associates riches, possessions, and honor with Solomon, gifts bestowed on the young king by God as rewards for unselfishness. Qohelet may allude to this tradition, but the combination could easily have occurred to him independently.

A literal translation of *le'ᵉkōl* (to eat) is not necessary; perhaps "to enjoy" is the best translation, since it applies to honor as well as to riches and possessions.

[3] This verse seems to introduce another example of misfortune, presenting a hypothetical case of someone who receives the traditional signs of the good life (many children and a long life; cf. Gen. 25:8; Job 42:17), but does not derive satisfaction from them.

The syntax is difficult. An iterative *šᵉ* on *šeyyihyû* continues the sense of *'im* (if, although). The chief difficulty lies in the clause about a burial. To whom does it refer? The person who lived long and had many children but did not find any satisfaction in the goods? The stillborn? It seems better to understand *lô* as anticipatory; it refers to the stillborn infant, who would normally receive no burial. Even such an unfortunate creature is better off than the man who looked upon children and long life without satisfaction.[88] The preposition *min* (from) after the verb *lō'-tiśba'* ("it does not find satisfaction") is also found in Isa. 66:11 (*ûs^{e}ba'tem miššōd,* "and you will be satisfied by the breast").

[4] The coming and going of 5:15 [16E] returns here with reference to the stillborn. The birth of a dead infant thrusts it into a realm characterized by both futility and brevity (the two meanings of *hebel*). The stillborn enters a transient stage and departs promptly for a permanent abode in darkness. The verb *yēlēk* (Qere *hlk*) has a solemn sense (die); the Qumran fragment has *hlk,* confirming *poreuetai* in the Septuagint.

The repetition of *ûbaḥōšek* ("and in darkness") has a lingering effect, emphasizing the only reality the stillborn experiences. To cover its name implies completely forgetting the child. Job's initial lament also describes an untimely birth as never seeing light (Job 3:16).

[5] In Job 3:16 the stillborn never sees light *('ôr);* Qohelet refers to the source of light, the sun (without the article, which is unusual). Elsewhere he combines the two, sun and light (11:7, "sweet is the light [*hā'ôr*], and it is good for the eyes to look on the sun [*haššāmeš*]"). For Qohelet, to see light and the sun is to live (cf. Eccl. 7:11, "an advantage to those who see the sun").

What is the object of *w^{e}lō' yādā'* ("and has not known")? Some interpreters assume that both verbs govern *šemeš* (sun). However, the verb *yāda'* can mean "to have knowledge" (as in Isa. 44:9, "their witnesses neither see nor have knowledge"; Ps. 73:22, "I was stupid and did not have knowledge"). The translation of Symmachus construes *naḥat* (rest) with the verb *yādā'* ("and has not known rest").

The noun *naḥat* means "pleasure, satisfaction" in rabbinic usage. Gordis (259) refers to *Erub.* 13b ("It would be better [*nôaḥ*] for man not to have been created than to have been created"). Whitley's example (58) from Eccl. 4:6 is less convincing, for Qohelet uses *ṭôb* followed by the *min* of comparison. The rabbinic text dispenses with both in favor of *nôaḥ* (an extended meaning of "pleasure").

"This one" refers to the stillborn, and "that one" to the man who had possessions but did not enjoy them. Job 3:17–19 exaggerates the advantage that the one has over the other. Although Qohelet does not elaborate, he could not emphasize the rich man's plight more strongly than by this comparison. The stillborn lies at rest while the rich man continues in frustration.

[6] The sentence begins with a protasis and concludes with a rhetorical

---

[88]Some interpreters relocate this clause (for example, after *w^{e}lō' yādā'* in 6:5), while others repoint *lō'* to *lu'* (if). The first view refers the clause to the stillborn, the second to the miserable man.

question. This unusual structure introduces an element of surprise, but there is no doubt about the correct answer to the question. Yes, all go to the same place, the gaping hole, the open mouth that has no satiation. Like the frustrated rich man, Sheol is never satisfied (Prov. 30:16; Isa. 5:14; Hab. 2:5).

Qohelet now questions the traditional belief that long life was a blessing, a reward for virtuous conduct. For Qohelet, length of days could be frustrating under certain circumstances, so that an incredibly long life was not necessarily good. His expression for longevity *(šānîm paʿamayim)* is as rare as the accomplishment; the idea is normally expressed by *'alpayim šānāh.*

Aramaic influences the form *'illû* (if), which is a combination of *'im* and *lû.*[89] The unusual form *'illû* occurs in Esth. 7:4 (*we'illû laʿabādîm welišpāḥôt nimkarnû,* "if we had been sold for slaves, male and female"). In Ezek. 3:6 *'im-lō'* should probably read *'im lû'* (cf. Peshitta and Targum, which have *'illû*). Whitley (58) points to two rabbinic uses of *'illû* (*Mak.* 1:10, "If we had been in the Sanhedrin"; *Ned.* 9:2, "If I had known").

[7] To whom does the suffix on *lepîhû* refer? If it alludes to the wealthy man in 6:2, whose appetite was never filled (6:3), this verse summarizes that argument in different language (*hā'ādām* rather than *'îš; timmālē'* instead of *tiśbaʿ*). More likely, this verse is an aphorism with universal application. The sentiment still applies to the person less fortunate than a stillborn.

An alternative interpretation for the suffix on *lepîhû* refers it to Sheol (the one place mentioned in the previous verse).[90] All human toil is for Sheol's appetite. The idea of Sheol's open mouth fits the context nicely, but so does the sense of toiling for one's own appetite, the subject of another proverb ("The appetite of a toiler works for him, for his mouth urges him on," Prov. 16:26). Qohelet may have crafted his syntax to invite both interpretations.

[8] The first half of the verse presents no difficulty. The rhetorical question functions as a strong denial: the wise have no advantage over fools. The initial *kî* may be asseverative (indeed, truly). Qohelet associates traditional types of people spoken of by earlier sages, the wise and the foolish, with a favorite idea: profit or advantage. Previous teachers took for granted the absolute superiority of wisdom over folly. Qohelet does not.

But what does the second half of the verse mean? The versions do not help, for they attest to the Massoretic Text. Are "the poor" and "who knows" the same person or two different types of people? If the preposition *min* carries over from the first half of the verse, a comparison is made between the *'ānî* and the *yôdēaʿ*, making *'ānî* equivalent to *ḥākām,* which

---

[89]The Qumran fragment of Qoh. 6:6 has *w'm lw'.*

[90]Peter Ackroyd, "Two Hebrew Notes," *ASTI* 5 (1967) 82–86. Mitchell Dahood moved beyond Ackroyd's suggestion and translated *nepeš* as throat rather than appetite ("Hebrew-Ugaritic Lexicography," *Bib* 49 [1968] 368).

parallels it. The usual translation for *ʿānî* is unsatisfactory, for "the poor" were rarely considered wise by Qohelet or his predecessors.[91] Whitley (59) proposes the unlikely meaning "intelligent man" for *ʿānî* on the basis of *ʿnh,* "to answer," citing Job 9:14–15 ("Would that I could answer him effectively, that I could choose my words with him; though I am innocent, I cannot express myself [*ʾeʿeneh*]") and Sir. 9:14 ("According to thy ability answer [*ʿnh*] thy neighbor"). Kroeber (118) understands the word *ʿānî* on the basis of *ʿnh,* "to be humble," hence a reserved person.[92]

Despite the pointing of the Massoretic Text, *yôdēaʿ* seems to be in apposition with the definite *leʿānî.* What does this person know? The expression, "to walk before the living," is an idiom for conducting one's affairs successfully, perhaps in the face of opposition (the hostile sense of *neged*). Yet Qohelet says even this individual has no advantage. Possessing insight into the way one ought to act does not assure success, for imponderables offset the positive effect of knowledge.

[9] The meaning of this "better saying" is elusive, despite the ease of translation. The verb *rāʾāh* has two meanings in Ecclesiastes: to see and to enjoy.[93] According to 11:9, "the ways of the heart and the sight of the eyes" are desirable, for Qohelet urges young people to walk in them. On the other hand, 5:10 [11E] downplays the privilege of looking on one's wealth. Perhaps in 6:9 Qohelet refers to the things that are immediately attainable (a bird in the hand).

By contrast, a roving appetite seeks what one desires but has no realistic means of obtaining. Qohelet has referred to restless striving for wealth and endless appetite for food in 5:9–11 [10–12E] and 6:7. Better what one can look on and enjoy than fantasizing about eminently desirable things outside one's grasp.

Qohelet often uses *hlk* with reference to death (3:20; 5:14 [15E]; 6:4; 9:10), a usage found elsewhere in the Bible (cf. Ps. 39:14 [13E], *beṭerem ʾēlēk weʾênennî,* "before I go and am not"). Whitley (60) translates the entire

---

[91] In Eccl. 9:13–18 an anecdote about a poor wise man shows that at least in Qohelet's mind there was such a thing as poverty and wisdom in the same person. If one follows many manuscripts and the Targum, which add a *waw* before *ḥākām,* one can see this as an anomaly (poor but wise). It is noteworthy that Qohelet uses *ʾîš miskēn* rather than *ʿānî* in this story. The reference in 4:13 ("a poor but wise youth") is less apt, for the youth later became a king.

[92] Among the many emendations, one of the most interesting is *ʾanî* for *ʿānî,* yielding "Why do I know how to conduct myself before the king?" (Galling, 104). See also F. Ellermeier, "Die Entmachtung der Weisheit im Denken Qohelets," *ZTK* 60 (1963) 1–20. He emends to *lāmāh ʾanî yôdēaʿ,* "Why am I knowledgeable as to walking before men?"

[93] Whitley (59) writes that *rāʾāh* means "to perceive, to discern" in 2:3 and 5:17 [18E]; "to enjoy" in 2:1 and 6:6; "to experience" in 2:12. The meaning in 6:9 is "to attain pleasure," both senses of "experience and enjoy." These two nuances are also present in 11:9 ("the sight of your eyes"). He finds the same understanding of *rāʾāh* in *Yoma* 74b (*mrʾh-ʿynym bʾšh,* "the pleasure of looking at one's wife").

verse along those lines: "Better the pleasure of the moment than the departing of life."

The full futility formula occurs here for the last time.[94] If the comparison in the verse is between immediate pleasure and illusory desires, the image of chasing the wind applies to a roving desire. The whole formula aptly characterizes momentary pleasures and insatiable desires.

A Transitional Unit
6:10–12

> 6:10 That which is, its name has already been called, and it is known that it is; man cannot indeed argue with one who is stronger than he. [11]If there are many words futility increases; what advantage does anyone have? [12]Who knows what is good for a human being in life the few days of his empty life that he spends like a shadow, because who can tell one what will occur afterward under the sun?

This section returns to the idea that nothing new ever occurs and ironically alludes to the name of the first human creature, who cannot compete with God. The reference to multiplication of words reinforces the suspicion that the comment has Job in mind. The fundamental orientation of ancient wisdom—the discovery of what benefits human beings—becomes an impossible goal.

[10] This verse contains two examples of *casus pendens,* isolating "that which is" and "man" from their immediate context. This understanding of *'ādām* does not reflect the view of the Massoretes, who connected the noun with the preceding words. Their accentuation yields "and it is known that he is a man." This might play on Adam's name. (The references to pronouncing the name of whatever comes into existence has parallels in the Babylonian creation epic.[95] To name a thing was tantamount to bringing it into existence. Deutero-Isaiah praises the creator in these words: "the one who brings out their host by number, calling them all by name" (*l*^{e}*kullām b*^{e}*šēm yiqrā',* Isa. 40:26). A pun on the name Adam and his association with the ground would reinforce the observation in the second half of the verse that a mere human cannot contend with the creator. A similar reminder of

---

[94] The Massoretes locate the midpoint of the book between verses 9 and 10 of this chapter.

[95] "When on high the heaven had not been named, firm ground below had not been called by name . . . uncalled by name, their destinies undetermined—Then it was that the gods were formed within them" (*ANET,* 61).

finitude occurs in Isa. 45:9–11, which compares human striving with God to a vessel's contention with a potter *(ḥarśê ʾadāmāh).*

The adjective *taqqîp* (strong) occurs only here,[96] but Qohelet uses the verb *yitqepû* (emended text) in 4:12. Although the Ketib can be understood either as an adjective with the article or as a Hiphil form of the verb, the Qere identifies *taqqîp* as a predicate adjective.[97] A comparable form appears in 10:3 *(kšhskl).* If the *waw* in *welōʾ* is asseverative (indeed), it means that no one can argue with someone who is stronger. Perhaps Qohelet has Job in mind, observing that attacks on God are useless.

[11] Continuing the thought of the previous verse, which dismissed wordy litigation[98] and harangue against a stronger person as ineffective, Qohelet observes that numerous words increase the emptiness and futility already present. Words, however eloquent, only widen the gulf between weak and strong, making the act of forming words counterproductive and leaving no profit or advantage. Ironically, Qohelet uses alliteration in this observation about the futility of careful speech: *debārîm harbēh marbîm hābel.*

The quest for eloquence fails for two reasons: first, echoing a theme he has already emphasized more than once, the predetermination and recurrence of all events, and second, the fact that in the last resort power rests in God, not in the human tongue. Human beings regularly confront their limits, both among other humans and in the face of death and the one who determines when to send forth the death angel.

[12] This verse, like 6:8, has two rhetorical questions.[99] Zimmerli (1933) thinks the question, "What is good for human beings?" expresses the fundamental concern of Israelite wisdom. If Zimmerli's assessment of the situation is correct, Qohelet dismisses the essence of the tradition to which he was heir, for he virtually asserts that no person really knows the good. But he does not follow an anthropological orientation in his dismissal of the quest for what is good, nor does he substitute a religious pursuit for an anthropological one.

In Qohelet's description of life two qualifying adjectives stand out: brief and empty. The Septuagint speaks of men and women spending their few days of empty existence in the shade, furnishing a fine contrast with the final phrase, "under the sun." But this does not accord with Qohelet's negative

---

[96]Biblical Aramaic uses *tqp* several times (Dan. 2:40, 42; 3:33; 7:7; Ezra 4:20).

[97]The form seems to be a conflation of *štqyp* and *htqypʾ* but some interpreters follow Driver (*Textus* 4 [1965] 79) in viewing it as an abbreviation of *šwʾ tqyp.*

[98]The essential meaning of *dîn* is to adjudicate; Eccl. 6:10 has a wider connotation that approximates the development in the meaning of the related verb *rîb* (from "contend at law" to "strive").

[99]In 6:8 the sequence is *kî mah . . . mah,* whereas it is reversed in 6:12 *(mî . . . ʾašer mî).*

comments about transience and futility. Spending time in the shade was eminently desirable. For this reason, it seems best to retain the Massoretic Text ("like a shadow"). Individuals move toward darkness, like a shadow that lengthens until lost in evening.

Many interpreters discern Greek influence in *w^{e}ya^{ʿa}śēm,* that is, *poieō* in the sense of spending time. This usage, common in Hellenistic Greek, has made its presence felt in the Septuagint of Prov. 13:23 (*dikaioi poiēsousin en ploutō etē polla,* "The righteous will spend many years in wealth"); in Tob. 10:7 (*poiēsai auton ekei,* "that he should spend there"); and in Josephus' *Antiquities* 6.1.4 (*poiēsasa . . . mēnas tessaras,* "having spent . . . four months"). Whitley (61) also adduces Thucydides 7.28 for earlier use (*tēn nykta eph' hoplois poieisthai,* "to spend the night under arms"). Gordis cites Ruth 2:19, but there the three uses of the verb probably mean "work."

Some commentators understand God as the subject of *w^{e}ya^{ʿa}śēm:* God makes them like a shadow (cf. NAB).

A Collection of Proverbs 7:1–14

7:1 Better is a good name than fine ointment,
And the day of death than the day of birth.
2 Better to go to a house of mourning
Than to go to a house of feasting,
For that is the end of every person,
And the living should take it to heart.
3 Better vexation than laughter,
For in a sad face the heart is made well.
4 The heart of the wise is in a house of mourning,
But the heart of fools is in a house of levity.
5 Better to hear the rebuke of the wise
Than to hear the praise of fools.
6 Surely the laughter of fools resembles the sound
of nettles under a kettle,
This is also absurd.
7 Surely oppression makes the wise foolish,
And a bribe corrupts the heart.
8 Better the end of a thing than its beginning;
Better a patient spirit than a proud spirit.
9 Do not be quick in your spirit to take offense,
For resentment lodges in the bosom of fools.

10 Do not say, "How was it that the former days were
better than these?"
For it is not from wisdom that you ask about this.
11 Wisdom is good with an inheritance,
And an advantage for those who see the sun.
12 For the protection of wisdom is the protection of money,
And the advantage of knowledge is that wisdom gives life
to those who possess it.
13 Consider the work of God,
Indeed, who can straighten what he made crooked?
14 On a good day be happy, and on a bad day take thought:
God made both this day and that day in order
that nobody could find out anything afterward.

This unit emphasizes the relative worth of many things, using the key word "better," sometimes in the sense of "good." Alliteration finds expression in a play on similarities between the Hebrew words for oil and name, as well as nettles and kettle (perhaps also laughter). Qohelet characterizes God's works, whether good or evil, as unalterable, and advises persons to visit the house of mourning rather than a place of festivity because the end of everyone beckons.

[7:1] In the better saying of 7:1a we find an exquisite example of chiastic alliteration: *ṭôb šēm miššemen ṭôb.* Proverbs 22:1 had argued: "A name is to be chosen over great wealth, and favor over silver and gold." Unfortunate beyond description were the persons whose name stank, whose reputation was sullied, who were "senseless, disreputable offspring" (*b^{e}nê-nābāl gam-b^{e}nê b^{e}lî-šēm,* Job 30:8). A concern for a good reputation was not restricted to human beings. Even God sought to make a reputation through delivering the Israelites from bondage, zealously guarding it from profanation (e.g., Deut. 28:58–59). When Amos attacked father and son for cohabiting with the same young woman, he accused them of sullying God's holy name (*l^{e}maʿan ḥallēl ʾet-šēm qodšî,* Amos 2:7bβ).

Song of Songs relates a favorable name and fragrant perfume ("As for scent, your oils are good: 'Oil of Turaq' is your name; that's why maidens love you," S. of Songs 1:3).[100] Qohelet's association of name and oil is not simply the product of a punning imagination. Reflection on the fragrance or stench of a reputation leads naturally to thoughts about precious ointments.

But how did Qohelet arrive at the observation in 7:1b? Perhaps this alteration of traditional wisdom is just another instance of Qohelet's preoccupation with death. One's reputation is not complete until one dies ("Call

---

[100]The translation is taken from Michael V. Fox, *The Song of Songs and the Ancient Egyptian Love Songs* (Madison, Wis., University of Wisconsin Press, 1985), p. 96.

no one happy before his death," Sir. 11:28a). The tone of 7:1b typifies Qohelet's attitude toward life, and the difficult syntax in expressing the impersonal is also characteristic of his style.[101]

[2] Qohelet now introduces the mourning that accompanied death. (According to Sir. 22:12, the official period of mourning lasted seven days [cf. Gen. 50:10].) The occasion for feasting is not specified, whether a birth, marriage, or another joyous event. This "better saying" may be traditional wisdom, encouraging the obligation to show proper respect for the dead and discouraging extravagant feasting. However, it might equally well be an original expression of Qohelet's attitude to reality.

The reason for preferring grief to revelry resembles the thought in Ps. 90:12 ("So teach us to number our days that we may get a heart of wisdom," RSV). By pondering the implications of life's brevity and death's inevitability, we may acquire insight or even real wisdom. Qohelet advises one to face death squarely, without drowning awareness of mortality in endless drinking bouts and parties.

[3] In 1:18 Qohelet associates vexation with knowledge, acknowledging the painful thinking that generates new insights, while 2:2 links laughter with madness. Wisdom's relative advantage over folly leads Qohelet to prefer vexation over laughter.

But what reason does Qohelet give for his preferences? The idiom for a downcast countenance is widespread (Gen. 40:7, Joseph's companions in prison; Neh. 2:2, *maddûa' pāneykā rā'îm . . . 'ên zeh kî-'im rōa' lēb,* "Why is your countenance disconsolate . . . ? This is nothing but sadness of heart"). The expression for a merry heart also occurs frequently in the Bible (e.g., Ruth 3:7, "now Boaz ate and drank and made his heart merry"; cf. Judg. 19:6, 9). This is also the sense in which Qohelet uses *w^{e}yiṭab libb^{e}kā* in 11:9 (emended text). Does the heart thrive on serious thinking that causes the face to frown? This recalls the strange proverb: "The heart is sad even in laughter, and the end of joy is grief" (Prov. 14:13).

Gordis (268) takes *yîṭab lēb* to mean "the understanding improves," despite the common biblical idiom of *ṭôb lēb,* meaning "joy and gladness." (Qohelet does use *lēb* to mean "understanding" [as in 10:3, *libbô ḥāsēr,* "he lacks understanding"], but does he shatter the idiom *ṭôb lēb?*) Gordis' interpretation retains the earlier connection between vexation and wisdom.

[4] A natural bond exists between feasting and mirth (cf. Esth. 9:17, *w^{e}'āśōh 'ōtô yôm mišteh w^{e}śimḥāh,* "and they made it a day of feasting and joy"). This association of ideas is not explored in 7:2, but the thought flows

[101]Gordis (267) remarks that "in general, Koheleth has difficulty in expressing the impersonal." Gordis refers to the suffix on *hiwwāl^{e}dô* (one's birth), which he compares to 8:16 (*šēnāh b^{e}'ênâw 'ênennû rō'eh,* "there is no seeing sleep with one's eye"), and 7:5 (*mē'îš šōmēa' šîr k^{e}sîlîm,* "than for one to hear the praise of fools").

logically from 7:1 to 7:4. In these "better" sayings Qohelet seems captivated by death's finality. Since everyone eventually dies, a realist prepares for that moment. In considering that unwelcome event one encounters an astonishing paradox: suffering can instruct, purge the spirit, and offer increased learning. An astute observer of life makes a path for the house of mourning, anticipating an encounter with the essence of human existence.[102] The fool takes up residence in the place of mirth.

[5] Gladness now takes the form of singing rather than the earlier feasting, while sadness also persists here, though indirectly, as a result of correction. Traditional wisdom recognized the value of a timely chiding ("A wise son hears his father's instruction, but a scoffer does not hear a rebuke," Prov. 13:1).

The usual sense of *šîr k^e^sîlîm* need not be sacrificed in this verse, although "flattery" would offer a better contrast with rebuke. Perhaps the word *šîr* has both senses here, boisterous singing (cf. Amos 6:5) and praise (see the parallel use of *šîr* and *t^e^hillāh* in Isa. 42:10 and Ps. 149:1 [*šîrû layhwh šîr ḥādāš t^e^hillātô,* "Sing to the Lord a new song, his praise . . ."], and the parallel expressions in Jer. 20:13 [*šîrû layhwh hal^e^lû 'et-yhwh,* "Sing to the Lord, praise the Lord"]).

In the unusual syntax of the second half of the verse, *mē'îš* distinguishes the individual who hears the song of fools from the person mentioned in 7:5a. That half verse contains the only use of *ga^ʿa^rat* in Ecclesiastes, despite its frequency in other biblical texts (Psalms, Proverbs, Job, Isaiah). The emphasis is not so much on the value of correction but on mocking lighthearted songs of fools.

[6] Another instance of alliteration occurs in this verse: *k^e^qôl hassîrîm taḥat hassîr.* Barton (138) reproduces the wordplay by translating: "As the crackling of nettles under kettles." This wordplay gives an apt description of the spontaneous bursts of laughter among fools, where there is more noise than substance. Thistles provide quick flames, little heat, and a lot of unpleasant noise. The singing of fools was equally cacophonous; Qohelet seems to develop the idea of *šîr* in 7:5, which gave rise to the similar-sounding *sîr* (thorn).

To what does the concluding observation, "This also is futile," refer? The rebuke of the wise, the laughter of fools, or the statement that follows? The formula usually comments on the absurdity or ephemerality of what precedes it. But here 7:5–6 may present the apparent advantage of wisdom over folly, whereas 7:7 points to the weakness inherent to wisdom. Qohelet argues similarly in 2:13–14 and 15–17.

[7] Wisdom does not always succeed; it can be nullified by brute

---

[102]Gordis (269) quotes Abraham Ibn Ezra: "Even when the wise do not go to the house of mourning, the house of mourning is always within them."

strength or by subterfuge. Thus the relative advantage of wisdom over folly varies with the situation, and one cannot always rely on wisdom. This understanding of the text is possible despite the signs of disjuncture: (1) the futility formula, which normally occurs at the end of a unit, but which seems to set off verse 6 from verse 7; (2) the use of *kî* in 7:7 without an initial observation, which the *kî* clause elaborates; and (3) evidence from the Qumran fragment that a full line may have dropped out before this verse.

The position of the futility formula may vary in the second half of the book because other formulas replace it for the most part. As for the use of *kî* without an initial statement, there are instances of an asseverative *kî*, which can be translated "surely" ("Surely vexation slays a fool and jealousy kills an innocent," Job 5:2; "Surely I am stupid beyond a human being, and I do not have understanding appropriate to a person," Prov. 30:2). The evidence from Qumran would carry more weight if the ancient versions confirmed the existence of an extra line in 7:7. Of course, the loss may have occurred prior to these versions. Recovery of the line seems impossible.

The noun *mattānāh* (gift = bribe) does not agree in gender with the verb *wî'abbēd,* but this phenomenon occurs elsewhere in the Bible (GKC, 145o). Whitley (62–63) thinks the *waw* would have been attached to the noun *mattānāh* if the two halves of the verse were parallel. He takes *mattānāh* to be an adjective *(motnāh)* and translates the verse as follows: "For oppression stupefies the wise man, and destroys[103] his strong heart." The Greek translations of Aquila and Theodotion, as well as the Vulgate, have "strong heart."

[8] Although the idea in the first half of this verse accords with that in 7:1–2 (the day of death is preferable to the day of birth), the relationship with 7:8b gives the observation a different sense. One cannot know whether a matter will be successful until it has run a full course, for obstacles tend to retard, if not frustrate, informed efforts. The stupidity of presuming too much is ridiculed in an old proverb in I Kings 20:11 ("Let not the person putting on armor brag like the one taking it off").

Elsewhere Qohelet uses *sôp* (end), but *'aḥ^{a}rît* has this meaning in Prov. 25:8 (*pen mah-ta'aśeh b^{e}'aḥ^{a}rîtāh,* "lest what you do in its end"). Normally, the expression for patience is *'erek 'appayim;* Eccl. 7:8 is the only occurrence of *'erek-rûaḥ.* But the phrase *q^{e}ṣar-rûaḥ* (shortness of spirit) appears several times in the Bible (e.g., Job 21:4, *w^{e}'im-maddûa' lō'-tiqṣar rûḥî,* "why should I not be impatient?"; Prov. 14:29, "Whoever is slow to anger

---

[103]The fragment from Qumran has *wy'wh* (pervert) instead of *wî'abbēd* (destroy). One may compare Prov. 12:8b (*w^{e}na'^{a}wēh-lēb yihyeh lābûz,* "but a person of perverse mind will be despised").

[*'erek 'appayim*] has great understanding," and "Whoever is short-tempered [*ûqᵉṣar rûaḥ*] exalts folly").

Both halves of 7:8 express conventional wisdom in a "better than" saying. The repetition of *ṭôb* and *rûaḥ* is unusual in so short a verse. The spatial imagery is noteworthy. Length of spirit is a positive image, whereas an upward stretching of the spirit is negative, an apt expression for haughtiness. According to Prov. 16:5 the heart can also be exalted, hence arrogant ("Every arrogant heart [*kol-gᵉbah-lēb*] is an abomination to the Lord").

[9] Qohelet continues the thought of 7:8 by emphasizing the damaging effect of a quick temper. Knowing that anger generates strong resentment within the innermost being, the individual who possesses a patient spirit will not become angry without prolonged cause. The sages observed that fools take quick offense but prudent persons shrug off an insult (Prov. 12:16).

In Eccl. 1:18; 2:23; and 7:3 *ka'as* has the connotation of sorrow and affliction. But the meaning in 7:9 is close to that of Prov. 17:25a ("A foolish son is an exasperation to his father") and Prov. 27:3b ("And a fool's provocation is worse than both of them"). According to Prov. 14:33a, wisdom lodges in the mind of a person of understanding *(bᵉlēb nābôn tānûaḥ ḥokmāh).* This metaphor is more felicitous than the image of resentment resting *(yānûaḥ)* in the bosom of fools, for anger is ever restless.

[10] The temptation to glorify the past was present in various segments of Israelite society, inspiring the prophetic admonition to forget the splendors of a bygone era in favor of anticipated deliverance from exile. By its very nature, wisdom venerated the insights that earlier teachers gained from examination of daily experience. Each generation tested these insights in light of a new set of realities; in doing so, it was often tempting to trust the intelligence of predecessors over personal insight. Qohelet advises against the assumption that things were once better than now. This formula of debate mocks sapiential warnings to persons struggling against divine justice.

If there is nothing new under the sun, the past is not superior to the present. Verse 10 criticizes traditional wisdom as it appears in 7:8–9 (so Lohfink). The person who favors the culmination of something over the anticipation associated with the inauguration of the project refuses to take risks. The result is safe but dull. In some circumstances what passes for patience may actually be lethargy. Therefore, it is not from wisdom (the Septuagint has "in wisdom") that such an attitude about a venerable past is articulated. The usual preposition after *šā'al* is *lᵉ*; *'al* is a late idiom (*wā'eš'ālēm 'al-hayyᵉhûdîm,* "and I asked them concerning the Jews," Neh. 1:2).

[11] The book of Proverbs associates wisdom and wealth, a combination partly responsible for the choice of Solomon as fictive author of Ecclesiastes. Intelligence was certainly desirable, but understanding and wealth together were eminently more desirable. Thus one can read this verse in the usual sense of the preposition *'im* (with). But in 2:16 *'im* has the meaning "as, as good as"; if this is the sense in 7:11 ("Wisdom is as good as an inheritance"), the point then shifts to a downplaying of riches.

"Those who see the sun" are the living as opposed to the dead and stillborn. The idiom occurs in other texts as well (Ps. 58:9 [8E], *bal-ḥāzû šāmeš,* "they do not gaze on the sun"; Ps. 49:20 [19E], *lō' yir'û-'ôr,* "they do not see the light"; Job 3:16, *kᵉ'ōlᵉlîm lō'-rā'û 'ôr,* "like infants who never see light"). In Eccl. 11:7 Qohelet uses *hā'ôr* and *haššāmeš* in parallelism.[104]

The Peshitta has probably conflated this verse and 9:18 ("Wisdom is better than weapons of war"). If so, the comparative *min* in the Peshitta has no bearing on the Massoretic Text.

[12] The ancient versions offer little help in understanding this difficult text. The Septuagint reads *bᵉṣēl* ("in the shadow") in the first occurrence of the word, and this reading is followed by the Syro-Hexaplar and Coptic. But Symmachus, Peshitta, and Vulgate seem to have read a *kap* instead of a *bet* in both instances. The Massoretic Text can be understood by viewing the *bet* on *ṣēl* as *bet essentiae* in both cases. Alternatively, one can follow the Septuagint and read the first *bᵉṣēl* as a *bet essentiae* plus *ṣēl* and take the second as a *kap* (*kᵉṣēl,* "like the protection").

The problem with the second half of the verse concerns the relationship between *da'at* and *haḥokmāh.* Although the Septuagint and Peshitta understood these nouns as genitives following *wᵉyitrôn,* the Vulgate has them as subjects ("but learning and wisdom excel in this"). The accentuation in the Massoretic Text separates *da'at* from *haḥokmāh.* Furthermore, the form of *da'at* is the same as an infinitive, which can be translated as follows: "and the advantage of knowing that wisdom gives life to those who possess it."

Commentators have offered many emendations. Some drop *wᵉyitrôn da'at* and insert it in 7:11 in place of *wᵉyōtēr.* Others substitute the verb *bṣl* for the two instances of *bᵉṣēl,* yielding "he who possesses wisdom possesses money." A Ugaritic parallel for *bᵉṣēl hakkāsep* ("the sheen of silver") has given rise to the supposition that Qohelet plays on the meaning of "glitter" in this saying about money.

The verse reinforces the claim that wisdom and money are desirable (7:11) by claiming that wisdom provides protection in the same way riches secure one's existence, thus bestowing life. Zimmerli subjects these com-

[104]Gordis (273) cites *Ned.* 3:7 ("He who takes a vow to enjoy no benefits from 'those who see the sun' may not enjoy a benefit even from the blind").

ments about wisdom and money to Qohelet's skepticism, finding beneath the surface a hint that wisdom is in the final analysis as unreliable as possessions.

[13] Lest those who possess wealth and wisdom become complacent, Qohelet invites them to consider the divine achievement (the Septuagint and Vulgate have a plural for the Hebrew *maʿăśēh*). Neither money nor insight can make any difference in the things God has made. This concession undercuts the claim that property and education give power to hold on to life.

There is another admission here, frank recognition that the universe has wrinkles. Some things were twisted in the act of creation itself, and nothing can effectively transform them now. This attitude to the order of nature and human society differs sharply from later claims that a harmonious universe encourages virtue, a view that surfaces in Sirach and Wisdom of Solomon.[105]

Although an Egyptian school text describes the remarkable achievements of teachers, stating, among other things, that a crooked stick can be straightened, Qohelet has no such optimism about changing society.

[14] One cannot change things. One can only enjoy the good things that come along and use misfortunes as occasions for reflecting on divine mystery. Both the good and the evil that God sends conceal any pattern or any trend useful for predicting the future.

The conjunction *ʿal-dibrat šᵉ* is used only here, but its meaning is clear from the Aramaic *ʿal-dibrat dî* (Dan. 2:30; 4:14). Elsewhere Qohelet uses *ʿal dibrat* in the sense of "concerning" (Eccl. 3:18; 8:2).

An attractive variant occurs in the Vulgate, which reads: "that man may not find just complaint against him." Probably the translator read *mᵉʾum* (or *mûm*) as in Job 31:7 (*ûbᵉkappî dābaq mʾûm,* "and any spot has stuck to my palm") and Dan. 1:4 (*ʾên-bāhem kol-mûm,* "without blemish"). A similar reading occurs in Symmachus: "that one may not find complaint against him." Whitley (66) points to a Syriac idiom in the Peshitta of John 19:4 and Acts 28:18 ("to find fault with"). It is not clear how this reading of Eccl. 7:14 improves the meaning, for the bewildering array of good and evil hardly prevents human beings from finding fault with the creator.

Verses 13–14 have been called "an admirable epitome of Koheleth's thought" (Gordis, 274–275). Before an all-powerful God, human beings must resign themselves to ignorance about the ebb and flow of events. They can enjoy the good and consider the nature of reality when misfortune strikes. Nothing can challenge God's sovereign power or secure human existence.

---

[105] The twisted character of things also contradicts Qohelet's view in 7:29 that God made humankind straight *(yāšār),* but they sought out devious means.

On Moderation
7:15–22

7:15 I have seen everything in my brief life; there is a righteous person
who perishes in his righteousness, and there is a wicked person who
lives long in his evil. [16]Do not be too righteous and do not be excessively wise; why should you be ruined? [17]Do not be too wicked and do
not be a fool; why should you die before your time? [18]It is good that
you hold on to this and also that you do not let go of that, for the person
who fears God will come out well with respect to them both. [19]Wisdom
is stronger for the wise than ten rulers who are in the city. [20]Surely
there is no righteous person on earth who does good and never sins.
[21]Moreover, to all the words that they speak do not pay attention lest
you hear your servant cursing you. [22]For your heart also knows that
you too have cursed others many times.

This unit deals with the dangers of excess, whether good or evil. Qohelet argues that extreme virtue produces self-righteousness and excessive vice endangers one's life. He does not specify the agent of punishment, but Qohelet probably implies that human beings will destroy the proponent of violence. In any event, Qohelet does not believe the universe operates according to a principle of reward for virtue and punishment for wickedness. For this reason, he urges a moderate course that does not call God's attention to one.

[15] Qohelet grounds his attack against the cherished convictions of the sages in personal experience, turning their own method against them. He acknowledges perversion in the human arena. The thought of the verse links with previous verses, and *hakkōl* may be retrospective or anticipatory, or both (a meaning *hakkōl* sometimes has; cf. 2:14). *Heblî* carries a nuance of futility, although here the emphasis falls on the brevity of human days.

The particles of existence *(yēš)* can be dispensed with in the translation. Qohelet uses standard terms for good and evil persons, but the use of *'ōbēd* with *ṣaddîq* and *ma'*^{a}*rîk* with *rāšā'* is wholly untraditional. The categories of the righteous, hence wise, and the wicked, hence fools, have been reversed here. Qohelet reports that his experience has not confirmed traditional promises of long life for the good person and an early death for the sinner. Good persons perish in, or despite, their virtue (as in Deut. 1:32, *ûbaddābār hazzeh,* "and despite this word"). With *ma'*^{a}*rîk,* one must supply "days" *(yāmîm),* as in Prov. 28:2 *(kēn ya'*^{a}*rîk).*

[16] If just individuals sometimes perish and villains prolong their days, why should anyone strive for the goals of virtue and wisdom? Does Qohelet advise moderation in everything one does, adopting the Greek concept of the middle way? Since he later insists that no one attains justice (7:20), this human failure implies that a warning against excess righteousness is unneccessary. But Qohelet's advice may be ironic, for justice is an unattainable ideal.

Whybray (1978) argues forcefully against the prevailing interpretation of this verse and those that follow; he claims that the unusual construction of the verb (*'al-tᵉhî ṣaddîq* instead of *'al tiṣdaq*), and the parallel to *'al-titḥakkam* in Ezek. 13:17 (*hammitnabbᵉ'ôt,* "who play the prophet"), suggests that Qohelet attacks pretense, exalted estimation of one's intellectual achievements. This interpretation of the verse emphasizes the traditional warning against moral and intellectual hypocrisy.

Sirach 7:5 seems to denounce calling attention to one's righteousness in God's presence, or one's wisdom in a king's presence. Sirach 10:26 warns against putting one's wisdom on display and exhibiting one's accomplishments at inappropriate times (cf. 32:4).

The apparent reason for Qohelet's advice is that excessive conduct (or self-righteousness) leads to ruin. Qohelet does not say whether the destruction[106] originates with God or with human beings. In this regard the verse differs from 5:5, which asks why one should make God angry.

[17] The ancient curse in Deut. 27:24 ("Cursed be whoever slays his neighbor in secret") does not suggest that it is all right to do so in public. In the same way, Qohelet's warning against excessive wickedness does not endorse moderate evil. Rather, it accepts villainy as a harsh fact, one which Qohelet articulates in 7:20 and 7:29 ("no one is righteous"; "everyone searches for ways to do wrong"). Nevertheless, Qohelet advises against perfidy and stupidity, for they increase one's chances of being slain by angry fellows or executed by the authorities despite the earlier observation that some wicked people escape punishment. The conservative attitude to reality requires sensible behavior. Qohelet was no iconoclast in matters dealing with ethical conduct. He could scarcely have said, "Do not be evil," for that would have been an impossible task.

The *harbēh* (greatly, too) continues the parallel with 7:16. But why does Qohelet omit *yôtēr,* breaking the structural symmetry? Like wickedness, folly is omnipresent. No one can achieve complete knowledge (7:23–24), so it would seem appropriate to attach a qualifying adverb to *sākāl.* But Qohelet has not done so.

The final question, "Why should you die before your time?" uses an idiom that occurs in Job 22:16 (*'ᵃšer-qummᵉṭû wᵉlō' 'ēt,* "who were snatched away prematurely"). The expression appears in *Ahiqar* 7:102 (*wthk bl'*

---

[106]The word *tiššômēm* is a shortened Hithpoel. In Sir. 43:24 *ništômēm* has the meaning "surprised." Such a reading in Eccl. 7:16, if allowed, would call attention to the embarrassment that occurs when pretenders are exposed.

bywmyk, "and you go away before your time") and in the Phoenician Eshmunazar inscription (*bl 'ty,* "not at my time").

[18] The indefinite language of this verse raises two questions: (1) what do "this" and "that" refer to? and (2) what does *kullām* signify? In context, *zeh . . . zeh* (this . . . that) point to the extremes of righteousness and wickedness, zealotry and criminality. The same meaning probably underlies *kullām,* although it is also possible to translate "all of them, in every respect." The point would then be much broader: the god-fearer would go forth in all eventualities.

An alternative interpretation of the verb *yēṣē'* derives from Mishnaic usage. In *Ber.* 2:1 *(hyh qwr' btwrh whqy' zmn hmqr' 'm kwn lbw yṣ' 'm l'w l' yṣ')* the idiom *yṣ'* means to be released from the power of an obligation. The same sense of *yṣ'* appears to be found in Sir. 38:17 (*wśyt 'blw kywṣ' bw,* "and arrange his mourning according to his merit"). The Vulgate *nihil neglegit* approximates this rendering of *yēṣē' 'et-kullām.*

The optimism in the final clause does not agree with Qohelet's experience in 7:15 ("Good people perish, wicked ones prolong their days"). If the observation is authentic, it must be full of irony. No assurance is forthcoming that the person who avoids excessive wickedness or goodness will receive rewards appropriate to such conduct.

[19] The idea that wise counselors were particularly important in defending a city occurs in biblical proverbs (Prov. 24:5–6; cf. 21:22). Of course this teaching enhanced the status of the sages themselves. Qohelet also introduces traditional concepts about relative power, casting his vote for intelligent strategists rather than administrative officials. Although it is not clear what he meant by ten rulers, one may compare the ten rulers *(deka prōtoi)* mentioned by Josephus (*Antiquities* 20.8.11) as residing in Jerusalem as well as in Hellenistic cities.

The verb *tā'ōz* used transitively has caused problems for many interpreters, despite Ps. 68:29 [28E] (*'ûzzāh 'ᵉlōhîm,* "strengthen that which . . . , O God") and possibly Prov. 8:28 *(ba'ᵃzôz//bᵉ'ammᵉṣô).* (The normal use of the verb *'zz* is intransitive.) This translation of *tā'ōz* as "is stronger" gives the most natural meaning to the *lamed* as well, for it serves as a dative. However, in Aramaic the *lamed* can indicate the direct object, yielding the following translation: "wisdom strengthens the wise."

There is some evidence for another verb in place of *'zz.* The Septuagint has *boēthēsei,* which presupposes *ta'ᵃzōr* (helps), and the Qumran fragment has this verb *('zr).* The principle of *lectio difficilior* favors the Massoretic Text.

[20] The language recalls the prayer attributed to Solomon in I Kings 8:46 (*kî 'ên 'ādām 'ᵃšer lō'-yeḥᵉṭā',* "for there is no one who does not sin"). The idea that everyone occasionally falls into evil is widespread (Ps. 143:2, *kî lō'-yiṣdaq lᵉpāneykā kol-ḥāy,* "for no living person is righteous in your presence"; Prov. 20:9, *mî-yō'mar zikkîtî libbî tāhartî meḥaṭṭā'tî,* "who can say, 'I have cleansed my heart, I am pure from my sin'?"; Sir. 19:16b, "who has never sinned with his speech?"). Job's friends carried this notion to an extreme; they intended to exalt God and force Job to admit his offense before the deity.

How does this verse relate to what precedes it? The *kî* can refer to 7:18 ("hold on to both"); if so, this gives the basis for that advice. Because no one can ever achieve full justice or avoid sinning, the prudent path is to be realistic and not try to deceive oneself. But if the *kî* is emphatic, there may not be a causal connection with what precedes.

The syntax of the verse is strange, but Ex. 5:16 resembles it (*teben 'ên nittān,* "straw was not given"). Gordis (279) thinks *ṣaddîq bā'āreṣ* is anticipated by the subordinate clause.

[21] The practical consequence of sin's inevitability is tolerance when one encounters pettiness in others. Qohelet advises against listening too closely to the conversation among servants, for the principle that everyone sins implies that they will do so and that the object of their anger will also err in ways that provide fuel for their fire.

The verb *yᵉdabbērû* is impersonal (GKC, 144f.). The expression *'ᵃšer lō'* has the same meaning as *pen* (lest). In Gen. 11:7 *'ᵃšer lō' yišmᵉ'û 'îš śᵉpat rē'ēhû* means "so that they may not understand each other's speech," and in I Kings 22:16 *'ᵃšer lō'-tᵉdabbēr* means "that you do not speak." Whitley (68) compares the Aramaic *dî lā' yᵉhōbᵉdûn* ("lest they perish," Dan. 2:18).

The reference to servants cursing their owner in Prov. 30:10 has no apparent connection with Eccl. 7:21. Note, however, that the advice is directed toward the masters in each instance. Such allusions offer indirect evidence that the sages belonged to the privileged slave-owning class.

[22] Qohelet's argument rests on an honest evaluation of one's inner thoughts. Reverse sentence order emphasizes the frequency of the cursing. The accusative "many times" precedes the verb *yāda'*. Use of *libbekā* (your heart) directs the attention within. Qohelet does not merely say, "You know." Instead, he insists that the inner being[107] knows how often idle and inflammatory remarks have come to expression.

The second *gam* implies that servants have let their hearts and tongues do their damage. Qohelet does not condone the scurrilous talk so much as he advises against exposing oneself to it. The point seems to be that hearing unpleasant remarks only angers a person, prompting vindictive acts that

[107]The word for conscience *(syneidēsis)* occurs for the first time in Wisd. of Sol. 17:11 ("For wickedness is a cowardly thing, condemned by its own testimony; distressed by conscience, it has always exaggerated the difficulties").

accomplish nothing worthwhile. After all, the slaves are no more culpable than their owner, who curses others with impunity.

The Septuagint either mistook *yāda'* for *yāra'* (abuse), or it had *yr'* in the *Vorlage.* Confusion of similar *dalet* and *reš* is natural, but the result here is hardly felicitous. The verb *qillaltā* need not have the grave meaning of imprecation. One could render it as "belittle, demean."

Seeking and Finding 7:23–29

> 7:23 I have tested all this by wisdom; I said, "I shall be wise," but it was far from me. [24]Distant—whatever is—and extraordinarily deep; who can find it? [25]My heart and I turned to know, to investigate, and to search out wisdom and the sum of things, and to recognize that evil is folly and foolishness is madness. [26]And I found more bitter than death the woman who is a snare, whose heart is a net, whose hands are bonds; whoever God favors will escape from her, but the errant person will be taken by her. [27]"Look, this I found," says Qohelet, "one to one to find the sum. [28]That which I sought continually I did not find: one man in a thousand I found, but a woman in all these I did not find." [29]Only see what I found—that God made humankind upright but they have sought after numerous devices.

This section discusses two profound mysteries: wisdom and woman. Both mysteries defy understanding, wisdom because of its remoteness, and woman because she cannot be found. Qohelet acknowledges the limits of knowledge, regardless of how hard one tries to master its secrets. The discovery that the notorious seductress is more bitter than death and that lucky persons escape her trap breaks no new ground. A similar judgment applies to the gloomy description of humanity. Less than kind to women, it judges men almost as negatively. God alone escapes responsibility for the sorry mess that Qohelet observes.

[23] In 1:13 Qohelet spoke of searching and of spying by means of wisdom *(lidrôš wᵉlātûr baḥokmāh).* Here he uses the verb *nissāh* (to test).[108] To what does *kol-zōh* refer? It may point back to the conclusions in 7:1–22, particularly concerning human nature. Alternatively, "all this" may point forward to the comments about wisdom's inaccessibility and the impossibility of finding a good woman (7:24–29). Or "all this" may restrict itself to

[108]Gordis (280) thinks *nissāh* governs the accusative and translates accordingly ("I tested concerning wisdom"). He refers to the interchange of direct object and *bet* of means, and cites GKC, 119q.

the observation that wisdom lies beyond him, so that 7:23–24 constitute an independent unit (Lauha 1978).

This verse contains the only cohortative in the book, *'eḥkāmāh* ("I shall be wise"). It expresses strong resolve, indicating that the determination to acquire wisdom was no flippant remark. Qohelet intends to submit to personal discipline in order to reach a worthy goal. But he achieved only the recognition that he had set his sights too high. The elusive goal, wisdom, remained out of reach. In this judgment Qohelet concurs with the author of the poem on wisdom's inaccessibility in Job 28 and with the skeptic Agur, who was responsible for the sayings in Prov. 30:1–4.

[24] Not only is wisdom par excellence, as opposed to practical knowledge, beyond Qohelet's grasp, but the future also defies comprehension. The adjective *rāḥôq* (distant) is emphatic. The Septuagint, Peshitta, and Vulgate presuppose a comparative *min* instead of *mah* ("deeper than what is").

The two verbs in 1:13 *(dāraš* and *tûr)* indicate searching horizontally and vertically. These spatial categories appear in 7:24 also. In line with the meaning of the verb *tûr,* the adjective *rāḥôq* shifts the emphasis to the depths beneath the rays of the sun. Repetition of the adjective *'āmōq* amounts to a superlative (GKC, 133k). The twofold use of *rāḥôq* and *'āmōq* in 7:23–24 emphasizes the distance and depth of wisdom.

The final rhetorical question, "Who can find it?" acts as an assertion that no one can reach out far enough to touch wisdom or penetrate deeply enough to lay hold of it. Qohelet generalizes from his own experience: if I cannot be wise, no one can. The theme of wisdom's inaccessibility occurs frequently in Israelite wisdom literature (Job 28:12–22; Sir. 24:28–29; Baruch 3:14–23). Of course, God is the exception, and sages stress the deity's access to wisdom (Job 28:23–28; Baruch 3:29–37).

[25] The extra subject may be a virtual personification of the heart, which occurs also in 2:1, where Qohelet talks to his heart (Ginsburg). On the other hand, 79 manuscripts, together with Symmachus, Targum, and Vulgate read *belibbî* (in my heart). Against this easier reading is the witness of the Septuagint and Peshitta.

The verb *sbb,* which in 1:6 referred to the endless circling of the wind, now describes Qohelet's vain effort to discover the extent of human knowledge. The singular noun *ḥešbôn* appears in Eccl. 7:25, 27; 9:10; the plural *ḥiššebōnôt* in 7:29 and in II Chron. 26:15.[109] In Sir. 42:3 the noun *ḥešbôn* refers to reckoning or keeping accurate accounts. The same meaning attaches to it in *Šabb.* 150a (calculations). Coupled with wisdom, *ḥešbôn* constitutes the substance of human thought, the sum total of all knowledge.

The four nouns in the second half of the verse caused a problem for some

[109]The plural refers to contrivances invented through rational calculations. BDB takes this plural as a different word entirely.

versions. The Septuagint has "the folly of the wicked," and Peshitta has "the wickedness of the fool," adding the copula (and) after "foolishness." The nouns can be understood as double accusatives after the verb of cognition (Gordis), or they may simply be four objects of the twice-used infinitive *lāda'at* (to know).

[26] The theme of the woman who ensnares men is standard in ancient Near Eastern wisdom. It echoes the book of Proverbs' persistent warning against the "foreign" woman. But this unflattering attitude toward women is balanced by awareness of the joys of a happy marriage. Qohelet also encourages enjoyment of the woman whom one loves (9:9).

In Ezek. 3:14 the word *mar* means "stronger," (*wā'ēlēk mar baḥᵃmat rûḥî,* "and I went forth strong in the fervor of my spirit"). Dahood (1958, 308–309) appeals to the Aramaic use of *mryr'* in connection with a chain, *'yswr',* as well as Ugaritic *mrr,* to strengthen (*ltbrkn 'alk brkt tmrn 'alkn mrrt,* "bless me and I shall go forth blessed; strengthen me and I shall go forth strengthened").[110] Nevertheless, I Sam. 15:32 has *'ākēn sār mar-hammāwet* ("surely the bitterness of death has passed"), and this sense fits the context in Eccl. 7:26.

In the cumbersome expression *'ᵃšer-hî' mᵉṣôdîm, hî'* seems to be a copula, hence "who is a snare." If *'ᵃšer* is taken as causal, *hî'* is the subject, giving smoother syntax ("because she is a snare"). A third approach connects this phrase with the one that follows (whose heart is a snare and net), as the Massoretes have done.[111]

The opposites in the second half of the verse *(ṭôb lipnê hā'ᵉlōhîm* and *ḥôṭē')* are not moral categories. They refer to lucky and unlucky (as in 2:26) rather than to virtuous as opposed to wicked. The word *ḥôṭē'* signifies a person who misses the mark, the original meaning of the verb.

Proverbs 5:4 compares the bitterness associated with a wicked woman to wormwood, and Prov. 6:26 speaks of an adulteress stalking a man *(tāṣûd).* Qohelet employs this image for the active pursuit of a man and for the laying of hidden traps in which to take him. The emphasis falls on the hunter rather than the hunted (some of whom are fortunate, others not).

What did Qohelet discover *(ûmôṣe')?* That certain types of women are more bitter than death, or that fortunate people escape her whereas errant ones do not? Neither discovery is original or profound. If the assertion about woman is an aphorism with which Qohelet takes issue (Lohfink 1980, 58–59), the discovery then must be his observation based on the traditional saying that woman is stronger than death.

---

[110]The passage may be antithetical instead of synonymous, and then the meaning "embitter" makes sense. But the opposite of bless is normally curse.

[111]Perles (131) reads "her steps" *('ᵃšureyhā),* which would agree with "her heart" and "her hands."

[27] In the interest of consistency, most commentators follow the Septuagint and Peshitta, reading *'āmar haqqōhelet* ("says the Qohelet," as in 12:8). The feminine noun *qōhelet* commonly takes a masculine verb (1:12; 12:8, 10). This third-person reference to the writer is unique in the body of the book.[112] It may subtly hint at the name's meaning, since it appears in connection with the collecting of discrete objects (item by item). The idiom, "one to one to find the sum,"[113] may also play on the tradition about Solomon's collection of women. His experience in gathering a thousand wives is thus given a worthy purpose. The two uses of the verb *mṣ'* (find) in this verse constitute the second and third in a series of seven within 7:25–29.

[28] The relative *'ᵃšer* may refer to *ḥešbôn* in the previous verse, pointing to the sum of all Qohelet's itemization ("the sum, which I sought again and again but did not discover"). Or *'ᵃšer* may refer to *zeh māṣā'tî,* anticipating the statement in 7:28b about one man and no woman. If the former, Qohelet failed to find the solution to reality despite a valiant effort at adding up the insights that came to him. If the latter, Qohelet identifies his discovery as the slight discrepancy between men and women (men are one tenth of one percent better than women!)—or it connotes infinity, because 1/1000 is infinitely more than zero.

Another possibility exists. The relative *'ᵃšer* may anticipate the saying in 7:28b without reflecting backward to *zeh māṣā'tî* ("this I found"). The meaning thus would be: "This I sought but did not find (true): that women are worse than men" (Lohfink 1980).[114] The assertion in 7:29 that God made humankind upright favors this interpretation. But this understanding of woman does not seem to harmonize with the misogynism underlying 7:28b, where women are responsible for their own distortion.

Regardless of the view one adopts, one must deal with the juxtaposition of *'ādām* and *'iššāh* in 7:28 and the ostensibly generic use of *'ādām* in the next verse. Some explain the inconsistency via abstraction: when a general term and a specific term are used, the latter abstracts from the former, and *'ādām* takes on the meaning "all human beings *except women,* hence, males" (Gordis).

One can easily document unflattering attitudes toward women in ancient literature. Qohelet added his voice to the choir that sang about the weaknesses of women, but he viewed men as only slightly better than women.

Why did Qohelet use the number "a thousand"? It occurs elsewhere in wisdom literature where an association with Solomon's thousand wives is

---

[112]Galling (1969) thinks the gloss was added to indicate that the view expressed here is Qohelet's private opinion.

[113]The expression is an adverbial accusative of manner (GKC, 118q).

[114]Perles (131) emended the relative *'ᵃšer* to *'iššāh,* but there is no manuscript evidence for this reading.

out of the question (Job 9:3). The idiom may simply be a round number. But allusion to Solomon's harem is perhaps apropos here, an ironic suggestion that the king's addition of one to one until he reached a thousand did not introduce him to a good wife (Prov. 31:10, *'ēšet-ḥayil mî yimṣāʾ;* cf. Prov. 20:6b, *wᵉʾîš ʾᵉmûnîm mî yimṣāʾ,* "and a trustworthy man, who can find?").

[29] Qohelet has now made three discoveries: (1) women of a certain type are more bitter than death (7:26); (2) men are only slightly less wicked than women (7:28); (3) this perversity is not God's fault, but results from human contrivances (7:29). In 3:11 Qohelet asserted that God made everything beautiful in its time; now the descriptive adjective is *yāšār* (straight, upright). Qohelet's search for the sum *(ḥešbôn)* has failed, but humankind's search for many devices or intrigues *(ḥiššᵉbōnôt)* has succeeded admirably.

In II Chron. 26:15, the only other use of this noun, it signifies devices for use in warfare. On the basis of the Septuagint and Vulgate,[115] Whitley argues for a meaning here of "questionable things." This interpretation accords with the primary meaning of calculation or questioning, and provides an appropriate contrast to *yāšār* (straight).

The sequence of *rᵉʾēh-zeh māṣāʾtî ʾᵃšer* in 7:27–28 and in 7:29 appears to argue against the interpretation that Qohelet rejects the truth of the saying about one woman in a thousand. In any event, the third observation places responsibility for evil on human beings. Gordis cites *Ber.* 33b (*hkl bydy šmym ḥwṣ myr't šmym,* "Everything is in the hand of Heaven [i.e., God] but the fear of Heaven").

Rulers and Subjects
8:1–9

8:1 Who is like the wise, and who knows the interpretation of a thing? A person's wisdom illumines his countenance and changes the hardness of his face. [2]Keep a king's command because of a sacred oath. [3]Be not dismayed. Leave his presence; do not persist in an unpleasant situation, for he does as he pleases. [4]Because a king's word has authority, and nobody can say to him, "What are you doing?" [5]Whoever obeys a command will not experience harm, for a wise heart knows a time and procedure. [6]Indeed, for everything there is a time and procedure, but the evil of human beings is heavy on them. [7]For nobody knows what will happen, because who can tell him when it will be?

---

[115]*Logismous pollous* ("many arguments") in the Septuagint, *infinitis quaestionibus* ("with many questions") in the Vulgate.

> [8]No one has control over the life so as to retain the breath, and no person rules over the day of death; and no man has release during war; and evil will not save those who practice it. [9]All this I have seen and I have given my attention to every deed that is done under the sun while one person rules over another for harm.

This section examines the complex issues involving rulers and subjects. It emphasizes the absolute power of a monarch and the consequent necessity for caution in his presence. However, Qohelet concedes that careful individuals can escape royal fury by loyal adherence to the king's will as expressed in decrees. The unit ends with some reflection about the great imponderables that render all human beings subject, specifically life-breath and the moment of death. Where does the unit begin? The initial verse may be a clever allusion to the previous section, or it may ask whether anyone knows the true meaning of the aphorism about wisdom illuminating one's face. One thing seems clear: Qohelet thinks that those who exercise authority do so with little thought about persons who may be hurt in the process. Furthermore, he insists that no one can catch a glimpse of the future, despite the certainty about the cruel wielding of power.

[8:1] Two rhetorical questions introduce a traditional wisdom saying. The first question asserts that no one is like a sage, and the second denies that anyone knows the meaning of a matter. In late Hebrew the article is not always assimilated, hence the form *k^e^heḥākām.* Although the word *pēšer* occurs only here in Biblical Hebrew, it appears often in Biblical Aramaic (cf. Dan. 2:4, 5, 6, 7, 9, 16, 24, etc.) and in the literature from Qumran.[116] In Gen. 40:5, 8 the phonetic equivalent is used *(k^e^pitrôn; ûpōtēr; pitrōnîm).*

The idiom "to cause the face to shine," with reference to God, refers to a gracious response toward humans (cf. the Levitical blessing in Num. 6:25, *yā'ēr yhwh pānāyw 'ēleykā wîḥunnekā,* "the Lord make his face to shine on you and show favor to you"). On this analogy, Qohelet means that a wise person's depth of experience gives tolerance of faults, enabling the sage to look on others with favor. Alternatively, and more probably, wisdom leads the wise to dissimulate, to hide their true feelings under a pleasant demeanor. The second image, a changed countenance, shows wisdom transforming an angry look into a gentler and less threatening one (cf. Sir. 13:24 [25E]).

The ancient versions had considerable difficulty with this verse. The Septuagint has *tis oiden sophous* ("who knows like the wise?") and *misthēsetai* (hates = *yiśśānē*). The Peshitta also has the verb "hate" instead of "change," conjugated like *lamed alep* verbs. Furthermore, the versions

---

[116]Whitley (71) notes that in Egyptian Aramaic *hpšr* occurs with the meaning "to settle an account."

understood *'ōz* as an adjective *('az),* as in Deut. 28:50 (*gôy 'az pānîm,* "a harsh nation" = of stern demeanor) and Prov. 7:13 (*hē'ēzāh pāneyhā,* "impudent is her face").

Does this traditional saying refer back to the search for the sum and to the assertion that God made humans *yāšār* (note the similarity to *pēšer*)? The use of the equivalent term *pitrôn* in Gen. 40:5 in the setting of discovering the answer, as well as the meaning of *hšpr* in Egyptian Aramaic, suggests that a relationship with what precedes is not out of the question. However, the second part of the verse anticipates the discussion of behavior in the royal court (8:2). Probably the reference to one's countenance concerns conduct before the king and his officials.

[2] The initial *'ănî* constitutes the major problem of this verse. Solutions vary from adding *'āmartî* (cf. 2:1; 3:17, 18) to emending *'ănî* to the sign of the direct object *'et* or to *bᵉnî* (my son), which occurs regularly in Prov. 1–7 but elsewhere in Ecclesiastes only in the epilogue (12:12). Another interpretation reads *'npy* (in the presence of), which occurs in a remarkably similar passage in *Ahiqar* (7:101–102, *hzy qdmtk mnd'm qšh* [*'l* ']*npy m*[*lk*] *'l tqwm* . . . *'nt 'štmr lk*).[117] Whitley thus reads: "Take heed in the presence of a king," comparing this text to Prov. 25:6 (*'al-tithaddar lipnê-melek,* "Do not put yourself forward in the king's presence"). However, Lindenberger has raised serious objection to this interpretation of the *Ahiqar* text. There remains the Aramaic expression *mn 'npy tym'* ("from the face of Tema") in a fifth-century inscription.

The sacred oath (oath of God) can be either an objective or a subjective genitive, an oath of loyalty to the king taken in God's name or God's oath regarding kingship. The *waw* is emphatic (and that), whereas *'al dibrat* is an idiom meaning "because of" or "on account of." The attitude of wisdom literature toward royalty is ambiguous, but there is never any refusal to recognize the awesome power resting in a ruler's hands. The sages advise caution, encouraging persons to avoid a king's wrath.

[3] The first two words may belong to the preceding verse, yielding "and be not dismayed on account of a sacred oath" (cf. the Septuagint and Peshitta). Some interpreters take the two words with 8:3, reading the first verb as an adverbial qualification of the second: "Do not leave his presence precipitately."[118] The advice continues: do not delay when the matter is unpleasant. This word of counsel seems to stand in opposition to the previous one, although one can view the first advice as encouragement to tarry long enough to assess a potentially explosive situation (contrast Sinuhe's

---

[117] J. M. Lindenberger (*The Aramaic Proverbs of Ahiqar* [Baltimore, Johns Hopkins University Press, 1983], 81) translates as follows: "Here is a difficult thing for you: do not stand opposed to the king . . . look out for yourself."

[118] Elsewhere Qohelet uses the verb *bhl* in the sense of "hasten" (5:1 parallel to *mhr;* 7:9).

hasty flight from the Egyptian court; although it saved his life, it required later justification), and the second advice as the thing to do when it is determined that the matter will lead to royal recrimination.

The final clause offers the reason for leaving a dangerous situation. Like God, the king does as he pleases and none can say, "What are you doing?" According to Prov. 16:14–15, a king's anger is a messenger of death but the light of his face (his favor) is life, like clouds that bring spring rain. (A sage is said to be able to appease the king's wrath.)

In late Aramaic use, *'md bᵉ* ranges in meaning from "rebel against" to "persist in." Lacking a stronger verb, it seems better to retain the nuance of tarrying.

[4] Job 9:12 asks this very question concerning the sovereign of the universe. The same idea occurs in Isa. 45:9 ("Can the pot say to the potter, 'What are you making?' "), and in Dan. 4:32 [35E] ("none can . . . say to him, 'What are you doing?' "). As before, the rhetorical question "Who can say to him?" amounts to a firm denial: "No one can say to him."

The word *šilṭôn* (power) occurs only here and in v. 8 (although the root *šlṭ* appears in Eccl. 7:19 and 10:15). A predicate nominative, it is paralleled in the Egyptian Instruction of Sehetepibre, which encourages submission to the king because "the king is Vital Force and his mouth Abundance."

[5] This traditional wisdom saying picks up the language of the previous verses (*šmr* in 8:2; *dbr r'* in 8:3), tempting us to relate the saying to the royal court. The *miṣwāh* (command) is then a royal decree. The basis for such confidence rests in the intelligence of one who understands the proper time and manner for action. But *miṣwāh* is also a divine command, and the saying may also relate to religious obligation. In neither instance does the view represent Qohelet's understanding of reality, for he introduces traditional wisdom to challenge it (8:6b–7).

The Septuagint and fifteen manuscripts omit the *waw* before *mišpāṭ*, which yields the construct "time of judgment" or a hendiadys *kairon kriseōs* ("time and judgment"). However, the Septuagint has *kairon kai krisin* in the next verse, which may be evidence for reading "time and judgment" in 8:5. In Judg. 13:12 the word *mišpāṭ* means "procedure" or "stipulation." The ancient versions (Septuagint, Peshitta, and Vulgate) understood *lēb ḥākām* as construct ("heart of the wise"), but in the absence of an article it seems best to view *ḥākām* as an adjective. The verb *yd'*, which also occurs in 8:1, has nuances of "experience" and "recognize" or "discern."

[6] The four occurrences of *kî* in this verse and the next pose an interpretative problem. The translation above takes the first *kî* asseveratively and the second adversatively. This reading may separate the verse too sharply from the previous one, for which it offers the reason. In this case it says that the discerning mind escapes harm because every matter has its own proper moment and correct procedure, which the astute observer seizes. The second part of the verse relates to the evil that lies heavy on kings, which suggests that even royal anger can be avoided by taking precautionary measures (Lauha 1978).

On the other hand, the first half of the verse may state traditional wisdom comparable to 3:1 ("a time for everything"), applying to much more than the royal court. The claim that everything has its proper time and procedure implies success in using this knowledge for one's own benefit. Qohelet refutes this implicit assumption by observing that human evil burdens the mind, making it incapable of knowing the right time for action. Qohelet leaves this final consequence unspecified, but he has already said much on the subject (3:21; 6:12).

The Septuagint, Theodotion, and Aquila read *da'at* for *rā'at;* similarity between *dalet* and *reš* explains the mistake in their *Vorlage.*

[7] The first *kî* is resultative, the second causative. The verse explains why no one can declare the right time for action: no one can acquire information about the future. Although Peshitta and Targum expand the text ("what will happen in the end"), the Massoretic Text is perfectly clear. For *ka'ᵃšer* Symmachus, Peshitta, and Vulgate read *'ᵃšer* (that which). Some commentators understand *ka'ᵃšer* as "how," but "when" makes good sense (cf. 4:17 [5:1E]; 5:3 [4E]; 8:16).

[8] The reference to *rûaḥ* is ambiguous, referring to the wind (cf. 1:17; 11:4) and denying that anyone is strong[119] enough to resist the powerful force of the wind or to contain it in any way, or *rûaḥ* may indicate life-force, which no one can hold at the moment of death. Either meaning fits the context, but juxtaposition with the day of death shifts the balance of probability toward the meaning "life-breath" (cf. 3:19, 21; 12:7).

Deuteronomy 20:5–8 and 24:5 give certain circumstances in which release from military service should be granted. Perhaps we must distinguish between release prior to an engagement and release during battle. No one can take furlough once the battle begins. Soldier and civilian alike feel the effects of war. The unusual word *mišlaḥat* occurs elsewhere only in Ps. 78:49 and in the Aramaic Midrash to Numbers. Because wickedness carries destruction in its very nature it cannot save its masters.[120] Some interpreters read *'ōšer* (wealth) by rearranging the Hebrew letters or by attributing an extended meaning to *reša'* (wickedness gets wealth, hence *reša'* means

---

[119]The word *šallîṭ* is an adjective, whereas it is a noun in 7:19 (plural); 10:5; and Gen. 42:6. The adjectival use occurs in Biblical Aramaic (Dan. 4:14 [17E], *dî šallîṭ 'illā'ā bᵉmalkût 'ᵃnāšā',* "that the Most High rules the human kingdom").

[120]Whitley (73–74) appeals to the Ugaritic use of *b'l* to mean "work" and argues that Hebrew *b'l* has this sense in Prov. 1:19 (*'et-nepeš bi'ālâw yiqqāḥ,* "and the life of his workers he claims") and 3:27 (*'al timna'-ṭôb mibbᵉ'ālâw,* "do not withhold good from the one who produces it"). Whitley points *mibbō'ᵃlâw,* construing it as a participle.

riches). Qohelet's point seems to be that no amount of energy, whether directed toward worthwhile or questionable ends, can actually yield the desired results. Knowledge will not bring success, for there are always great imponderables, the chief of which is death.

[9] The use of *šālaṭ* links this verse with the preceding ones (8:4, 8). Qohelet has observed the way people use their power to hurt others. The ambiguous Hebrew *lᵉra' lô* may include a sense that those wielding power harm themselves, but more probably it means they use their power to hurt others. Septuagint, Peshitta, and Targum all read unambiguous *lᵉhāra'* (to cause harm, injure) or *lāra'*.

Does *'ēt* refer to a specific period of stress or to all times? The idiom *'ēt 'ᵃšer* means "while,"[121] probably referring to human existence at all times, rather than a specific period. The sweeping language recalls earlier texts in which Qohelet describes God's sovereignty and human impotence.

The Mystery of Divine Activity 8:10–17

8:10 Then I saw the wicked, approaching and entering the holy place, walk about and boast in the city that they had done right. This is also absurd. [11]Because sentence is not passed quickly on evil deeds, therefore the heart of human beings is full to do evil. [12]Although a sinner does evil a hundred times and prolongs his days, yet I know that it will be well with those who fear God, because they are afraid in his presence. [13]And it will not be well for the wicked, and they will not prolong their days like a shadow, for they are not afraid in the presence of God. [14]There is an absurdity that is done on earth: there are righteous people whose reward is appropriate to the recompense of the wicked, and there are wicked people whose recompense is appropriate to the reward of the righteous. I say that this is also absurd. [15]And I praised pleasure, for there is nothing good for a human being under the sun but to eat, drink, and be happy, and it will accompany him in his toil the days of his life that God gives him under the sun. [16]When I applied my mind to know wisdom and to see the business that is done on earth—for neither by day nor by night do anyone's eyes see sleep— [17]then I saw all God's work—that a person is not able to fathom the work that is done under the sun, on account of which he works to seek, but will not discover; and even if a wise man claims to know, he is not able to find it.

---

[121]In Jer. 51:33 *'ēt hidrîkāh* means "when it is trodden." There is no reason to follow Septuagint, Peshitta, Syro-Hexaplar, and Coptic in reading *'et* for *'ēt*.

This section introduces the problem of delayed punishment for evil deeds, which encourages further villainy. An example of gross hypocrisy or of popular ignorance sets the stage for Qohelet's observations, which are promptly undercut by a secondary reaffirmation of divine justice even in the face of such apparent inequity. Qohelet, however, considers the traditional conviction with regard to reward and punishment unwarranted. Naturally, he endorses the best response to such inequity, grabbing all the pleasure one can afford. Qohelet repeats the claim that human beings are unable to discover absolute wisdom. The sharp tone of his denial opposes every contrary assertion.

[10] Interpretations of this verse have one thing in common: tentativeness. It begins clearly enough; *ûbᵉkēn* (then) occurs in Esth. 4:16 (*ûbᵉkēn 'ābô' 'el-hammelek,* "then I will go to the king"). On analogy with this text in the book of Esther, *ûbᵉkēn* continues the observation in the preceding verse. Others take the *waw* to be like that in *wayᵉhî* in Ruth 1:1 and Jonah 1:1 and see a new section starting at Eccl. 8:10.

What has Qohelet seen? A burial of wicked persons, or the coming and going of the wicked. On the basis of the Septuagint *(asebeis eis taphous eisachthentas)* some interpreters read *qᵉbārîm mûbā'îm* ("the wicked being carried to their tombs"). But the Vulgate, Peshitta, and Targum read "buried." Driver has proposed to read *qᵉrēbîm ûbā'îm* ("approaching and entering"), as in the translation above.

The use of *wᵉyištakkᵉḥû* is equally unclear. The Septuagint and many ancient versions read *wᵉyištabbᵉḥû* (and were praised). Furthermore, there is no agreement over whether the verse refers to the wicked throughout or to the wicked in the first half and to the righteous in the second half. In the former instance, wicked persons were buried and praised despite their deeds, or they came and went in the temple,[122] boasting of their accomplishments, without paying for their wickedness. In the latter instance, the wicked received a proper burial or pretended righteousness while the righteous were forgotten by the community in which they had acted justly, and in which they had regularly worshiped at the holy place.

[11] Qohelet continues the idea that wicked persons sin with impunity, now adding that delay in punishing them actually encourages evil people to carry out their nefarious deeds. The negligent officials may be civil authorities, or Qohelet may have God in mind. Another possible translation of the first half of the verse does not change the meaning appreciably: because sentence is not passed, evil deeds hasten.

---

[122]Gordis thinks "the holy place" is a euphemism for the cemetery, while Humbert proposes "the embalming place" (cf. the Admonitions of Ipuwer, which mentions the lords of the embalming place being thrown on the ground). An "unclean" place could hardly be referred to euphemistically as the holy place. On hearing the phrase *māqôm qādôš* one naturally thought of the temple, and in postbiblical times, of the synagogue.

The Persian loanword *pitgām* (sentence, decree, edict) has come into Hebrew by way of Aramaic.[123] It is found elsewhere only in Esth. 1:20 (*wᵉnišmaʿ pitgām hammelek,* "when the king's decree is heard") and in Aramaic literature (Ezra, Daniel, Egyptian texts, and the Targum). The accent on *pitgām* sets it apart from *maʿᵃśēh,* for which the Septuagint and Peshitta read *mēʿōśê* (on the doers). In the second half of the verse *bāhem* (in themselves) is redundant. The expression *mālēʾ lēb* ("the heart is full") occurs only in late Hebrew (Eccl. 9:3; Esth. 7:5; Ex. 35:35).

This blanket statement about human perversity shifts responsibility away from sinners to those entrusted with punishing them. People are guilty of evil, but God must take some blame, since a breakdown has occurred in the scheme of reward and punishment.

[12] The causal use of *ʾᵃšer* occurs frequently in this unit (cf. 8:11, 13, 15, and the probable two uses in 8:12). Qohelet recognizes the perplexing fact that some sinners continue in their evil deeds for a long time. The unusual construct *mᵉʾat* may presuppose *paʿam* (time), or it may be an archaic absolute modifying *rāʿ* ("hundredfold evil," so Gordis). The Septuagint has *apo tote kai* (from then and); Aquila, Symmachus, and Theodotion have *apethanen kai (mēt wᵉ).* Ellipsis occurs after *ûmaʾᵃrîk;* perhaps the missing word is *ʾap* (wrath). The point is that God's anger delays its punishment. Another possible way to read the ellipsis is to assume that *yāmîm* has been presupposed ("and prolongs his days").

The second half of the verse presents a view that Qohelet does not otherwise endorse, in language normally used for his own insights. The *kî gam-yôdēaʿ ʾānî* (yet I know) introduces a subordinate clause that extends to verse 14. Either this affirmation of traditional belief about the fate of sinners and good people is a secondary gloss or it constitutes a concession to tradition that Qohelet boldly undercuts in verse 14. In this instance, the verdict "gloss" seems justified.

Gordis understands Qohelet to be introducing a quotation in order to challenge it. Galling (1969) and others achieve the same thing by labeling this an example of "yes . . . but" reasoning. No satisfactory solution to the problem exists. Because it is almost universally recognized that an epilogist has added the final verses of the book, it is quite possible that the same person inserted 8:12b–13.

[13] This verse continues to articulate traditional belief about the fates of those who do good and those who do evil. In 8:12 Qohelet complained because sinners prolong their days (this is the result even if one assumes an ellipsis of *ʾap,* divine wrath). Now he says that sinners will not do so, and he adds the image of shadow (The Septuagint has *en skia* [in a shadow]).

[123]Rabinowitz (*Bib* 39 [1958] 82, n. 2) suggests that *pitgām* is a transliteration of the Greek *epitagma* (command).

The expression "like a shadow" *(kaṣṣēl)* can be understood with reference to days or to the sinners, either way envisioning a lengthening shadow as the sun goes down.

"The fear of God" has several meanings in Ecclesiastes (E. Pfeiffer). In 3:14; 5:6 [7E]; and 7:18 fear of God comes close to awe in the presence of dreadful power, the numinous. Here the idea resembles that in 12:13, where religious devotion is central.

This reaffirmation of traditional belief indicates a refusal to give up the conviction of an orderly universe. Whether one views this optimism as Qohelet's inability to abandon dogma altogether or as the religious community's inability to do so, the presence of 8:12b–13 demonstrates the force of the belief that good people fare well and bad people suffer. The impact of the Joban attack on this belief is difficult to assess.

[14] Qohelet strikes down the traditional belief of 8:12b–13 with a crushing blow, stating that glaring exceptions to the theory of reward and retribution, so dear to Deuteronomy, had penetrated the soul of the nation. Whoever dispenses reward and punishment has gotten things mixed up. This perversion of justice occurs everywhere. Here Qohelet uses *'al-hā'āreṣ* instead of *taḥat haššāmeš,* but the meaning is the same.

This long verse contains three particles of existence *(yēš),* three relatives *('ašer),* and two references to futility. The idea of *hebel* encloses the entire verse, which begins with an example of futility and concludes by asserting that the particular example shows the absurdity in abuse of justice. Furthermore, Qohelet repeats the key words: *ṣaddîqîm* and *rᵉšā'îm, maggîa' 'alēhem,* and *kᵉma'aśēh* ("righteous" and "wicked," "their reward," and "like the recompense").

The strange use of *ma'aśēh* here is found also in Isa. 32:17 *(wᵉhāyāh ma'aśēh haṣṣᵉdāqāh šālôm,* "and the effect of righteousness will be peace," RSV) and Hab. 3:17 *(kî . . . kiḥēš ma'aśēh-zayit,* "though . . . the produce of the olive fail," RSV).

[15] Qohelet's experiment led him to dismiss joy because it accomplished nothing of consequence (2:1–2), hence was futile. Yet he advocates a life of pleasure, insofar as possible. This praise for joy (contrast 4:2) does not mean, however, that he has abandoned the view that the house of mourning outranks the place of festivity. Qohelet knows that eating and drinking provide some pleasure in an imperfect world, and he therefore urges people to enjoy life. The repetition of *taḥat haššemeš* reveals the power of stereotypical language.

The use of *yilwennû* (Qal of *lwh*) is unusual, but the verb came to be used in the sense of "be joined to, accompany." This root *lwh* occurs in the Niphal with the meaning "join" (Isa. 14:1, *wᵉnilwāh haggēr 'alêhem,* "and the sojourner will join them"; Esth. 9:27, *wᵉ'al kol-hannilwîm 'alêhem,* "and all who joined them"). In Gen. 29:34 there is a pun on the name Levi (*'attāh happa'am yillāweh 'îšî 'ēlay . . . š^emô lēwî,* "now this time my husband will be joined to me . . . his name Levi"). Whitley observes that *lāwāh* is used in Sir. 41:12 (Hiphil *ylwk*) of a name accompanying a person, and it occurs in *Abot* 6:9 (*m^elawwîm,* Piel participle) of pearls and precious stones accompanying someone to the grave.[124]

[16] This verse begins with a traditional formula and familiar vocabulary (to apply the mind, 2:12 and 7:25; business, 1:13 and 3:10), but Qohelet's concluding thought has its closest parallel in Latin texts. The poet Terence wrote *somnum hercle ego hac nocte oculis non vidi meis (Heauton Timorumenos* 3.1.82), and Cicero observed that *somnum non vidit (Epistulae ad Familiares* 7.30). Gordis points out that the expression for not seeing sleep is used idiomatically in *Tos. Sukk.* 4:5 *(l' hyynw rw'yn šynh).* Barton underlines the rarity of Qohelet's image by pointing to the usual expression (Prov. 6:4, *'al-tittēn šēnāh l^e'êneykā,* "do not give sleep to your eyes"; Ps. 132:4, *'im-'ettēn š^enat l^e'ênāy,* "if I give sleep to my eyes": Gen. 31:40, *wattidad š^enātî mē'ênāy,* "and my sleep fled from my eyes").[125]

Several features of this verse require elucidation. The indefinite pronominal suffix seems to anticipate *hā'ādām* in the next verse. Furthermore, the entire verse is a protasis, with verse 17 serving as the apodosis ("When I applied my mind . . . then I saw . . ."). The parenthetical statement *kî gam . . . rō'eh* interrupts the natural sequence of thought. Qohelet seeks not only to know wisdom but also to *see* the business done on earth (not *taḥat haššemeš*). This juxtaposition of wisdom and *hā'inyān* is unprecedented, whether contrastive or explicative (one acquires wisdom by paying close attention to events and human interactions).

[17] This verse explicitly equates God's work with activity on earth—elsewhere Qohelet only implies that whatever occurs is God's doing. The idea that humans cannot fathom divine activity occurs also in 3:11, and Qohelet repeats it in 11:5. In its most extreme form, the idea of human limitation before ultimate truth appears in 7:25–29.

Who searches in 8:17? Humanity in general? Or humanity in general and the professional wise man in particular? Qohelet observes that all who endeavor to fathom God's work are destined to fail, however diligently they toil. The *b^ešel 'ašer* ("on account of which") is an Aramaism corresponding to *b^edîl d^e* (cf. *bdyl d'nwn bśr',* "because they are flesh," Targum on Gen. 6:3). In Jonah 1:7 the expression *b^ešell^emî* ("on whose account") occurs,

---

[124]Ginsberg, *Studies in Koheleth* (4) offers the plausible explanation, although textually unsubstantiated and orthographically distant, that *yilwennû* is a corrupted *ḥelqô* (his portion).

[125]The comprehensive expression "by day and by night" occurs here as well as in Eccl. 8:16. In the case of Gen. 31:40, the allusion to lack of sleep may refer only to the result of being cold during the night.

followed in 1:12 by *kî yôdēa‘ ’ānî kî b^e^šellî* (“for I know that because of me”).[126]

The use of the verb *’āmar* in the sense of “claim” is attested in II Chron. 13:8 (*w^e^‘attāh ’attem ’ōm^e^rîm l^e^hitḥazzēq,* “and now you claim to withstand”). Such application of *’āmar* to the thoughts of an individual occurs elsewhere, for example in Exodus 2:14 (*wayyō’mar,* “and he [Moses] thought”).[127] Alternatively, *’āmar* may have the meaning “intend” (cf. 7:23). This interpretation emphasizes the impossibility of anyone’s achieving an understanding of God’s actions on earth.

The Shadow of Death
9:1–10

9:1 For all this I took to heart, and I examined all this, that the righteous and the wise and their works are under God’s control; no one knows whether it is love or hate; everything is before them. [2]Everything is the same for everybody: a single fate for the righteous and the wicked, the good, the clean and the unclean, whoever sacrifices and whoever does not sacrifice; as the good person, so the sinner; as the person who takes an oath, so the one who is afraid to take an oath. [3]This is an evil in all that is done under the sun, that a single fate is for all, and also the heart of human beings is full of evil, and madness is in their heart during their lives—and afterward off to the dead. [4]For whoever is chosen among all the living has hope, for a living dog is better than a dead lion. [5]For the living know that they will die, but the dead know nothing, and there is no longer any reward for them, because the memory of them is forgotten. [6]Their love, their hate, and their passions have already perished, and they no longer have any portion ever in all that is done under the sun. [7]Go, eat your bread with joy and drink your wine with a glad heart, for God has already approved your actions. [8]At all times let your clothes be white and do not lack oil on your head. [9]Enjoy life with a woman you love all the days of your empty life that God has given you under the sun all your fleeting days, for that is your portion in life and in your wages for which you have toiled under the sun. [10]Whatever your hand finds to do, do mightily, for there is no work, or thought, or knowledge, or wisdom in Sheol, to which you are going.

---

[126]There is no compelling reason to follow Septuagint, Peshitta, and Vulgate in reading *b^e^kōl ’^a^šer* (in all that).

[127]Galling emends to *w^e^gam ’im yō’mar ’eḥkam lāda‘at.*

A lengthening shadow extends throughout the book, becoming especially dark in this unit. Qohelet thinks no one can ascertain the deity's disposition toward humans, for a common fate befalls everyone regardless of religious performance or its absence. Alternatively, Qohelet observes that even human passions remain a dark secret until death stills them. In an exquisite phrase the syntax breaks off like life itself. Qohelet employs irony in conceding that the living have an advantage over the dead, for the sequel negates the aphorism about a living dog and a dead lion. The logic of Qohelet's argument that human beings have no control over their lives elevates chance to a supreme position. Unfortunately, this arbitrary power does not take worth into consideration, thus effectively destroying the foundation on which the sages built so confidently. Drawing the conclusion that one should live it up, Qohelet encourages pleasure before Sheol claims its prize.

[9:1] The chief textual problem in this verse concerns *w^{e}lābûr.* Many witnesses (Septuagint, Peshitta, Syro-Hexaplar, Coptic) read *w^{e}libbî rā'āh 'et-kol-zeh* ("and my heart perceived all this"). Although this reading seems preferable to the Massoretic Text, the principle of *lectio difficilior* favors the rare *w^{e}lābûr,* an infinitive that receives the pointing of an *ayin waw* verb rather than that of a double *ayin* verb *(bārar).* Substitution of the infinitive *lātûr* (to spy out) for *lābûr* has no textual warrant. The pointing of *wa-ʿ^{a}bādêhem* (and their works) is unique; it is treated like an Aramaic noun (Whitley compares Ezra 4:17, *k^{e}nāwāt^{e}hôn,* "their colleagues"; and Targum on Eccl. 8:11, *ʿôbādêhôn,* "their works").

The Peshitta reads, "everything before him is futile," and the Septuagint of 9:2 has *mataiotēs en tois pasin* ("futile in all things"), taking the initial *hakkōl* as *hebel,* an attractive reading of the verse. Nevertheless, the Massoretic Text makes good sense and should probably be retained.

Qohelet looks ahead, announcing that he has carefully examined everything (*kol-zeh* twice) that he is about to discuss concerning the fate of human beings. This destiny of just people, and wise, is entirely at God's disposal, contrary to the sage's belief that they controlled their own destiny. The term "and their actions" refers either to what the wise and just think they accomplish in their own strength, or to their inability to do anything apart from the deity's prior approval. Qohelet adds that no one really knows what God's disposition is, whether positive or negative.[128] Because everything lies in the future, no one knows beforehand whether God will treat a given individual with favor or disdain. Hebrew sometimes uses polarities

[128]The Instruction of Ptahhotep concludes with a thematic parallel: "He whom God loves is a hearkener, (but) he whom God hates cannot hear" (*ANET,* 414). Qohelet rejects this optimism about divine favor for the wise, for he thinks the correlation between one's good deeds and divine favor no longer exists. As 8:17 asserts, human beings cannot fathom God's actions, hence they have no assurance that a virtuous life will call forth divine favor.

like love and hate in the sense of "everything," but that does not seem to apply here. The reference to passions could be applied to *hā'ādām,* but this reading does not commend itself. The expression "everything is before them" may be spatial or temporal.

[2] As Gordis has recognized, the idiom *hakkōl ka'ašer lakkōl* vaguely resembles *'ehyeh 'ašer 'ehyeh* ("I shall be what I shall be") in Ex. 3:14. There is thus no compelling reason to read *ba'ašer.* If one refers *hakkōl* to the previous verse and reads *hebel, ba'ašer* can be read. Qohelet declares that there is no difference in the way God treats a sinner and a moral person. Everything is the same regardless of one's conduct.

The series lists good persons first, with the exception of the last pair, which may have been reversed on the principle of concluding on a favorable note, but more likely is simply a stylistic variation.[129] Within the series a shift occurs from prefixed *lamed,* which is attached to the first seven categories, to the preposition *kᵉ.* The reference to the good *(laṭṭôb)* lacks an opposite, which is supplied in the Septuagint, Peshitta, and Vulgate. The contrast between a good person and a sinner later in the series argues for deletion earlier, although Qohelet is not afraid to repeat (note *kol-zeh* twice in the previous verse). *Hannišbā'* dispenses with the prefixed *kap,* although Septuagint, Peshitta, Targum, and Vulgate witness to its presence.

A person's behavior does not affect the way God treats that person. All are treated the same: the just and the wicked, the moral, the ritually clean and the defiled, the one who offers a sacrifice and the one who neglects that duty, the innocent and the guilty, the oath taker and the one who avoids swearing. This attitude contradicts virtually everything in Qohelet's heritage, which taught that a correlation existed between one's deeds and one's time and manner of death. Yet he asserts this unique view as if none could disprove it.

[3] The reality of our common fate, regardless of moral worth, issues in human madness (cf. 8:11). The sentence breaks off like life itself—"and then off to the dead" (Wildeboer). The contrast between the living and the dead continues to verse 5, which discusses the dubious advantage one has over the other.

Although ancient witnesses understood *wᵉ'aḥarāyw* as "after them" (Septuagint and Peshitta), "their end" (Targum and Symmachus), and "after these things" (Vulgate), the Massoretic Text may reflect an archaic ending (cf. 3:22). Some scholars emend *rā'* to *hārā',* but Qohelet normally uses the adjective without an article when expressing a "neutral evil" (Zimmerli 1962).

[4] The Qere *yᵉḥubbar* ("is associated with") has strong witnesses in 20

---

[129]Gordis explains the lack of a balancing term for *laṭṭôb* and the reversal of positive and negative terms for the oath taker as the result of concern for rhythmic evenness.

Hebrew manuscripts, Septuagint, Peshitta, Vulgate, and Targum. On this reading, those who are still alive have confidence; however, Qohelet has earlier praised the dead over the living. This secondary Qere reading removes the sting of Qohelet's denial of reward and punishment in 9:3. The original Ketib is ironic.

The rare word *biṭṭāḥôn* (hope) occurs elsewhere in the Hebrew Bible only in II Kings 18:19 and its parallel (Isa. 36:4), *māh habbiṭṭāḥôn hazzeh ʾašer bāṭāḥᵉtā,* "what is this confidence that you trust [in]?") Lohfink's (1980, 65–66) suggestion that *biṭṭāḥôn* in Eccl. 9:4 has its later sense of trust, perhaps in God, has nothing to commend it.

The second half of the verse is probably an aphorism that Qohelet composed, or more likely, quotes. In the ancient Near East "dog" (a scavenger) was a metaphor for a contemptible or worthless person, whereas "lion" designated a prince or person of great worth. Qohelet emphatically asserted (the *lamed* on *keleb* is emphatic) that a live dog is preferable to a dead lion. The next verse reveals a hidden sting in the aphorism.

[5] Once again Qohelet uses a wordplay: *śākār* and *zeker.*[130] The ending on *zikrām* is an objective genitive; those who survive soon forget the persons who preceded them, an idea that seems to have troubled Qohelet deeply. The only advantage of the living is knowledge that they, too, will die. Although many commentators view this theoretical knowledge as positive, Qohelet's words appear ironic. No comfort derives from knowing that the dead have already received their rewards and are completely forgotten, for the living will experience the same oblivion. Awareness of such grim prospects can hardly form a basis for hope. In this instance, ignorance is preferable.

The suffix on *ʾênām* focuses attention on the dead ("the dead, they do not"), a characteristic usage of Mishnaic Hebrew, for which Whitley gives the following example: *ʾlw šehēm srykym* ("these that require," *Miqw.* 10:4).

[6] Recalling the affective language in 9:1, where divine love and hate could not be predicted, Qohelet now turns to human passions, which are easily perceived. Death stills even the most violent emotions, those of love and hate. Lest it be thought that more moderate passions survive death's calming effect, he adds the word *qinʾātām* ("their zeal" = passions of rivalry; cf. 4:4). Perishing feelings squander one's portion among the living. Qohelet expresses the real tragedy of death, which separates an individual from any portion of joy and pleasure that has been granted.

The succession of three *gam*s in this verse recalls Isa. 48:8 (*gam lōʾ*-

---

[130]Gordis thinks the assonance also contains a poignant idea: the one thing that a living person might hope for as a reward, namely a living memory, is ruled out in principle. An attack on the sentiments expressed here may occur in Wisd. of Sol. 2:1–9, especially 2:4, but Skehan attempts to refute the claim that Qohelet's views lie behind this passage in Wisdom of Solomon.

šāmaʿtā gam lōʾ yādaʿtā gam mēʾāz lōʾ-pittᵉḥāh ʾoznekā, "you have not heard, you have not known, your ears have not been opened at all [lit., from then]"). The effect of the three particles and the pronominal endings attached to the three nouns for affections is deadening: *gam . . . ām . . . gam . . . ām . . . gam . . . ām.* The syntactically redundant use of *lᵉʿôlām* ("into the ages") after *ʿôd* reinforces the permanence of the darkening of hope's ray (i.e., possessing a portion of life [*ḥēleq*]).

[7] Until now, Qohelet's comments on enjoying life have taken the form of advice (2:24–26; 3:12–13, 22; 5:17–19 [18–20E]; 8:15; but note 7:14, "be happy"). Now he switches to imperatives *(lēk, ʾᵉkōl, šᵃtēh),* conveying a greater sense of urgency issuing from Qohelet's reflection on the power of death to extinguish powerful emotions. Although the sentiments of this verse and the three that follow are universal, the similarity with Siduri's advice to Gilgamesh is so great that Qohelet's familiarity with the Epic of Gilgamesh has often been proposed.

> Gilgamesh, whither rovest thou?
> The life thou pursuest thou shalt not find.
> When the gods created mankind,
> Death for mankind they set aside,
> Life in their own hands retaining.
> Thou, Gilgamesh, let full be thy belly,
> Make thou merry by day and by night.
> Of each day make thou a feast of rejoicing,
> Day and night dance thou and play!
> Let thy garments be sparkling fresh,
> Thy head be washed; bathe thou in water.
> Pay heed to the little one that holds on to thy hand,
> Let thy spouse delight in thy bosom!
> For this is the task of [mankind]!
>
> (*ANET,* 90)

Justification for joyous eating and drinking rests in the divine disposition, which 9:1 declares to be unfathomable. Since one's capacity to enjoy life depends on a divine gift, anyone who can eat and drink must enjoy divine favor. (The corollary is that persons who lack the means or the disposition to enjoy life lack that favor.) Divine approval precedes human enjoyment.

[8] The value of white clothes in a hot climate was widely known, and the frequent application of oils to combat the deleterious effect of dry heat on skin was widely practiced by those who could afford it. According to Esth. 8:15, Mordecai wore a combination of bright clothes and white garments on a festive occasion.[131] The mention of soothing oil occurs frequently

[131] Jewish and Christian eschatological literature states that the righteous will wear white garments in the world to come (Rev. 3:4, 5; 7:9; cf. *Šabb.* 114a).

in the Bible (e.g., Pss. 23:5; 45:8 [7E]; 104:15; Prov. 27:9). The author of Wisd. of Sol. 2:7–8 combats those who make a caricature of this verse in Ecclesiastes.

[9] The word for woman *('iššāh)* lacks a definite article. Did Qohelet urge enjoyment of any woman one desired, or pleasure with one's wife? Whitley argues that the absence of the article does not imply sexual union outside marriage, inasmuch as *'iššāh* occurs elsewhere without the article when designating a wife. But his examples from Gen. 21:21; 24:3, 37 refer to taking a woman for the purpose of marriage (this may also be true of Lev. 20:14), at which point she was not yet a man's wife. Would Qohelet have advocated lasciviousness of the sort that Wisd. of Sol. 2:9 attacks? Probably not.

The imperative to enjoy one's woman offers a clue that Qohelet's audience was exclusively male, unlike the broader audience (*hā'ām,* the people) envisioned by the first epilogist in 12:9. Qohelet's use of the verb *'āhab* (love) stands out, for he has despaired of discerning whether God loves or hates individuals and has noted that human feelings of love will subside. The command to enjoy life with a woman whom one loves seems a defiant attempt to beat death itself, at least for a fleeting moment (cf. Adam's response to the divine curse). The repetition of the idea of fleeting existence *(kol-yᵉmê ḥayyê heblekā . . . kōl-yᵉmê heblekā)* reinforces the utter futility of this effort to escape death's clutches.[132] The Oriental Ketib has *hî'* for *hû',* perhaps identifying the woman as one's portion in life.

[10] The idiom *kōl 'ᵃšer timṣā' yādᵉkā* means "everything one is able to do." The Massoretic accentuation construes the infinitive *la'ᵃśôt* with *bᵉkōḥᵃkā* rather than with the imperative *'ᵃśēh.* Following this lead, one should translate: "whatever you are able to do in your strength, do." However, the ancient versions (Vulgate, Targum, and several Hebrew manuscripts) read the words differently, connecting *bᵉkōḥᵃkā* with *'ᵃśēh.* The point follows naturally from Qohelet's observation about death's power. Enjoy a woman as long as that is possible, and do zealously whatever you can. Knowledge that such intensity of feeling will quickly diminish, subsiding completely in Sheol, motivates intense living.

Qohelet depicts Sheol as lacking any promising feature, whether achievement, mental calculation, knowledge, or wisdom. The participle *hōlēk* underlines the fact that human beings are already going that direction. The personal pronoun *'attāh* (you) personalizes the point. Qohelet saw no basis for optimism about the next life, either in its Hebraic expression, the resurrection of the body, or in its Greek expression, the immortality of the soul. For Qohelet, Sheol was a place of nonbeing.

---

[132]The entire phrase from the first *heblekā* to the second is missing from the Peshitta, probably because a scribe's eye jumped from the first to the second. This explanation seems to support the originality of both references to life's ephemerality in the Massoretic Text. The repetition, which varies in form, functions rhetorically.

Time and Chance
9:11–12

9:11 Again I perceived under the sun that the race is not to the swift nor the battle to the strong, nor yet bread to the wise and riches to the astute, nor favor to the informed, for time and mischance meet them all. [12]Indeed, nobody knows his or her time; like fish that are caught in an unwelcome net, and like birds that are caught in a trap, human beings are ensnared at a bad time when it suddenly falls on them.

Chance governs human lives, according to Qohelet, and it does no good to strive for excellence in the belief that pleasant results will follow. No one can plan for the unexpected or compensate for randomness. In the end, an unwelcome intrusion will suddenly terminate life, so that human beings resemble fish taken in a net and birds captured in a trap.

[11] This verse mentions five areas in which the principle of merit collapsed entirely. "Runner" probably means courier, not athlete, given the late date for the introduction of Greek contests into Palestine (probably during the time of Antiochus Epiphanes IV, 174–164 B.C.E.). (On the other hand, Qohelet may have heard about such races before their entrance into Jewish life.) The mightiest soldier does not win every skirmish, for strategy also plays an important role, as the story about David and Goliath demonstrated. Sages were not always well paid, nor were persons of discernment inevitably wealthy. Finally, not all who were "in the know" succeeded in gaining favor from persons who had authority. Over everything hangs the element of chance, and the combination of time and event often produced misfortune (cf. I Kings 5:18 [4E], *'ên śāṭān wᵉ'ên pega' rā',* "there is neither adversary nor misfortune").

The expression *taḥat-haššemeš* anticipates what follows, examples under the sun. The variation in the means of expressing negation, two uses of *lō'* and three instances of *wᵉgam lō',* indicates Qohelet's penchant for stylistic variety, just as the placing of the subject at the end throughout these five examples, and the use of the preposition *lᵉ* with all types of persons, shows his fondness for stylistic regularity. Delitzsch observed that the same sequence occurs also in Isa. 11:2 *(ḥokmāh, bînāh, da'at),* but Isaiah combines the intellectual categories with others *(rûaḥ ḥokmāh ûbînāh rûaḥ 'ēṣāh ûgᵉbûrāh rûaḥ da'at wᵉyir'at yhwh),* "a spirit of wisdom and understanding, a spirit of counsel and power, a spirit of knowledge and fear of the Lord"). Although some interpreters emend *ḥēn* (favor) to *hôn* (wealth), there is no need for a parallel to *'ōšer* (riches).

[12] Because misfortune strikes individuals indiscriminately, none can prepare for it. Qohelet has already ruled out virtue and knowledge as reliable means of protecting people from harm. No person can anticipate the moment of calamity, for the seasons roll relentlessly, oblivious to those crushed under the weight of their heavy wheels. The sequel requires the meaning "death" for *'ittô* (his time), for the similes describe the events that lead to the death of fish and birds. The adjective *rā'āh* characterizes the net from the standpoint of fish caught by it. Accordingly, the adjective also occurs with reference to the time *('ēt)* that spells doom for persons (cf. *Abot* 3:15, "All is given on pledge, and a net is spread over all the living").

Whereas Qohelet uses the same verb, although in different forms, to describe the capture of fish and birds *(šenne'eḥāzîm* and *hā'aḥuzzôt),* he opts for another verb to signify the snaring of human beings *(yûqāšîm).* This observation about inability to ascertain times is the most poignant yet, for Qohelet's earlier comments lacked the finality and pathos of this one. The images of captured fish and birds give specificity to previous remarks. The effort to find the right time for an action fails, and the trap closes unexpectedly and swiftly.

Wasted Wisdom 9:13–18

9:13 Also this I have seen as wisdom under the sun and it appeared significant to me. [14]A little town, and few people in it, and a great king came against it, invested it, and built huge siegeworks against it. [15]And they found in it a poor, wise man, and he could have delivered the town by his wisdom, but no one remembered that poor man. [16]And I said, "Wisdom is better than might, but the wisdom of the poor man is despised and his words are not heard." [17]The words of the wise spoken quietly are heard better than the shout of a ruler among fools. [18]Better is wisdom than implements of war, but one sinner destroys much good.

This section offers an example, perhaps hypothetical, of skill that did not bring the expected success. A poor but wise man could easily have saved a village under siege by a powerful king, but the residents of the small town forgot him (or they consulted him and were rescued, only to forget him after all danger had passed). Qohelet praises wisdom over weapons, but admits that people easily overlook it, thereby rendering wisdom ineffectual.

[13] The word *ḥokmāh* (wisdom) is in apposition to the demonstrative *zōh* (this). Because the story hardly demonstrates wise actions, some interpreters have emended *ḥokmāh.* The word can be a kind of explanatory comment on *zōh.* The adjective *gedôlāh* has also been emended by some critics, but late usage approaches the meaning of "significant, important." In Jonah 3:3 one finds *'îr-gᵉdôlāh lē'lōhîm* ("an important city to God"), and in Esth. 10:3 one reads *wᵉgādôl layyᵉhûdîm* ("and significant to the Jews"). Whitley points out that *gādôl* is used of Moses (Ex. 11:3) and of Mordecai (Esth. 9:4) as outstanding or distinguished. Perhaps it is significant that *gādôl* and *gᵉdōlîm* are used with reference to a king and siegeworks in the story that follows.

[14] In 7:26 *mᵉṣôdîm* signifies "snares" and in 9:12 *mᵉṣôdāh* means "snare." This interpretation of the word *mᵉṣôdîm* in 9:14 does not fit the context, for *ûbānāh 'āleyhā* ("and built against it") requires the meaning "siegeworks." Two manuscripts have *mᵉṣûrîm,* a reading that may be implied by several ancient versions (Septuagint, Symmachus, Peshitta, Vulgate).

Sages recognized a poor person's difficulty in being heard. According to Sir. 13:23 everyone listens to a rich person and praises what is said, whereas the people respond to a poor person's speech with an arrogant question: "Who is this fellow?" Because the poor are disliked by their neighbors (Prov. 14:20), they must use entreaties (Prov. 18:23). The rich speak roughly and obtain a hearing anyway. Qohelet tells a hypothetical story illustrating the dangers of such reasoning. Given the power of the conviction about divine reward and retribution, this attitude toward the poor is understandable. (Note that there seems to be a slight element of criticism in the proverbial observations themselves.)

The twofold reference to the size of the town (*qᵉṭannāh,* tiny; *mᵉ'āṭ,* few) contrasts with the two uses of *gādôl*, once in the singular and once in the plural. The phrase "great king" probably reflects Persian court protocol, although such language was not limited to the Persian era.

[15] The verb *ûmāṣā'* ("and they found") is impersonal, the equivalent of the passive (GKC, 144d). Its meaning appears to be "there was found," just as *ûlᵉ'ādām lō' māṣā' 'ēzer kᵉnegdô* in Gen. 2:20 means "and for the man there was not found an appropriate helper." The phrase "poor man" has received an apposition "wise," almost as a contrastive element (poor but wise). The only other use of this word (besides 9:16) in Biblical Hebrew occurs in 4:13, but it is used often in Aramaic.

A potential sense seems to adhere to the verb *ûmillaṭ* ("and he could have saved"; compare GKC, 106p). The same meaning occurs in I Sam. 13:13 (*kî 'attāh hēkîn yhwh,* "for now the Lord would have established"). Gordis objects to this understanding of the story, largely on the basis of the verb *zākar,* which he insists cannot mean "give thought to." But *zākar* must have this meaning in 12:1. To be sure, Qohelet knows the verb *ḥšb,* but there is no way to be certain that he would have used this word instead of *zākar.* The use of *zākar* in the sense of remembering someone during an emergency is strange, but for the town to forget the man if he actually delivered it is stranger still.

[16] Qohelet's conclusion seems to suggest that the poor, but wise, man's advice was not heard but despised. This strong participle *(bᵉzûyāh)* implies that his counsel was not even solicited. Otherwise Qohelet's point about despising wisdom and paying no attention to wise words would have been contrary to fact. If the people had listened to the man's advice and escaped harm, there would be no reason to complain about their failure to consult poor counselors.

Again Qohelet qualifies traditional wisdom. Like the sages he exalts wisdom over strength, but he points out that even wise counsel may not be heeded. Hence one cannot predict an outcome even when superior intelligence exists.

[17] The incident about the people's neglect of the poor but wise man gives occasion to draw a general conclusion, perhaps couched in a proverb. Calm advice accomplishes much more than loud shouting by an authoritative person. If the poor man was not consulted, the emphasis on the shouting ruler seems particularly appropriate.

The accent connects *bᵉnaḥat* (in quiet) with *dibrê ḥᵃkāmîm* (words of the wise) rather than with *nišmāʿîm* (heard). Just as in 4:17, *ṭôb* is presupposed by the *min* of comparison. The expression *môšēl bakkᵉsîlîm* does not mean "arch fool." Instead, it indicates an actual ruler. Barton refutes the claim that the idiom is borrowed from Greek. He cites II Sam. 23:3 (*môšēl bāʾādām ṣaddîq môšēl yirʾat ʾᵉlōhîm,* "he who rules justly among humankind, who rules in the fear of God"); Job 41:26 [34E] (*hûʾ melek ʿal-kol-bᵉnê-šāḥaṣ,* "he is king over all the children of pride"); and Prov. 30:30 (*layiš gibbôr babbᵉhēmāh,* "the lion, strongest among beasts"). Although Galling's (1969) emendation of the second half of the verse to read "but the parables of fools [are heard] with shouting" provides a better contrast, there is no textual warrant for this change.

The verb *zāʿaq* occurs frequently with reference to the anguished cry of persons in distress, and that nuance may underlie Qohelet's use of it to characterize a frantic ruler whose capital is under siege.

[18] Continuing the idea that sound counsel possesses the power to deliver a threatened town, Qohelet remarks that intelligent action is actually superior to sword and shield, a conviction that the sages who wrote the book of Proverbs shared, although they employed the usual word for war (*milḥāmāh;* cf. Prov. 20:18). Qohelet uses a late word that occurs also in Zech. 14:3 (*bᵉyôm qᵉrāb,* "on the day of battle"); Pss. 55:19 [18E] (*miqqᵃrob-lî,* "from the battle involving me"); 68:31 *(qᵉrābôt yeḥpāṣû);* 78:9 (*bᵉyôm qᵉrāb,* "on the day of battle"); 144:1 (*hamᵉlammēd yāday laqrāb,* "who teaches my hand for war"); Job 38:23 (*lᵉyôm qᵉrāb ûmilḥāmāh,* "for the day of war and battle"); Dan. 7:21 (*'ăbᵉdāh qᵉrāb,* "made war"); and often in the Targum.

The repetition of *ṭôbāh* provides a kind of balance that would be strengthened if one read *wᵉḥēṭ'* ("and errancy"). This reading would yield two abstractions, wisdom and errancy. However, reference to the effect of one bungler offers a transition to the following verse.

A Collection of Proverbs on Wisdom and Folly 10:1–20

10:1 Dead flies corrupt and ferment the perfumer's oil; weightier than
abundant wisdom is a little folly. 2The heart of the wise is to the right,
and the heart of the fool is to the left. 3And also when the fool walks
on the way he lacks sense and says concerning everyone: "He is a fool."
4If the anger of a ruler rises against you do not leave your post, for
submissiveness assuages great offenses. 5There is an evil I have seen
under the sun, indeed an error that issues from the presence of the
ruler.

6 Folly is set in high places and the rich dwell
in a low place.
7 I have seen slaves on horses and princes walking
like slaves on the ground.
8 Whoever digs a pit may fall into it,
And whoever tears down a wall—a snake may bite.
9 Whoever quarries stones may be hurt by them,
And whoever chops wood may be endangered by it.

10If the ax is dull and no one sharpens its edge, then more effort must
be put forth; and the advantage of skill is wisdom. 11If the snake bites
before it has been charmed, then there is no advantage to being a
charmer. 12The words of the mouth of the wise are gracious, but the
lips of a fool swallow him. 13The beginning of the words of his mouth
is folly, and the end of his talk is evil madness. 14For the fool multiplies
words; a person does not know what will happen, for that which will
occur after him, who can tell him? 15The toil of a fool wearies him so
that he does not know how to go to the city. 16Woe to you, O land,
when your king is a youth and your princes feast in the morning.
17Happy are you, O land, when your king is wellborn, and your princes
eat at the proper time, with self-control and not with drunkenness.

18 Through indolence the beams sink,
And through falling of hands the house leaks.

19 They prepare a feast for pleasure,
And wine makes the living jovial,
But money pays for both.
20 Even in your thought do not curse the king,
And in your bedroom do not curse the wealthy,
For a bird of heaven will carry the sound,
And a winged creature will declare the matter.

This section, not fully integrated into the book, lacks obvious connections between the individual sayings, although word associations do occur in some instances. The fool proclaims his own stupidity, or he considers everyone else devoid of intelligence. Qohelet complains about reversals in society such as servants riding horses like princes, who are relegated to walking. He also warns about hidden dangers lurking in domestic chores, expresses dismay over rulers who drink too much, mentions the function of bribes, and alludes to a proverbial saying about birds carrying slander to the ears of its object.

[10:1] This verse is not easy to understand. In the first half verse, the plural subject does not agree with the singular verbs, and the second verb *(yabbîaʿ)* seems out of place here. The second half verse has two words that are used in an unusual manner *(yāqār* and *kābôd*). The ancient versions had considerable difficulty with the verse, but do not appear to preserve the clue to rendering the Hebrew.

Qohelet's carelessness with respect to agreement between subject and verb has already been noted (cf. 1:10, 16; 2:7). The phrase *z*^{e}*bûbê māwet* can mean "deadly flies" (Pss. 18:5; 116:3, *ḥeblê-māwet,* "deadly snares"; Ps. 7:14 [13E], *k*^{e}*lê-māwet,* "deadly weapons"; Prov. 14:27, *mimmōq*^{e}*šê māwet,* "from deadly snares"), or it can mean "flies of death," that is, "dead flies." The asyndetic verb *yabbîaʿ* (ferment) is often called a gloss. On the basis of the Septuagint and Peshitta some interpreters read "vessel." (The word is not rendered in Symmachus, Vulgate, and Targum.)

In Dan. 2:11 *yaqqîrāh* means "weighty" in the sense of "difficult." On the analogy of Job 36:31 (*'ōkel l*^{e}*makbîr,* "abundant food"), one could emend *mikkābôd,* but the change is not necessary. By extension of meaning, something heavy may be construed as abundant. An ounce of folly weighs more than weighty wisdom.

A few dead flies spoil the perfumer's ointment by causing scum on the surface. So an ounce of folly undoes a pound of wisdom. The verse therefore states the same general idea as 9:18, that wisdom is easily canceled by its opposite.

[2] In ancient Israel the right hand connoted power and deliverance; the right side, moral goodness and favor. Hence the place of honor was on the right side. The left hand usually symbolized ineptness and perversity. Like attitudes are reflected in the language of ancient Greece (*skaios,* awkward;

aristeros, clumsy) and Rome (*sinister,* sinister), and in modern French (*gauche,* awkward). The moral sense of right and left is also found in *Šabb.* 63a, where the two verbs mean to study the Torah properly and improperly.

Qohelet observes that the sage's understanding tends to a favorable outcome, in contrast to the fool, whose inner disposition brings ruin. This praise of wisdom over folly resembles that in 2:14, which also uses anatomical language ("the wise person has eyes in the head").

[3] Perhaps the last half of the verse should be translated "and he declares to everyone that he is a fool," meaning that a fool cannot hide inadequacy, for it inevitably reveals itself in public places. An absence of intelligence makes the fool vulnerable to discovery. The reading that is adopted above emphasizes the fool's contempt for everyone else.

It is immaterial whether one adopts the Ketib or the Qere *(kᵉšehssākāl* or *kᵉšessākāl),* for the difference is mainly euphonic. The Septuagint, Peshitta, and Vulgate interpreted *wᵉʾāmar* as "consider," which supports the view that the fool thought everybody else a fool. However, the opposite view seems to gain support from parallels in Prov. 12:23 (*wᵉlēb kᵉsîlîm yiqrāʾ ʾiwwelet,* "and the heart of fools declares folly") and 13:16 (*ûkᵉsîl yiprōś ʾiwwelet,* "and a fool flaunts folly"). To retain the ambiguity of Qohelet's observation, we might render "he says to all that he is a fool."

[4] Qohelet's concern in 8:25 was with an unpredictable and irrepressible royal fury, before which an intelligent courtier will take cover. The present argument extols the virtue of deference under different circumstances, when the best response to anger is self-effacement, pacifying the angry ruler.

The verbs *tannaḥ* and *yannîaḥ* (Hiphil of *nûaḥ*) represent extended meanings of the root *nûaḥ* (to rest). Elsewhere Qohelet uses this verb in the sense of letting go, withholding (7:18; 11:6). The noun *marpēʾ* may blend the roots *rāpāʾ* (to heal) and *rāpāh* (to sink, relax); such confusion of *lamed he* and *lamed alep* verbs occurs in late Hebrew.

The sages recognized the advantages of remaining calm in all circumstances. This attitude led to the praise of a gentle or tranquil spirit (*ḥayyê bᵉśārîm lēb marpēʾ,* "a tranquil spirit gives life to the body," Prov. 14:30; *marpēʾ lāšôn ʿēṣ ḥayyîm,* "a gentle tongue is counsel of life," Prov. 15:4). The sinking of the passions conveyed by *marpēʾ* and *yannîaḥ* provides a sharp contrast with the rising fury of the ruler (*rûaḥ* plus the verb *ʿālāh,* to ascend).

[5] Once again Qohelet uses the particle of existence to state a grievous fact. In this particular instance, he complains that the inadvertent error derives from an unlikely source. A ruler was obliged to promote justice in society rather than encourage abuse of power and privilege by unscrupulous officials. But in this instance, the ruler sanctions injustice.

The *kap* on *šᵉgāgāh* (error) is asseverative (cf. GKC, 118x). Confusion of *lamed he* and *lamed alep* verbs occurs once more in *šeyyōṣā'* (Qal feminine participle from *yāṣā'*). There seems to be no special reason for Qohelet's shift from *hammôšēl* to *haššallîṭ* in 10:4 and 5. (In two related verses, 5:12 and 6:1, subtle differences exist. In 5:12 an adjective modifies the word "evil" [*rā'āh ḥôlāh,* "grievous evil"], and in 6:1 *rā'āh* is followed by the relative particle *'ašer.*)

[6] The versions render the abstract *hassekel* (folly) concretely as "the fool," but the Massoretic pointing should be kept on the principle of *lectio difficilior.* The lack of an article on *rabbîm* is unusual, but Qohelet's inconsistency in this regard warns against emending the text (especially in light of the versions). Other instances of a missing article on an adjective have been cited (Jer. 2:21, *haggepen nokriyyāh,* "a wild vine"; Ezek. 39:27, *haggôyim rabbîm,* "many nations").

Whitley argues for separating *rabbîm* from *bammᵉrômîm,* interpreting the former as "aged." He thus associates the aged and the rich at the lower end of the social stratum in a topsy-turvy world; the same result can be achieved by translating *rabbîm* as "mighty," an accepted use. Because Dahood (1966, 278–279) offered Ugaritic evidence for translating *rabbîm* as "aged" (*rbt ylm lḥkmt šbt dqnk ltsrk,* "you are aged, El, and truly wise; the grayness of your beard has truly instructed you"), Whitley finds this meaning of *rabbîm* in the Hebrew Bible as well (Job 32:9, *rabbîm//zᵉqēnîm;* 4:3, *rabbîm* and *yādayim* and *rāpôt,* "faltering hands"). He also notes that the senior members of the group at Qumran are designated as *rabbîm* in the Manual of Discipline.

A remarkable parallel to this text in Ecclesiastes occurs in the Egyptian Admonitions of Ipuwer.

> He who could not make a coffin owns a tomb.
> See, those who owned tombs are cast on high ground,
> He who could not make a grave owns a treasury. . . .
> See, the poor of the land have become rich,
> The man of property is a pauper.
> (Lichtheim I, 156–157)

Although this Egyptian text functions as political propaganda for a particular regime, Qohelet's social conservatism is not spoken on behalf of any ruler. Instead, he gives voice to the dominant attitude of those sages who enjoyed the advantages of privilege. How dare the ruler allow social upheaval to invert the upper and lower strata of society?

[7] Israel's sages believed in a sense of propriety, especially with regard to one's social class. The wealthy were entitled to certain privileges withheld from the poor, who were thought to have brought misfortune on themselves. Qohelet reveals this traditional attitude toward the well-to-do and their opposites. Something was inherently wrong when slaves enjoyed the privileges that belonged to nobility, and when princes were forced to travel on foot.

In early times royalty rode on mules and asses. At first, horses were used in warfare, hence were highly valued. References to riding on horseback are relatively late (contrast the use of asses or mules in Judg. 5:10; 10:4; II Sam. 18:9; I Kings 1:38; Zech. 9:9). This mode of transportation (mules and asses) may have been retained in royal ritual long after kings began to travel on horseback. The king's (Solomon's) multiplication of horses is criticized in Deut. 17:16. Qohelet's use of *'al-hā'āreṣ* has the sense of walking "on foot." A few manuscripts add *rōkᵉbîm* (riding) after *ʿᵃbādîm* as a contrast with the participle *hōlᵉkîm* (walking).

[8] A traditional saying expresses in graphic form the sages' understanding of retribution. The individual bent on destructive behavior will become the victim of such actions. (Similar convictions underlie the story of Haman's death on his own gallows in the book of Esther.) Here Qohelet endorses the view that misconduct bears its own fruit, although elsewhere he calls this dogma into question.

The word *gûmmāṣ* occurs only here in the Hebrew Bible. It is an Aramaic word that appears in the Targum as a translation for *šûḥāh* in Prov. 22:14 and 23:27 and for *šaḥat* in Prov. 26:27 (*kōreh-šaḥat bāh yippōl,* "whoever digs a pit will fall into it"). The sentiment is expressed elsewhere in Pss. 7:16 [15E]; 9:16 [15E]; Sir. 27:26 ("Whoever digs a pit will fall into it, and whoever sets a trap will be caught in it").

The prophet Amos mentioned the danger of being bitten by a snake in one's own home (5:19). Because mortar was often nothing more than mud, snakes easily found hiding places in the cracks. One who tears apart a wall may encounter a deadly obstacle. Conventional wisdom would have made a similar point, except that the victim would have been actively engaged in criminal behavior, such as breaking and entering for the purpose of stealing.

[9] This proverbial statement warns about hidden dangers in ordinary domestic chores (cf. Deut. 19:5). *Yēʿāṣēb* normally means "to be grieved," although it also means "to be pained" and hence "to be hurt." The verb *yissāken* (will be endangered) occurs only here in the Hebrew Bible, but is found in the Mishnah (e.g., *Ber.* 1:3, *sikkantî bʿṣmy,* "I was in danger") and Targum (e.g., Ps. 119:109, *npšy mstkn',* "my soul is endangered").

Participle balances participle, object balances object, Niphal imperfect verb balances Niphal imperfect verb, and preposition with pronominal object balances preposition with pronominal object in this aphorism. The addition of the conjunction *(waw)* in Peshitta, Vulgate, and many manuscripts breaks this perfect symmetry.

[10] Attempts to understand the language and syntax of this verse have not succeeded, but the context makes it possible to grasp the general meaning of the observation. Unless one uses practical knowledge, the expenditure of energy increases. Wisdom is useless if a person does not put it to work for some benefit.

The word *habbarzel* is literally "the iron," but in II Kings 6:5 the word clearly means "ax." The Piel verb *qēhāh* (to be blunt, dull) occurs only here in the Hebrew Bible, although in the Qal it is found in Jer. 31:29–30 and Ezek. 18:2. The pronoun *w^{e}hû'* ("and he") echoes the same word in the previous verse, but functions as an indefinite subject. The essential meaning of the Pilpel verb from *qll* is "to polish," but a derivative sense of "sharpen" is conceivable. On the basis of Ezek. 21:21 [16E] (*'ānāh pānayik mu'ādôt,* "where your edge is directed," RSV) *pānîm* is taken as the edge of an ax.

The expression *waḥ^{a}yālîm y^{e}gabbēr* occurs elsewhere in slightly different form (Job 21:7), *'āt^{e}qû gam-gāb^{e}rû ḥāyil,* "become aged and grow strong"). The second half of the verse is unclear. The word *hakšêr* is probably a Hiphil infinitive from *kāšēr,* a verb which Qohelet uses in 11:6 (*'ê zeh yikšār h^{a}zeh 'ô-zeh,* "whether this or that will succeed"). Its meaning in Esth. 8:5 *(w^{e}kāšēr haddābār)* seems to be "proper" or "right." In rabbinic usage the verb means "to prepare" or "make fit." But how do the three words in the second half of the verse relate to one another? Perhaps it is best to retain the ambiguity of the text and to translate somewhat literally: "and the advantage of success [skill?] is wisdom." Whitley renders the clause differently, construing *ḥokmāh* as an object of the infinitive. This yields the following: "but the development of skill is an advantage."

[11] Like the previous verse, this one makes the point that an unused skill is wasted. If a snake bites before the whispered spell takes effect, what reason is there for mastering the art of enchantment? The expression *b^{e}lô'-lāḥaš* functions as a temporal notation in Eccl. 7:17 (*lāmmāh tāmût b^{e}lō' 'ittekā,* "why will you die before your time?") and in Job 15:32 (*b^{e}lō'-yômô timmālē',* "it will be full before his time").

There is no reason to relate *ba'al hallāšôn* ("lord of the tongue") to the snake on the analogy with *ba'al hakk^{e}nāpayim* ("owner of wings," 10:20). Instead, the reference is to the master enchanter, the one with a skill that can influence the snake (cf. Isa. 3:3; Jer. 8:17; Ps. 58:6 [5E]).

In this observation Qohelet uses sound to full advantage: the resemblance of *yiššōk* to the hissing of a serpent; the similarity between *hannāḥāš* and *lāḥaš,* and perhaps *yitrôn* and *hallāšôn.*

Ben Sira acknowledges that none will pity a snake charmer whose skill does not protect him from the deadly creature. But Sirach uses this idea to warn against wrong associations, friends who will lead one into dangerous behavior.

[12] There are two possible meanings for the first half of the verse: the words of the wise obtain favor or they bestow favor. Both ideas occur in traditional wisdom. In 9:11 Qohelet denies the optimistic claim that persons of intelligence can count on obtaining favor *(ḥēn).* But here in 10:12 he seems to endorse the view that the wise speak only those things that result in harmonious relationships.

The fool does precisely the opposite. An inability to guard the lips results in a torrent of passionate speech that consumes the speaker. Qohelet's image is exquisite: the lips from which foolish utterances flow become the instrument of destruction, ultimately swallowing their owner. Although the subject is plural (*wᵉśiptôt,* lips), the verb is singular *(tᵉballᵉʿennû),* for which there is precedent in Job 27:20 (*taśśîgēhû kammayim ballāhôt,* "like water terrors overtake him"). On this linguistic phenomenon, see GKC, 145 k, n.

[13] This verse contains Qohelet's only use of *tᵉḥillat* (beginning); in 3:11 he uses *rō'š* and in 7:8 *rē'šît.* The contrasting word is *sôp* in 3:11, but *'aḥᵃrît* in 7:8 and in 10:13. In the book of Proverbs *rē'šît* and *tᵉḥillat* function as pregnant expressions for the essential ingredient and for the initial action, that is, first in rank and in time (Prov. 1:7, *yir'at yhwh rē'šît dāʿat,* "the fear of the Lord is the beginning [first principle] of knowledge"; Prov. 9:10, *tᵉḥillat ḥokmāh yir'at yhwh,* "the beginning of wisdom is the fear of the Lord"). The latter verse is the only instance of *tᵉḥillat* in the book of Proverbs.

In Hos. 1:2 one finds this introductory formula: *tᵉḥillat dibber-yhwh bᵉhôšēaʿ,* "when the Lord first spoke through Hosea." However, the Septuagint has *logou* ("of the word"; cf. also the Peshitta), which is closer to Qohelet's construction, apart from his redundant *pîhû* ("his mouth"). The second occurrence of *pîhû* in Eccl. 10:13 is metonymic, his mouth standing for the words that issue from it. The adjective *rāʿāh* may be emphatic, approaching the meaning "utter madness."

[14] If the first half of this verse does not continue the thought of the previous verse, the comment must be a fragment. The observation that fools talk constantly enlarges the horizon of 10:13; the self-destructive individual does not know enough to shut up. One could relate the rest of verse 14 to verbosity. Fools claim to know the unknowable.

With this observation Qohelet returns to a theme already discussed in 6:12; 7:14; and 8:7. Nobody knows what will occur in the future. Although the Septuagint, Symmachus, Peshitta, and Vulgate read *mah-šehāyāh,* which is found in a few manuscripts, this shift from the future to the past represents a leveling of the Massoretic Text to remove a seeming redundancy. It is better to retain the Massoretic Text. Qohelet complained elsewhere that people forgot the past, so that the memory of accomplishments was obliterated. But here he denies that anyone can predict the future. The beginnings of astrology may or may not lie behind Qohelet's remarks. The rhetorical question *mî yaggîd lô* ("who can tell him?") is equivalent to *mî yôdēaʿ* ("who knows?" = "no one knows").

[15] Why does the subject disagree with the verb, and the pronominal suffix with its antecedent? Other words normally regarded as masculine occasionally take a feminine verb form (*kābôd* in Gen. 49:6; *hᵃmôn* in Job 31:34 and Eccl. 5:9). Thus the feminine prefix on *tᵉyaggᵉʿennû* is not entirely without precedent. Alternatively, Whitley adduces evidence from Ugaritic literature for a masculine *taqtul* type.

The disagreement between the pronominal suffix and the plural *hakkᵉsîlîm* may be distributive (Gordis) or a misunderstanding of an enclitic *mem* preceded by the old genitive case ending *yod.* Alternatively, the present text may conceal an original *ʿᵃmal hakkᵉsîl mātay yeyaggᵉʿennû,* "when will the fool's toil tire him?"

The second half of the verse seems to contain an aphorism about abysmal stupidity comparable to the English saying, "He does not know enough to come in out of the rain." The relative *ʾᵃšer* may be translated "who" or "because" as well as resultative. If one renders it by "because," the observation can be the initial remark that explains the following malediction. An Egyptian idiom for not achieving a goal is contrasted with "reaching land" in The Protests of the Eloquent Peasant (Fox, forthcoming commentary).

[16] In the Bible *ʾî* as a formula of malediction is paralleled only in Eccl. 4:10, but it occurs in rabbinic literature *(B. Taan.* 7a, *ʾy ḥkmh; B. Roš Haš.* 19a, *ʾy šmym).* The range of *nāʿar* (youth) is considerable, but here it must connote a ruler who is so young and inexperienced that he loses control over his kingdom. The meaning of *nāʿar* here may be "slave" or "lackey."

Such a situation results in total neglect of political responsibilities on the part of officials entrusted with the king's affairs. While they enjoy life, important business goes unattended. According to Acts 2:15 reasonable people do not drink in the morning. The prophet Isaiah pronounced a woe oracle against persons who rose early in the morning for the purpose of getting drunk.

Or Qohelet may imply an entire night of feasting that extends into the early hours of the next day. He urges people to eat and drink, but this verse acknowledges that even this good thing can be abused. Classical authors describe such practices as drinking in the morning (Cicero, *Philippic* 2.41, *ab hora tertia bibebatur, ludebatur, vomebatur,* "From the third hour [nine o'clock] they would drink, gamble, and vomit"; Juvenal, *Satire* 1.49–50, *exul ab octava Marius bibit et fruitur dis Iratis;* Catullus, *Carmen* 10.7.5–6, *vos convivia lauta sumtuose de die facitis*).

[17] The expected contrast with *nāʿar* does not appear here (unless *nāʿar* means "slave"). Instead Qohelet uses *ben-ḥôrîm* ("son of free men," hence "free"). The Old Testament uses the plural *ḥôrîm* (from *ḥrr*) in the sense of nobles (I Kings 21:8, 11; Jer. 27:20; 39:6; Neh. 2:16; 5:7). Although *ben-ḥôrîm* occurs only in Eccl. 10:17, *ben ḥôrîn* appears in *Git.* 4:6, and the Aramaic *br ḥrn* is found in *Ahiqar* 14:217. In addition, the word *ḥr(w)t* (freedom) appears on Jewish coins of the First and Second Revolts against Rome.

The word *baššᵉtî* (with drunkenness) occurs only here, but its meaning is clear (a similar form, *šᵉtiyyāh* appears in Esth. 1:8, *wᵉhaššᵉtiyyāh kaddāt 'ên 'ōnēs,* "and drinking was according to the law, without compulsion"). Both the Septuagint and Vulgate offer inferior readings ("and not to be ashamed" = *bōšet; ad luxuriam*).

The land is blessed with a ruler who belongs to nobility by birth and thus is not consumed by a passion to abuse newfound power the way a slave might do who assumes control of the highest office in the land (cf. Prov. 30:22). Because this freeborn king is fully in control, his princes exercise proper decorum and restraint, eating to keep up their strength and drinking in moderation. The necessity for a king to exercise self-control with regard to strong drink is no new emphasis in the sapiential literature (cf. Prov. 31:5–7).

[18] This verse contains two words that occur nowhere else in the Bible: *hammᵉqāreh* (beam-work) and *šiplût* (falling). The form *qōrāh* is usually found (Gen. 19:8, *bᵉṣēl qōrātî,* "under the shadow of my roof"; S. of Songs 1:17, *qōrôt bāttênû 'ᵃrāzîm,* "the beams of our house are cedar"). In *B. Meṣ.* 117a the word *tiqreh* appears. In the Targum on Jer. 49:24 the word *šiplûtā'* occurs, and this form is also used in *Sota* 48a.

Zimmerli (1962, 237) has plausibly suggested that the absolute form *šiplût* (sinking down) was balanced by *'aṣalût* (sloth, indolence; cf. Prov. 31:27), and the ending *(im)* resulted from dittography, a scribe writing the first two letters of *yimmak* twice. Otherwise, the dual form of *ba'ᵃṣaltayim* presents a problem. The ending can be understood as intensive, or it may anticipate the dual *yādayim* (hands) in the second half of the verse.

The verb *yimmak* (Niphal imperfect of *mkk*) occurs two other times in the Hebrew Bible (Ps. 106:43; Job 24:24). The meaning of *yidlōp* may be "to drop" (Job 16:20, *'el-'ᵉlôah dālᵉpāh 'ênî,* "my eyes drop [tears] to Eloah"; Ps. 119:28, *dālᵉpāh napšî mittûgāh,* "I melt away [bow down?] from sorrow"). The point would then be that idle hands cause the roof to sag. However, the figurative use of *dlp* may suggest the meaning "leak." This interpretation is strengthened by the Targumic use of *dlp* in Prov. 19:13 to indicate a continual dripping of rain. The noun *delep* (drip) seems to confirm this interpretation (Prov. 19:13; 27:15).

[19] In Ezek. 4:15 *wᵉ'āśîtā 'et-laḥmᵉkā 'ᵃlêhem* ("and you may prepare your meal on them") the verb *'śh* is used along with the noun *leḥem.* The verb *'bd* occurs in a similar phrase in Dan. 5:1 (*bēlša'ṣṣar malkā' 'ᵃbad lᵉḥem rab,* "Belshazzar the king made a great feast"). Qohelet uses *'ōśîm* as an indefinite subject, the equivalent of the passive (a feast is prepared for the purpose of enjoyment). The *lamed* is therefore purposive.

The chiastic structure of verb-subject-subject-verb is not used to maximum potential. Furthermore, the symmetry is broken by the Piel imperfect *y^e^śammaḥ* ("makes happy"), which the Septuagint corrects *(lśmḥ).*

The emphatic article on *hakkesep* draws attention to the item that makes feasting possible. Although the Septuagint and Vulgate render *ya'^a^neh* as *epakousetai* or *hypakousetai* and *obediunt* respectively, and the Peshitta takes the verb from the root *'nh* (to afflict, humble), there may be biblical precedent for the meaning "pay, provide for" (Gen. 41:16; Hos. 2:23–24 [21–22E]). (However, the verb can be translated "answer" in these texts.) The other pertinent text in Eccl. 5:19 *(kî hā'^e^lōhîm ma'^a^neh b^e^śimḥat libbô)* is unclear. Does God afflict him with fleeting joy, or provide a genuine source of joy?

The final *hakkōl* may mean "both" or "everything." In context, this verse may continue the thought of 10:16–17, but more probably the verse represents an independent saying. The observation about the power of money relates better to the drunken conduct of verse 16 than to the commendable behavior recorded in verse 17.

[20] The parallelism in the entire verse is highly unusual for Qohelet, who uses it sparingly. Here the parallel ideas are not strictly synonymous. The verse moves from the more powerful to the slightly less powerful: Do not even *think* ill of royalty or *speak* bad things of the rich. The king has more persons looking out for his interests than the wealthy, hence special care is needed. But one cannot afford to relax a guard where the rich are involved either, for they also have ample spies.

The word *b^e^maddā'^a^kā* is an Aramaized form that is found only in II Chron. 1:10–12 and Dan. 1:4, 17 within the Bible. The word appears in the Targum to Jer. 3:15; Ps. 34:1; and Prov. 1:5. The Aramaic equivalent is used often (e.g., Dan. 2:21; 4:31, 33; 5:12). Some interpreters emend the text to *b^e^maṣā'^a^kā* ("on your couch"), but this reading does not differ sufficiently from the following expression *ûb^e^ḥadrê miškāb^e^kā* ("and in your bedroom"). Winton-Thomas' suggestion (*JTS* 50 [1949] 177) that one read *mōdā'^a^kā* ("your repose," from *yd'* with the meaning "to be quiet, rest") is suggestive but unnecessary.

The inconsistent use of the article is noticeable in this verse, particularly because the article occurs with the word for voice *(haqqôl).* We also encounter one of the few jussives in Ecclesiastes *(yaggêd),* but for no apparent reason. The expression *ba'al hakk^e^nāpayim* (owner of wings) recalls the singular form *ba'al kānāp* in Prov. 1:17 ("For naught is a net spread in the sight of any bird"). Qohelet adjusts the expression to balance the plural *'ôp haššāmayim.* A similar expression occurs in Dan. 8:6, 20 *(ba'al haqq^e^rānayim,* "horned creature").

Modern proverbial sayings about walls with ears and little birds telling tales capture the point of Qohelet's advice. Elsewhere Aristophanes (*The Birds* 49f., 601) and Juvenal (*Satires* 60.95f.) use the motif of a communicative bird. Qohelet urges extreme caution lest one's true feelings become known to powerful persons whose fury will lead to avoidable suffering on the part of the offender.

The Element of Risk
11:1–6

> 11:1 Send your bread on the surface of the waters, for you will find it after many days. [2]Give a portion to seven or even to eight, for you do not know what misfortune may occur on earth. [3]If the clouds are full they pour rain over the earth, and if a tree falls in the south or in the north, in the place that the tree falls there it is. [4]Whoever watches the wind will not sow, and whoever observes the clouds will not reap. [5]Just as you do not know what is the way of the life-breath in the bones in a pregnant womb, so you do not know the work of God, who does everything. [6]In the morning sow your seed and in the evening do not withhold your hand, for you do not know whether this one or that one will succeed, or whether both of them will be equally good.

In this unit Qohelet observes that an element of risk always resides in commercial and agricultural enterprises, but intelligent people venture nonetheless. The image of sending bread on waters is also found in a late Egyptian Instruction, although its exact meaning eludes modern interpreters. Qohelet probably implies that the mystery of pregnancy does not preclude union between lovers, hence ignorance about the wind should not prevent the sowing of seed.

[11:1] This strange advice seems to relate to maritime commercial ventures; Qohelet urges the taking of risks, the sending forth to distant ports in the hope of obtaining a substantial profit. One should be willing to take risks, confident that surprising results may follow. The verb *šālaḥ* occurs in connection with *bayyām* and *'al-pᵉnê-mayim* in Isa. 18:2 (*haššōlēaḥ bayyām ṣîrîm ûbiklê-gōme' 'al-pᵉnê-mayim,* "who sends ambassadors on the Nile and in vessels of papyrus on the waters").

Diaz (in *Merkwürdigkeiten von Asien*) records a story that ends with an Arab proverb reminiscent of Qohelet's advice ("Do good, cast thy bread upon the waters, and one day thou shalt be rewarded"). It appears that Qohelet's advice was understood as referring to acts of charity. In ancient and medieval Jewish circles this interpretation became standard.

A remarkable parallel occurs in The Instructions of 'Onkhsheshonqy

19.10 ("Do a good deed and throw it in the water; when it dries you will find it"). Within the Bible, Prov. 31:14 compares the virtuous woman with merchants' ships, adding that *mimmerḥāq tābî' laḥmāh* ("she brings her bread from afar").

In light of the alliteration in *hammāyim* and *hayyāmîm* one may discern a reason for Qohelet's use of the verb *šālaḥ,* the final syllable of which is repeated in the initial syllable of the word for bread *(šallaḥ laḥmᵉkā).*

[2] The interpretation of this verse depends on that of the previous verse. Qohelet may advise diversifying one's investments in several ships, or he may counsel the befriending of several persons who would help if one's own circumstances were reversed. If one ship were destroyed in a storm or its cargo stolen, other vessels would return with wares intact. Alternatively, if a person places a number of people in debt by examples of kindness, some of them may be around to help in the event that their benefactor falls on hard times.

Numerical heightening, familiar from Ugaritic literature as well as Egyptian and Mesopotamian texts, sometimes is followed by an actual enumeration of the highest number of things, and at other times only one general idea is mentioned (cf. Job 33:14; Ps. 62:12 [11E] [once and twice]; Job 33:29 [twice and thrice]; Isa. 17:6 [two and three]; Amos 1:3, 6, 9, 11, 13; 2:1, 4, 6; Prov. 30:15, 18, 21; Ex. 20:5; 34:7 [three and four]; Isa. 17:6 [four and five]; Prov. 6:16–19 [six and seven]; Micah 5:4 [5E] [seven and eight]).

Together, 11:1 and 2 accord with Qohelet's emphasis elsewhere on the precariousness of one's actions and the inability to know the future. Both verses have a similar structure, and the meaning of *kî* is ambiguous in each instance (causal, concessive, or emphatic?).

[3] This verse asserts that hidden laws make certain things inevitable. Regardless of human effort, some things occur without fail. When clouds become full, they empty themselves. It matters little whether one follows the Massoretes and links *gešem* (rain) with *he'ābîm* (the clouds) or ignores the accents and associates *gešem* with the verb *yārîqû.*

The other example is less clear. Does Qohelet say that a tree lies where it falls and nothing can be done about it? That is palpably untrue. People can move a tree to another place. Or does he refer to our inability to know which way it will fall during a violent storm? Or, the word *'ēṣ* may refer to a divining rod (Hos. 4:12, *'ammî bᵉ'ēṣô yiš'āl,* "my people inquire with a rod"). No one can make the stick incline in a desirable direction, because stronger forces are at work to see that the rod functions properly.

The unusual reading *šām yᵉhû'* ("there it is") may echo *šām hû'* in Job 3:19 and *šām yihyeh.* Four manuscripts read *šām hû'* for *šām yᵉhû'.* On the basis of *lehᵉwē'* (Dan. 2:20) and *tehᵉwē'* (Dan. 2:40), Whitley takes *yᵉhû'* to be a Qal imperfect of the Aramaic verb *hāwāh* (to be), which is *wehweh* or *wehwē'.*

[4] The overly cautious individual is destined to fail, for optimal conditions may not materialize. The person who delays planting time for fear the wind will scatter the seeds unevenly is unrealistic, for every action contains a measure of risk and uncertainty. The same is true of the person who keeps watch over the clouds, waiting for a perfect time to reap without fear of an unseasonal rain spoiling the grain. Gordis calls attention to the chiastic relationship between verses 3 and 4 (clouds-falling tree-wind-clouds). In his view, the effects of the wind (a felled tree and irregularly scattered seed) are the link between 3b and 4a.

The image of watching wind compares vividly with Qohelet's earlier picture of the human occupation, a fruitless chasing after or herding the wind. The symmetry of 11:4 increases its effect (each half of the verse has a participle plus object, followed by a verb with the negative particle). According to Prov. 26:1, rain during the time of harvest and snow in summer are inappropriate—like bestowing honor on a fool. Qohelet portrays someone hesitating to harvest crops even when the chances of rain are remote. Such caution approaches stupidity.

[5] Does Qohelet refer to two things that defy explanation: the secret paths of the wind and the development of an embryo? Or is there a single example, the mysterious manner in which the life-breath functions within a pregnant womb? If two examples are intended, one would expect a *waw* before the *kap* on *ʿᵃṣāmîm* (bones). Although the syntax is rough, it is possible to understand the *kap* as an additional comparison, with implicit repetition of the verb *ʾênᵉkā yôdēaʿ* ("you do not know"). The Targum and many manuscripts have *bāʿᵃṣāmîm* ("in the bones"), which may be an attempt to remove a difficulty in the text. In any event, the Septuagint *(hōs osta)* and Vulgate *(qua ratione ossa)* support the Massoretic Text. Qohelet's point may be as follows: "As you cannot know the path of the wind—like the bones in a pregnant womb—so . . . ."

Emphasis certainly falls on human ignorance, whatever the number of mysteries. The miracle of birth is celebrated in Ps. 139:13–16; Job 10:11–12; 2 Macc. 7:22; and Qohelet Rabbah 5:10. Although the pointing on *bᵉbeṭen* makes it a construct with *hammᵉlēʾāh* ("in the womb of a pregnant woman"), it is also possible to construe the *hammᵉlēʾāh* as an adjective (the pregnant womb), as in *Yebam.* 16:1 (*yṣʾh mᵉlēʾāh,* "she went away pregnant"). Inability to know God's works is mentioned in Eccl. 3:11; 8:17; and 9:12. For the singular *maʿᵃśeh,* the Septuagint, Peshitta, and Vulgate have the plural, in accord with their understanding of two examples of divine mystery. If their interpretation is correct, the final *hakkōl* may refer to "both" rather than "everything."

[6] The juxtaposition of this verse and the previous one led ancient Jewish interpreters to an erotic understanding of *zᵉraʿ* (sow). Accordingly,

Qohelet was thought to have encouraged continuous begetting of children. If the *bet* on *bōqer* has the function of *mem* (from), as it does in Ugaritic, the idea is to be active in sowing from morning until evening (cf. Job 4:20, *mibbōqer lā'ereb,* "from morning until evening"). But the meaning may be to sow at two times rather than continuously: in the morning and in the evening. The *zeh 'ô-zeh* ("this or that") supports the latter sense *babbōqer . . . wᵉlā'ereb,* although "this" could possibly refer to sowing and "that" could allude to continuous work related to sowing.

The image of sowing need not be taken erotically, for 11:4 refers to actual planting of seeds. The word *zᵉra'* may symbolize a number of human activities. The sense is then to get on with one's work despite abysmal ignorance about divine mysteries such as the paths of the wind and the development of a fetus.

Youth and Old Age
11:7–12:7

11:7 Yes, sweet is the light, and it is good for the eyes to behold the
sun. [8]Indeed, let anyone who lives many years rejoice in all of them,
but remember the days of darkness, for they will be many; everything
that comes is absurd. [9]Rejoice, young man, in your youth and let your
heart be glad during the days of your prime, and walk in the ways of
your heart and in the sight of your eyes; but know that God will bring
you into judgment because of all these. [10]And remove vexation from
your heart and banish pain from your body, for youth and black hair
are fleeting. 12:1 And remember your wife in the days of your youth,
before the evil days come and the years approach of which you will say,
"I have no pleasure in them."

2 Before the sun is darkened and the light—and the moon
and the stars—
And the clouds return after the rain.
3 When the keepers of the house tremble and valiant men
are stooped,
And the grinding women cease because they are few,
And those who look through the windows are dimmed;
4 And the doors on the street are closed,
When the sound of the grinding is muted,
And one rises at the sound of the bird,
And all daughters of song are brought low.
5 Also they are afraid of heights,

And terrors are in the path,
And the almond blooms, the locust burdens itself,
the caperberry is useless;
For mankind goes to his eternal home,
And the mourners go about the street.
6 Before the silver cord is torn,
And the golden bowl is shattered,
And the jar by the fountain is broken,
And the pulley at the cistern is ruined.
7 And the dust returns to the earth as it was,
And the life-breath returns to God who gave it.

The contrast between youthful vigor and incapacitating old age that eventuates in death is vividly portrayed in this section. The image of light characterizes youth, whereas darkness functions as an apt description of waning years. Two verbs link the opposites as one: rejoice and remember. The youth is admonished to rejoice during the days of youthful energy but also to remember that quite different years are lurking beyond the horizon. A threefold allusion to life's futility *(hābel)* offers a sobering reflection (11:8, 10; 12:8). A refrain suspends the thought for a duration, concentrating all attention on the dreaded event *('ad 'ăšer lō',* "before" [12:1, 2, 6]).

The interplay of human and nonhuman images throughout this unit emphasizes the intimate association of humankind with nature. This link persists after the severing of the life-cord, the shattering of the pitcher from which came the water of life, and the separation of wondrously fashioned dust from the divine breath. Crumbling dust returns to the earth from which it came; spring has ended, and a permanent winter sets in.

Because of the somber nature of the material, Qohelet resorts to emphatic speech. Jussives occur in thematic statements about the advisability of rejoicing and remembering. These quickly shift to imperatives, the first of which is accompanied by an identification of the addressees as young men. Four additional imperatives elaborate the theme of pleasure during youth and of concomitant obligation (walk, know, remove, banish). The second use of *zākar* (remember) introduces a thought that continues for seven verses, with a parenthetical comment in verses 3–5.

The thin line between debilitating old age and death makes it difficult to know whether the description is terrestrial or subterrestrial. The first two instances of *'ad 'ăšer lō'* seem to introduce solemn descriptions of old age. The last use of this expression ushers in a powerful account of death. These exquisite images are preceded by a straightforward statement of departure to one's eternal home. Therefore it appears likely that the reference from first to last is to events on earth, and the verses do not portray the weakened existence characteristic of Sheol's inhabitants.

The subsection in 12:1–7 employs symbolic language as well as literal expressions, and this mixture presents problems. When is one to understand the text literally and when figuratively? Furthermore, there are several different images, no one picture continuing from beginning to end. Regardless of whether the thought is about (1) a storm that threatens a crumbling house, or (2) the undesirable features of advanced years, Qohelet addresses young persons once more, although indirectly ("when you will say, 'I have no pleasure in them' "). The section is therefore a fitting conclusion to Qohelet's words, hence the inclusio in 12:8 concerning life's complete futility.

[7] Before this reference to the sweetness of seeing the light, Qohelet has twice mentioned the subject in the context of a full life (6:5; 7:11). The idea appears elsewhere as well, for example, in Euripides (*Iphigenia in Aulis* 1.1219, *hēdy gar to phōs leussein,* "it is sweet to see the light") and in the Gilgamesh Epic ("Let mine eyes behold the sun that I may have my fill of the light! Darkness withdraws when there is enough light. May one who indeed is dead behold yet the radiance of the sun!" *ANET,* 89). One may also note Homer's observation: "And if our fate be death, give us light and let us die" (*Iliad* 17.1.647), but the sentiment of this thinker is closer to that of doomed persons in Isa. 22:13 who say, "Let us eat and drink, for tomorrow we die."

The *waw* on *mātôq* (sweet) may introduce a new section (cf. 3:16; 4:4; 7:26; 8:10; 12:1, so Gordis), or it may be emphatic.

[8] Even as Qohelet acknowledges the sweetness of the light, he anticipates a lengthy stay in darkness. Present enjoyment does not blot out less pleasant thoughts. One may enjoy a long life with its accompanying pleasantries, but one needs also to ponder dark days, because they are numerous.

In the following verses darkness will describe old age, but here it does not, for there is no assurance that these days will be many. Perhaps the symbol of darkness indicates that the dreaded failing years already participate in the essential feature of Sheol, an absence of the warmth of the sun. If this is true, the days of darkness may include old age while focusing on one's stay in Sheol.

It is not necessary to view *'et-yᵉmê haḥōšek* as anticipation ("remember that the dark days will be many"). The initial *kî* and its repetition may be causal rather than asseverative. There is no intended contrast between "many years" *(šānîm harbēh)* and "days of darkness . . . many" *(yᵉmê haḥōšek . . . harbēh),* for each expression denotes an indefinite period, a long time.

This verse has another instance of lack of agreement between a pronominal suffix and the noun to which it refers (*bᵉkullām* and *šānîm,* masculine and feminine respectively).

The final remark registers unrelieved pessimism: everything that the future holds in Sheol is utterly absurd.

[9] Gordis understands this verse as emphasizing the divine imperative to enjoy life, taking the conjunction on the imperative *dāʿ* as consecutive rather than adversative. Qohelet says "rejoice . . . be happy . . . walk . . . know." Know what? That God will call you to account if you do not enjoy life to the height of your capacity.

The verse gives us a whole set of words for youth. The first, *bāḥûr,* means "the chosen one," hence a youth in the prime of life. The abstract *yaldût* ("childhood," but more generally "youth") occurs three times in the Bible (Eccl. 11:9, 10; and Ps. 110:3 [*ṭal yalduteykā,* "the dew of your youth"]). Similarly, the feminine plural abstract form *beḥûrôtekā* ("in your youth") occurs only here and in 12:1.

Numbers 15:39 warns against following the organs of desire, the heart and the eyes. The second half of Eccl. 11:9 may well be a moralistic gloss, inserted to counteract Qohelet's shocking advice. The entire tradition was on the side of the glossator. But a consecutive reading of *wedāʿ* is unlikely.

The emphatic use of the personal pronoun on *wîṭîbekā* is a sign of late composition, typical of Qohelet's style.

[10] This verse continues Qohelet's advice in 11:9a, interrupted by 11:9b, and gives a motive for the action. These imperatives offer a negative counterpart to the positive counsel already given. A person cannot fully enjoy life without excluding certain kinds of annoyances. Qohelet specifies *kaʿas* and *rāʿāh,* sorrow and suffering. By removing all manifestations of these evils, and by positively replacing them with rejoicing, making one's heart happy, and following one's desires, an individual stands a chance of blotting out the terrible specter of death. But one can never quite achieve this goal. The period when you can do these things is brief, fleeting like a breath or a puff of smoke. Qohelet is concerned for the well-being of body and mind. Hence he mentions both mental anxiety and physical distress.

The hapax *haššaḥarût* posed a problem for the versions. The Septuagint has *anoia* (folly or ignorance), the Peshitta reads "ignorance," and the Vulgate has *voluptas* (desire). The essential sense of *haššaḥarût* is blackness, either the time of black hair or dawn. There is a metathesized cognate in Arabic (*šariḥ,* youth). In Job 30:30 (cf. Sir. 25:17) the root *šḥr* means "to be dark" (*ʿôrî šāḥar mēʿālāy,* "my skin is dark on me"). But the word also signifies the dawn (I Sam. 9:26, *kaʿalôt haššaḥar,* "at the break of dawn"), a meaning that is also found in the Mesha Inscription (1.15, *mbkʿ hšḥrt,* "from the break of dawn"). The Targum reads *yômê ʾûkkāmût śʿr* ("the days of the blackness of hair").

[12:1] Although the versions and some Hebrew manuscripts have the singular, the Massoretic Text has *bôreʾeykā* ("your Creator"); the plural, indicated by the *yod,* can be explained as a plural of majesty or as a mixing of *lamed alep* and *lamed he* verbs. But allusion to God the Creator ill fits this context. Both *beʾērekā* ("your well") and *bôrekā* ("your pit") have been proposed as alternatives. The first symbolizes one's wife (cf. Prov. 5:15, *šᵉtēh-mayim mibbôrekā,* "drink water from your own well," which 5:18 identifies as one's wife), and the second alludes to the grave. A third possibility is *bᵉrû'eykā* or *boryᵉ'ākā* ("your vigor, well-being"). A threefold interpretation of the difficult word *bôrᵉ'eykā* is attributed to Aqiba in explaining the saying of Akabya ben Mahalalel in *Abot* 3:1 ("know whence you came [*b'rk,* your source], whither you are going" [*bwrk,* "your grave"], and before whom you are destined to give an accounting [*bwr'yk,* "your Creator"]). A thinker of Qohelet's complexity might well have chosen a word that suggests one's greatest pleasure (the wife) and one's ultimate destiny (the grave). More probably, he urges young people to reflect on the joys of female companionship before old age and death render one incapable of sensual pleasure.

In 11:8 Qohelet used the sequence "years . . . days"; here in 12:1 he reverses the order. Both verses use the verb *zākar* (remember) and end on a gloomy note. The phrase *'ad 'ᵃšer lō'* (before) occurs here and in 12:2 and 6. It is related to the Mishnaic *'ad šellō'* (e.g., *Mak.* 2:4, *'d šl' nbḥrw,* "before they are chosen"). In Prov. 8:26 *'ad-lō'* is used in a similar sense.

Some commentators understand 12:1a as a gloss, citing (1) the unsuitability of the reference to Creator in the context and (2) the natural sequence of thought from 11:10a to 12:1b ("banish vexation . . . remove pain . . . before the unwelcome days arrive"). Qohelet does introduce a religious motive for caution in 5:6, but that is far removed from the piety of 12:1a.

[2] Qohelet now clarifies the nature of days and years that yield no pleasure. Every source of light becomes dark, from the powerful sun to the moon and stars. But where does the light *(hā'ôr)* belong in this context? Genesis 1:3, 16 distinguishes between the light *(hā'ôr)* and the sun, moon, and stars. This understanding of a separate entity that supplies the light for the greater lamp and lesser lamp, as well as the stars, can be achieved in Eccl. 12:2 by viewing *wᵉhā'ôr wᵉhayyārēaḥ wᵉhakkôkābîm* as hendiadys ("and the light of both the moon and the stars").

The image suggests both an approaching storm and failing sight during old age. Qohelet knows that the time will soon come when the brilliance of the sun will suffer permanent eclipse as one moves closer to the abode of darkness. If the sun's light is dimmed, the stars and moon will be affected all the more. Life becomes a long winter, dark and cold. In earlier times the rains came and then the clouds disappeared, leaving clear skies. But now reduced vision in advanced years gives the impression that it is always cloudy (which sounds like the symptoms of glaucoma).

[3] If Qohelet has in mind the ruin of a house, the verse alludes to the discomfiture of its guardians, the bending of old backs, the inactivity of the grinding maids, and the darkening of the women whose status granted them free time to watch from openings in the house. The four categories of people are arranged chiastically (slaves—free men—slave women—women of substance). But two problems remain. Why do the slaves cease grinding because they are few in number? One would expect them to work all the more diligently, unless the implication is that residents in the house are few and need little food. And what is the sense of saying that the women who look out the windows are darkened? That they are clothed in garments of mourning?

Because of these uncertainties on the literal level, many interpreters concentrate on the symbolic content of the expressions. They envision a body described as a house. For example, its keepers may be the hands, its valiant men the back, its grinding women the teeth, and the women who peer through the windows may be the eyes. But scholars cannot agree about the exact things represented by the several images.

The verb *zûaʿ* occurs in Biblical Hebrew in two other places (Esth. 5:9; Hab. 2:7); it is also used in Biblical Aramaic (Dan. 5:19; 6:27) and in the Mishnah (e.g., *Abot* 5:22). The root *bāṭal* occurs nowhere else in Hebrew, but it does appear in Biblical Aramaic (Ezra 4:21, 23, 24; 5:5) and in the Mishnah (*Abot* 1:5; 2:4). Whitley refers to a participial form *(mbṭl)* in an Aramaic Palmyrene inscription of the second century C.E.

[4] If Qohelet describes the gradual deterioration of a house, the dual form for doors *(dᵉlātayim)* presents a problem. Most houses apparently had only one door. The allegorical approach capitalizes on the dual, interpreting it to mean ears or lips. The word *šûq* (street) occurs outside Ecclesiastes (12:4, 5) in Prov. 7:8 (*ʿōbēr baššûq ʾēṣel pinnāh,* "wandering in the street near her corner") and in S. of Songs 3:2 (*ʾāqûmāh nāʾ waʾᵃsōbᵉbāh bāʿîr baššᵉwāqîm ûbārᵉḥōbôt,* "I will get up and wander in the city, in the streets and in the wide places"). It is also found in various Aramaic, Palmyrene, and Nabatean inscriptions.

The verb *šāpal* is used in a figurative sense in Prov. 16:19 (*ṭôb šᵉpal-rûaḥ ʾet-ʿᵃnāyyîm,* "It is better to have a contrite spirit with the poor"). The unusual noun for grinding *haṭṭaḥᵃnāh* is approximated in Lam. 5:13 (*baḥûrîm ṭᵉḥôn nāśāʾû,* "young men are forced to grind"). The literal reference to Samson's grinding in prison (Judg. 16:21, *wayᵉhî ṭôḥēn bᵉbêt hāʾᵃsîrîm,* "and he was grinding in the house of bonds") was understood figuratively in an erotic sense by ancient Jewish interpreters.

Because the verb *qûm* is an unsatisfactory parallel to the following *šḥḥ* (to be low), some commentators have proposed emendations, the closest orthographically being *wᵉyiqmal* (and it decays). Others understand the verb *yāqûm* to be impersonal (one rises), and interpret the *lamed* on *qôl* temporally. Still others view the bird as subject, stressing the singing of birds. Those who emphasize the figurative sense of these verses think of the rising pitch of elderly persons' voices; the critics who take the idea literally think of the light sleep of old people, who awake at the chirping of birds. Daughters of song are thought to be dancing women who brought pleasure, or the image is taken to be an allusion to the feeble quality of the voice. The former interpretation has a parallel in Ugaritic (*bnt hll,* "the daughters of praise"). But the phrase *b^e^nôt haššîr* can also refer to songbirds (Job 30:29, *b^e^nôt ya^ʿa^nāh,* "young ostriches").

[5] The Vulgate rendering, *timebunt,* supports the interpretation of *yirāʾû* as a defective for *yîr^e^ʾû* (from *yārēʾ* rather than from *rāʾāh,* to see), despite many manuscripts, Septuagint, Coptic, and Symmachus. The strange form *w^e^ḥatḥattîm* is a duplication of *ḥatat* like *ʿpʿpym* (eyelids), *tltym* (palm branches), *qśqśym* (scales), *slslwt* (baskets). The old person is terrified of high places and afraid of dangers along the path.

The next part of this verse is virtually impossible. Two interpretations are attractive: (1) it describes the rapid growth of spring, when almonds blossom, locusts eat so much that they can barely drag themselves along, and caperberries burst from growth; or (2) it characterizes the deterioration of the human body in three aspects—the hair turns white, the limbs are stiff and creak, and sexual desire fades. The first of these views emphasizes the stark contrast between the deterioration of a house and the fresh birth of nature. Human beings die and nature is unconcerned, indeed it mocks the decay of unfortunate inhabitants of earth. The second view focuses on the gradual encroachments of age. Naturally, this latter view takes the language as figurative.

The verbs pose many problems. The ancient versions (Septuagint, Peshitta, Vulgate, Coptic, Syro-Hexaplar) imply that *nṣṣ* lies behind *yānēʾṣ* (it blossoms), although some interpreters understand the unusual form (use of *plene* orthography) to derive from *ynṣ* (to despise). The meaning would then be that old people dislike most kinds of food because of the difficulty in digesting them.

The meaning of *sbl* is "to bear a load," and the Hithpael should mean "to burden oneself." An alternative reading from *skl* is found in numerous manuscripts, with the meaning "is confused." The normal sense of *heḥāgāb* is locust or grasshopper. Several versions render the verb *yistabbēl* by "swell, grow fat" (Septuagint, Peshitta, Targum). If the allusion is to an old person, the noun *heḥāgāb* must suggest fatness or a specific part of the body (ankles, Targum; buttocks, *Šabb.* 152a).

The verb *tāpēr* ("to break," from *prr*) should probably be *tuppar* (Hophal, so Septuagint, Syro-Hexaplar, Coptic, Symmachus), although Aquila implies a verb from *prh* (to bear fruit). The word *hāʾ^a^biyyônāh* is hapax, but it occurs in *Maas.* 4:6 with the meaning "caperberry." The versions (Septuagint, Vulgate, and Peshitta) understood the word as caperberry, a stimulant of the appetite. The Targum renders this word as a reference to sexual desire, which vanishes with age, and so does *Šabb.* 152a. The absence of any reference to dwindling sexual desire in the description of old age makes this an attractive reading: and sexual desire is broken.[133]

The second half of the verse is reasonably clear. It refers to the death of human beings, who go to the grave, their eternal home, and to the mourners who go about the streets. Although the phrase *bêt 'ôlāmô* occurs only here in Biblical Hebrew, the expression was well known in the ancient world. Whitley cites a Palmyrene inscription from the end of the second century C.E. (*bt 'lm' qbr' dnh dy bnh zbd'th,* "the house of eternity, that grave which Zabdeateh built"). The Egyptians referred to the grave as an eternal house, according to Diodorus Siculus. A Punic inscription has *hdr bt 'lm* ("the chamber of the tomb"). The pronominal suffix on *'ôlām* occurs only here in the Bible, but the Talmud has it (*Abod. Zar.* 10b). The expression "house of eternity" also appears in the Targum on Isa. 14:18 and in *Sanh.* 19a). Tobit 3:6 has *topos aiōnios.*

[6] Two images seem to occur here: the breaking of a bowl after the cord that held it on the wall has snapped, and the smashing of a vessel after the pulley that assisted in raising and lowering the jar has shattered. The relation between these metaphors is not clear.

The word *gullat* occurs in Zech. 4:2–3 with reference to a golden lamp. Proverbs 13:9 uses the image of an extinguished lamp for death (*w^e nēr r^e šā'îm yid'āk,* "but the lamp of the wicked will be extinguished"). In Greek mythology the severing of the cord or thread of life conveyed this idea.

The verb *yērāḥēq* (is distant) and the alternative Qere reading (*yērātēq,* is joined) yield little sense, prompting interpreters to read *yinnātēq* (is torn) with the help of Septuagint (overthrow), Peshitta, Symmachus (cut), and Vulgate (break). The verb *tāruṣ* derives from *rṣṣ* (to break) and is treated like an *ayin waw* verb. Many versions also read this verb in 6b (for *nārōṣ;* so Septuagint, Syro-Hexaplar, Peshitta, Targum). The Vulgate distinguishes between the two (*recurrat,* from *rûṣ,* to run; *confringatur,* from *rṣṣ*).

The noun *hammabbûa'* (the fountain) occurs elsewhere only in Isa. 35:7 (*w^e ṣimmā'ôn l^e mabbû'ê māyim,* "and the thirsty springs of water") and 49:10 (*w^e 'al mabbû'ê mayim ye nah^a lēm* "and will lead them by springs of water"). The picture of a fountain in disrepair suggests that the water of life can no longer be drawn, and the end has come.

[7] The allusion to Gen. 2:7 and 3:19 does not contradict Qohelet's earlier denial that the human spirit ascends to God and the animal life

[133]On Qohelet's attitude to old age, see my article "Youth and Old Age in Qoheleth," *HAR* 11 (1987), forthcoming.

principle descends to the earth. There is nothing comforting about Qohelet's acknowledgment that life comes from God, who breathed into the human nostrils and now sucks the breath back out. The jussive form *wᵉyāšōb* is unexpected in this verse, especially when the usual imperfect occurs in the second half of the verse.

Thematic Statement (Inclusio)
12:8

12:8 Absurdity of absurdities, says the Qohelet, everything is absurd.

[8] This verse forms an inclusio with 1:2 for the words of Qohelet, which end at 12:7. A few manuscripts and Peshitta repeat *hᵃbēl hᵃbālîm* after *haqqôhelet* to conform with 1:2. If 12:7 contained any word of hope, this refrain would be entirely inappropriate. Its presence here refutes the claim that Qohelet hoped for immortality of the soul.

The Epilogue(s)
12:9–14

12:9 In addition to being a wise man, Qohelet also taught the people knowledge, and he weighed, searched out, and arranged many proverbs. 10Qohelet sought to find pleasing expressions, and he faithfully wrote trustworthy words. 11The words of the wise are like goads, and like nails, planted tightly, are the collected sayings; they were given by one shepherd. 12In addition to these, my son, be on your guard; there is no end to the making of many books, and much study wearies the body. 13The end of the matter; all has been heard. Fear God and keep his commandments, for this is the whole duty of humankind. 14For God will bring every deed into judgment concerning everything that is secret, whether good or bad.

Two epilogues bring the book to a close, each beginning with *wᵉyōtēr* (besides, in addition to). The first epilogue focuses on the professional activity of Qohelet and the nature of his teaching. The second epilogue characterizes the intellectual process as endless and exhausting, offers some advice on what is really important, and warns that a judgment day is certain. The style is generally consistent with Qohelet's, although the content of the second epilogue differs sharply from his thought. Furthermore, the only occurrence of *b^e^nî* (my son) in the book takes place here (12:12). The point of view in the first epilogue is that of a devoted student who reflects on Qohelet's activity. The second epilogue seems to be the work of a detractor who thinks of Qohelet's teachings as inadequate and perhaps perverse.

The first epilogue ignores the earlier literary fiction of royal authorship and identifies Qohelet as a professional *ḥākām,* a sage. His audience is said to be all-encompassing *(hā'ām),* and his expertise beyond question. Three verbs describe his research that produced numerous proverbs (he weighed [or listened], examined, and arranged). In addition, he is praised for achieving compositional integrity and elegance. Recognizing the pessimistic tone and realistic truth inherent in Qohelet's teaching, this epilogist understands both aspects positively. They prod one to think more profoundly, and they act as fixed points of reference, for they derive from a single source (one shepherd). This observation extends to the achievements of others besides Qohelet (the words of the wise: *ḥ^a^kāmîm,* among whom he is but one).

An apologetic note may reside within this concession about sapiential teachings: they are like cattle prods. This feature becomes much more prominent in the second epilogue, which suggests the proper perspective within which to understand Qohelet's unusual reflections. Here the speaker claims the authority of a teacher over students ("my son, be warned") and sums up the essence of reality as religious devotion to God and the commandments. Qohelet had insisted that God's works remain concealed in mystery, but this epilogist asserts that all human works will be brought into the open. Imperatives return once more, after a brief absence in the remarks of the first epilogist. A sense of urgency fills the air ("be warned, fear, keep," and possibly "let us all hear").

[9] This verse describes Qohelet's professional activity. Not only was he a sage, presumably responsible for educating youth; he also communicated his teachings with ordinary people *(hā'ām).* The three verbs that characterize his work are not entirely clear. The first, *'izzēn* is the only instance of the verb *'zn* (to weigh), although *mō'z^e^nayim* (scales) occurs several times. On the basis of several versions that have a reference to the ear or hearing, Whitley proposes to translate "and he listened." The second verb, *ḥiqqēr,* refers to searching out the complexity of something, hence careful considering. The third verb, *tiqqēn,* rendered as a noun in the Septuagint, is used in 1:15 and 7:13 in the sense of setting something straight. This also appears to be its meaning in Sir. 47:9, although Gordis understands the verb to mean "he fashioned."

The punctuation on *w^e^yōtēr* suggests the meaning "furthermore," as if to introduce some additional comments. The *'ôd* can refer to continued activity. Although the expression *m^e^šālîm harbēh* has been taken to mean the entire book of Proverbs, that is less likely than a general statement about Qohelet's work as a sage. In its narrow sense of "proverb" *mᵉšālîm* applies poorly to the book of Ecclesiastes, but the word can have much broader range.

[10] The emphasis falls on elegance and truth: Qohelet devoted time and energy both to the aesthetic of his composition and to the reliability of what he said. The construct relationship *dibrê-ḥēpeṣ* means words that bring delight to those who hear them, hence pleasing expressions. The verb *wᵉkātûb* (and was written) is usually corrected to a Qal imperfect or to an infinitive absolute. Five Hebrew manuscripts and some versions (Aquila, Symmachus, Peshitta, and Vulgate) understood the verb as active, although the Septuagint has passive (*kai gegrammenon euthytētos,* "and that which is written is of uprightness").

The adverbial accusative *yōšer* means "faithfully." The final word *'ᵉmet* has the same force. A comparable use occurs in Ps. 132:11 (*nišba'-yhwh lᵉdāwid 'ᵉmet lō'-yāšûb mimmennāh,* "Yahweh swore to David a reliable oath from which he will not turn away"). Many readers have not concurred in the statement that Qohelet's observations are both pleasing and truthworthy.

[11] The opening words remind us of superscriptions in Prov. 24:23; 30:1; 31:1; and probably 22:17. The parallel hapax expression *ba'ᵃlê 'ᵃsuppôt* is very difficult. In *Sanh.* 12a it means "masters of assemblies," but Qohelet seems to use it with reference to words rather than people. The chiastic structure of the first half of the verse may not be the only rhetorical device here. It is possible that Qohelet's choice derives from the words' alliterative value *(dibrê* and *dārᵉbōnôt; nᵉṭû'îm* and *nittᵉnû).*

The epilogist compares the wisdom tradition (not just Qohelet's sayings) to oxgoads, which prodded animals in a desired direction. The word occurs only here, but *drbn* in I Sam. 13:21 indicates a sharp instrument, and in Judg. 3:31 *bᵉmalmad habbāqār* refers to an implement for training cattle. The word for nails or pegs, spelled with *samek,* is found in Jer. 10:4 and II Chron. 3:9. In *Šabb.* 6:2 one finds the expression *bsndl hammᵉsûmār* ("with a nail-studded shoe"). The word *nᵉṭû'îm* has the meaning "fastened" in Dan. 11:45 (*wᵉyiṭṭa' 'ohᵒlê 'appadnô,* "and he will pitch his state-tents").

The final clause may refer to Solomon or to God, since the image of a shepherd was used for royalty and for God, both in Israel and in Egypt (D. Müller). The claim of divine origin for wisdom literature goes beyond anything else in canonical wisdom. In the deuterocanonicals Ben Sira comes close to it.

[12] Does *mēhēmmāh* ("from these") apply to Qohelet's sayings or the entire wisdom tradition? The author probably intended the latter, warning against an open attitude toward the canon. Only here in the book does the standard expression for student *(bᵉnî)* appear. The author mentions the endless process of writing books; the use of the infinitive *ᵃśôt* is strange, for one expects *ktb.*

The word *lahag,* found only here, may result from haplography (for *lahāgāh*) or relate to the word *hag* (meditation). The Septuagint *(meletē)* and Vulgate *(meditatio)* confirm the general sense of the text. The verb *hāgāh* (to study) occurs frequently, and *hāgût* in Ps. 49:4 [3E] means "meditation." Some interpreters think the *lamed* on *lahag* is emphatic.

[13] This verse, along with the rest of the epilogue, sums up the contents of the book. But what does *sôp dābār* mean? Barton took the expression to be a colophon marking the end of the discourse, to which a pious glossator added the rest of the verse and the last verse of the book. Such markers, like the later Massoretic *sôp pāsûq,* are common in ancient Near Eastern literature. The Aramaizing word *sôp* occurs in Eccl. 3:11 and II Chron. 20:16, as well as in the Mishnah. The absence of an article on *dābār* is strange. The *sôp dābār* appears to be a sort of ascription.

The form of *nišmāʿ* is a Niphal imperfect or imperative. The Vulgate translates "let us all hear." The Greek and Coptic versions take *nišmāʿ* as an imperative in the singular: "hear everything." A similar singular third-person Niphal (*hakkōl niškāḥ,* "everything is forgotten") occurs in 2:16. Its pausal pointing suggests that 12:13 is also imperfect: "Everything has been heard."

The summary is alien to anything Qohelet has said thus far. The combination of fear toward God and observance of the divine commands would fit better elsewhere, particularly in Sirach. In the final clause, one must supply something like "duty." Similar pregnant expressions occur elsewhere, for example, Ps. 110:3 (*ʿammᵉkā nᵉdābōt,* "your people are freely offering themselves"); 109:4 (*waʾᵃnî tᵉpillāh,* "and I am at prayer"); 120:7 (*ʾᵃnî-šālôm,* "I am seeking peace"). Whitley notes that even the Talmudic teachers had difficulty understanding this phrase, for they asked what it meant in *Ber.* 6b. He thinks the original was probably *kᵉlāl* (general rule, principle) and the final *lamed* was lost by haplography.

Ben Sira seems to echo this verse, Sir. 43:27 (*ʿwd k'lh l' nwsp wqṣ dbr hw' hkl,* "Though we speak much we cannot reach the end, and the sum of our words is: 'he is the all,' " RSV).

[14] Using the same expression for divine judgment which appeared in 11:9, the epilogist insists that nothing will fall between the cracks. God will uncover the hidden villainies and the secret deeds of charity. This comforting word for good people and frightening word for sinners is, again, totally alien to Qohelet's thinking.

The Massoretes repeated v. 13 after 14 in order to make the book end on a positive note. They did the same thing at the end of Isaiah, the Minor Prophets, and Lamentations. Few people can endure words of relentless wrath. Or the conclusion that life is utterly futile!